PACHUCAS AND PACHUCOS IN TUCSON

Situated Border Lives

The Southwest Center Series

Joseph C. Wilder, Editor

Ignaz Pfefferkorn, *Sonora: A Description of the Province*

Carl Lumholtz, *New Trails in Mexico*

Buford Pickens, *The Missions of Northern Sonora: A 1935 Field Documentation*

Gary Paul Nabhan, editor, *Counting Sheep: Twenty Ways of Seeing Desert Bighorn*

Eileen Oktavec, *Answered Prayers: Miracles and Milagros along the Border*

Curtis M. Hinsley and David R. Wilcox, editors, *Frank Hamilton Cushing and the Hemenway Southwestern Archaeological Expedition, 1886–1889*, volume 1: *The Southwest in the American Imagination: The Writings of Sylvester Baxter, 1881–1899*

Lawrence J. Taylor and Maeve Hickey, *The Road to Mexico*

Donna J. Guy and Thomas E. Sheridan, editors, *Contested Ground: Comparative Frontiers on the Northern and Southern Edges of the Spanish Empire*

Julian D. Hayden, *The Sierra Pinacate*

Paul S. Martin, David Yetman, Mark Fishbein, Phil Jenkins, Thomas R. Van Devender, and Rebecca K. Wilson, editors, *Gentry's Rio Mayo Plants: The Tropical Deciduous Forest and Environs of Northwest Mexico*

W J McGee, *Trails to Tiburón: The 1894 and 1895 Field Diaries of W J McGee*, transcribed by Hazel McFeely Fontana, annotated and with an introduction by Bernard L. Fontana

Richard Stephen Felger, *Flora of the Gran Desierto and Río Colorado of Northwestern Mexico*

Donald Bahr, editor, *O'odham Creation and Related Events: As Told to Ruth Benedict in 1927 in Prose, Oratory, and Song by the Pimas William Blackwater, Thomas Vanyiko, Clara Ahiel, William Stevens, Oliver Wellington, and Kisto*

Dan L. Fischer, *Early Southwest Ornithologists, 1528–1900*

Thomas Bowen, editor, *Backcountry Pilot: Flying Adventures with Ike Russell*

Federico José María Ronstadt, *Borderman: Memoirs of Federico José María Ronstadt*, edited by Edward F. Ronstadt

Curtis M. Hinsley and David R. Wilcox, editors, *Frank Hamilton Cushing and the Hemenway Southwestern Archaeological Expedition, 1886–1889*, volume 2: *The Lost Itinerary of Frank Hamilton Cushing*

Neil Goodwin, *Like a Brother: Grenville Goodwin's Apache Years, 1928–1939*

Katherine G. Morrissey and Kirsten Jensen, editors, *Picturing Arizona: The Photographic Record of the 1930s*

Bill Broyles and Michael Berman, *Sunshot: Peril and Wonder in the Gran Desierto*

David W. Lazaroff, Philip C. Rosen, and Charles H. Lowe Jr., *Amphibians, Reptiles, and Their Habitats at Sabino Canyon*

David Yetman, *The Organ Pipe Cactus*

David Yetman, *The Great Cacti: Ethnobotany and Biogeography*

Gloria Giffords, *Sanctuaries of Earth, Stone, and Light: The Churches of Northern New Spain, 1530–1821*

John Messina, *Álamos, Sonora: Architecture and Urbanism in the Dry Tropics*

PACHUCAS AND PACHUCOS IN TUCSON
Situated Border Lives

Laura L. Cummings

The University of Arizona Press
Tucson

The University of Arizona Press

www.uapress.arizona.edu

Library of Congress Cataloging-in-Publication Data

Cummings, Laura (Laura Lee)
Pachucas and pachucos in Tucson : situated border lives / Laura L. Cummings.
p. cm. — (The Southwest center series)
Includes bibliographical references and index.
ISBN 978-0-8165-2737-3 (pbk. : alk. paper)
1. Mexican American teenagers—Arizona—Tucson—History—20th century. 2. Mexican American teenagers—Arizona—Tucson—Social conditions. 3. Mexican American teenagers—Arizona—Tucson—Ethnic identity. 4. Tucson (Ariz.)—History—20th century. 5. Tucson (Ariz.)—Race relations. 6. Tucson (Ariz.)—Social conditions. I. Title.
F819.T99M53 2009
305.235089'68720791776—dc22 2009017690

Publication of this book is made possible in part by the proceeds of a permanent endowment created with the assistance of a Challenge Grant from the National Endowment for the Humanities, a federal agency.

Manufactured in the United States of America on acid-free, archival-quality paper containing a minimum of 30% post-consumer waste and processed chlorine free.

14 13 12 11 10 09 6 5 4 3 2 1

To the memory of Fernando Argueta Cruz
May 24, 1954–October 30, 2002
Tijuana, Baja California

Contents

Illustrations

Acknowledgments

I wish to express my gratitude to all the individuals who graciously granted life history and linguistic interviews, sharing their personal and family histories, commentary, and memories. My gratitude also goes out to the following persons: my parents, Don and Evelyn Cummings, for their enduring support; my advisor, Jane Hill, for all she taught and exposed me to; Jose Cuellar, who taught me to do fieldwork and encouraged my interest in the culture; Macario Saldate IV, for his support of the research; and my committee members, Dick Henderson and Tom Sheridan. I thank my colleagues at the Instituto de Investigaciones Históricas at the Universidad Autónoma de Baja California in Tijuana for introducing me to the Mexican sources on U.S.–Mexico border history. Armando Trujillo, Mauricio Mixco, Antonio Rios Bustamante, and the late Charles Polzer, S.J., provided input; the late Ricardo Aguilar Melantzón kindly gave me a copy of his Cuidad Juarez glossary manuscript before it was published (1989); and Warren Allison graciously provided photos of his father. Helen and Dick Henderson provided support throughout the research. Maria Rodriguez and Mary Contreras helped with transcription and with the manuscript, and Albert Moreno generously provided office space and use of a computer to finalize the manuscript.

The research was supported by funding from the United States Department of Education, Office of the Director for Bilingual Education and Minority Languages Affairs; a Sigma Xi Grant-in-Aid of Research; and the following scholarships at the University of Arizona: a Women's Studies Advisory Council Graduate Student Stipend, an Edward H. Spicer Research Award from the Department of Anthropology, a Mexican American Studies and Research Center Research Grant, a Graduate College Research Grant, and a Barbara Curran Fellowship.

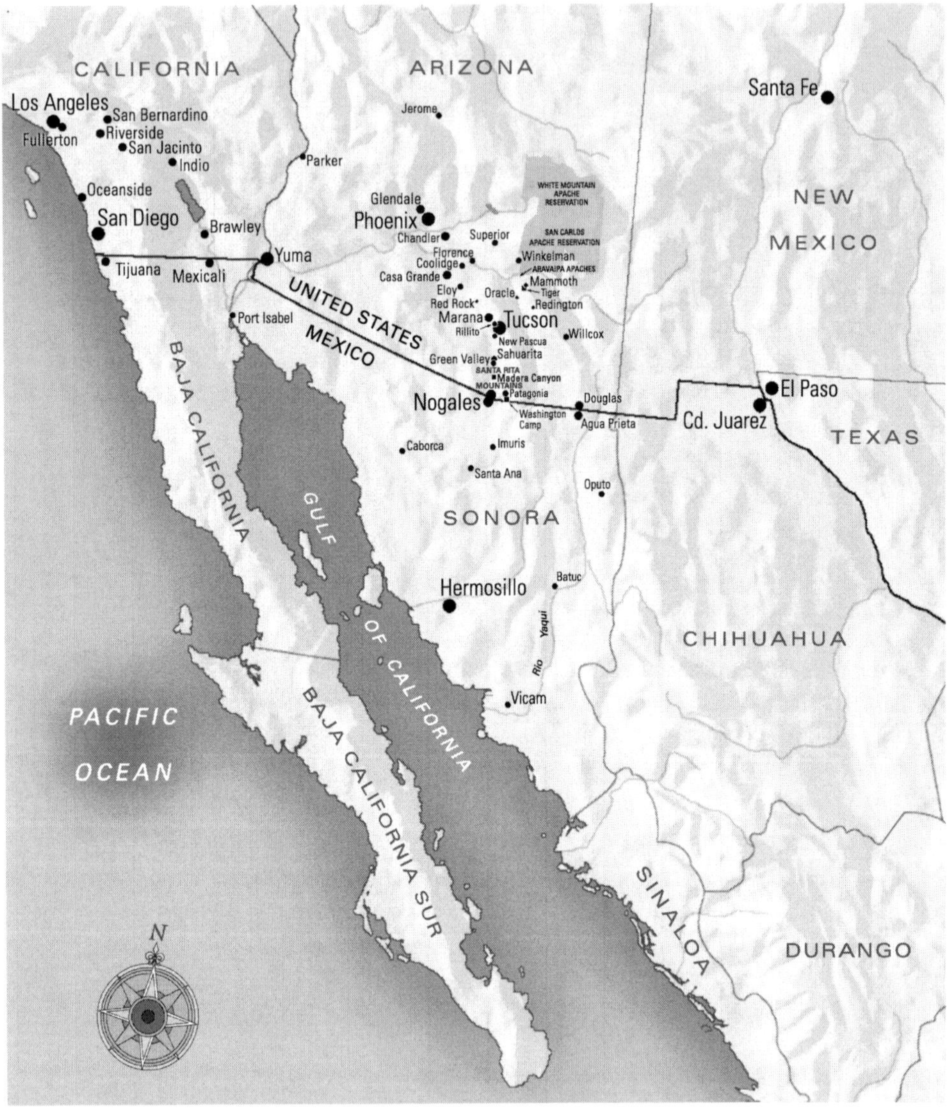

Figure 1. Map of the Greater Southwest with places mentioned by interviewees.

Introduction

The present study examines the *pachuco* phenomenon (*pachucos* were sometimes called zoot-suiters) as it developed in Tucson, Arizona. It combines ethnography, history, and sociolinguistics to contextualize the early years of the phenomenon, its diverse cultural roots, and its language variety in Tucson, situating the culture in the political, economic, and social contexts in which it is embedded. It examines the historical and cultural contexts of the culture's development and popularization, the arrival of the language variety in Tucson, and changes in socialization contexts, giving attention to internal variation in the culture. Family histories presented reveal that their economic and sociocultural activities both in Mexico and in the southwestern United States span indigenous lifeways, life in haciendas, in mining camps and towns, in subsistence agriculture, in labor on commercial farms, in ranch-hand work, in the military, and in urban employment in construction, service industries, small businesses, and factories.

The study is based on oral history, recollections, anecdotes, commentary, and linguistic observations of nineteen interviewees, and on extant literature and documentary sources about the culture. It is intended as a contribution to situated histories and ethnographies of the phenomenon. The study is based on research carried out in Tucson between 1984 and 1994 with ten female and nine male participants of Mexican, Apache, Mayo, Seri, Yaqui, and Spanish ancestry. Four of the consultants were born in the 1920s, five in the 1930s, and seven in the 1940s. Four teenagers and young adults (born 1966, 1967, 1968, and 1970) who were children and grandchildren of principal consultants were also interviewed. All but four of the interviewees were born in Tucson. Those four were born in towns in the region: Jerome, Redington, and Douglas, Arizona.

Over a period of five years, ongoing informal conversations with interviewees and others in the community about pachuco culture and language served as a prelude to recorded interviews. This was because when I first began to carry out the research and seek consultants, I found that many older people initially showed aversion to the topic, although at the same time there appeared to be much interest.

In 1991–92, formal tape-recorded interviews addressing life history and pachuco language and culture were carried out with the interviewees. Life history interviews were open-ended but elicited information on residential, occupational, educational, and linguistic history of family members. In the linguistic interviews, individuals, families and groups listened to a rare recording of Pachuco conversations made in Tucson by University of Arizona anthropologist George C. Barker in 1947.[1] Consultants commented extensively on the culture's creative, hybrid language variety. Their comments were simultaneously recorded on a second tape recorder. Language use in the interviews reflected the multiple varieties spoken in interviewees' communities and included standard and regional varieties of Spanish and English, Pachuco/*caló* (the language variety spoken by the pachucos), and Tucson's brand of code-switching.

As I conducted the research in the Tucson community, the cooperative construction of discourse and knowledge seemed to be the mode. People spoke with care, with awareness that theirs was not the only experience or perspective. They explicitly stated this, often couching their comments with a phrase such as, "Someone else might see it differently," thus placing their remarks in the context of their community's social conventions. There seemed to be an assumption that individuals possess partial knowledge; there was recognition of and respect for different perspectives and opinions. Authoritative statements or claims to definitive knowledge seemed absent. Even so, the comments, perspectives, and memories expressed often showed much agreement.

Ultimately, approximately fifty hours of tape-recorded interviews were collected. These were then transcribed. The interviews and the 1947 Barker recordings constitute the database. The five-year prelude of informal conversations also provided data and contextual information.

I was relatively familiar with Pachuco/caló and other registers of southwest Spanish because I had previously worked as a volunteer at an orphanage in northern Baja California, Mexico, in 1964, 1965, and 1972–73. The orphanage children used quite a bit of Pachuco/caló vocabulary, as did high school students I worked with in California in the Migrant Education program in the 1970s, so I had learned some vocabulary. I had also lived for a number of years in two of Tijuana's informal-sector and working-class neighborhoods while employed at the Universidad Autónoma de Baja California, commissioned to Mexico's Instituto Nacional de Antropología e Historia. Before beginning the formal research in Tucson in 1985, I had spent time in Tijuana learning the caló presently spoken by that city's *cholos* while carrying out research with those groups. I had also conducted research with contemporary cholo groups in Chihuahua and Ciudad Juarez in the state of Chihuahua, Mexico; in Nogales, Sonora, Mexico; El Paso, Texas; and Los Angeles, California. The Tijuana caló was unintelligible using my everyday border Spanish, with the exception of a few words and phrases. I later found that it was quite intelligible with the caló used in the Pachuco conversations of the 1947 Barker recordings.

In the United States the pachuco phenomenon has been described as a Mexican American subculture. Early pachuco forms probably jelled in the El Paso–Ciudad Juarez area between 1910 and 1920 and spread during subsequent migrations. The violence, upheaval, and famine in the wake of the Mexican Revolution of 1910 had occasioned large population displacements and migrations to the U.S.–Mexico border area, especially through El Paso, which at that time was a center of labor contracting for the western United States. The caló spoken in central Mexico probably came north with these migrations and combined with Southwest regional and border influences. In 1943, the so-called zoot-suit riots in Los Angeles brought national notoriety to the youth culture. Initially emerging in the United States in southwestern border towns, Pachuco forms have been present for years in Texas, New Mexico, Arizona, California, Colorado, Nevada, and the Midwest. Contemporary chuco and cholo forms have now appeared in diverse places distant from the border in the United States and in Mexico, where in addition to their occurrence in border towns and cities, they can be found in the states of Michoacán, Sinaloa, Chihuahua, and Zacatecas. For some years now, contemporary cholo forms have also been influencing youth-culture forms in Central America.

As I looked into the literature on Pachuco when beginning the Tucson research, I noted two major currents: one aligned with deviance perspectives and another that presents a cross-cultural focus on experience and identity. Works from the deviance perspective tend to identify as core elements of the pachuco phenomenon: lower socioeconomic class, criminality, maladjustment, a problematic nature, and in some cases, immorality (Bogardus 1943; Griffith [1948] 1973; Coltharp 1965; Alvarez 1967; Trejo 1968; Barrera Bassols 1979; Vigil 1988). Works comprising the second trend tend to stress history, social class, power relations, sociopolitical and economic processes, biculturalism, language, and the formation and maintenance of identity (Barker 1950; Gonzáles 1967; Trejo 1968 [Trejo has elements of both trends]; Saiz 1973; Madrid-Barela 1973; Trujillo 1974; Hinojos 1975; Ortega 1977; Moore 1978; Peñalosa 1980; Galindo 1981, 1992; Webb 1982; Sanchez 1983; Sanchez-Tranquilino 1987; Mazón 1984; Limón 1989; Sanchez-Tranquilino and Tagg 1992).

Many of the deviance-oriented approaches seem to aim to explain *why* the youth are deviant, taking deviance as a given. However, the construct of deviance itself must be scrutinized and contextualized, historically, socioculturally, and politically. Some studies on the pachuco phenomenon have sought subjects in jails and youth detention facilities. One must ask what effect that can have on a study's conclusions. One must also ask why there are so many minority youth, especially males, in jails and youth facilities in the first place. We must look candidly at the history of policing practices with these populations, at the history of institutional racism. One must also ask if it is just a coincidence that only groups of ethnic minority youth have been labeled "gangs." The deviance school of thought has had a profound influence on scholarship on pachuco and on how the culture has been perceived.

Any given focus, of course, may result in a particular characterization of a culture. For example, a focus on the hardcore gang element in contemporary Los Angeles cholo culture produces a snapshot that is not representative of most people conversant with the culture in the United States and Mexico. It is important not to extend the findings of such a focus to the culture as a whole and to all places, because that would be grossly inaccurate. Vigil points out that even in Los Angeles "many individuals copy the style without joining the gang" (1988:3).

The present study takes an anthropological approach, examining the pachuco phenomenon as a syncretic or hybrid culture, investigating its sociocultural and linguistic dynamics in historical perspective. The focus is on a specific locale and region: Tucson, Arizona, viewed in the context of the greater Southwest. Rather than depart from presumptions of deviance or a focus on the highly visible hardcore gang element, I focus on the more widespread and less sensational culture, which I view in the same way Ortega (1991) and others (Barker 1950; González 1967) have described the culture's language variety (*caló*): "It may be that a more significant distributive feature of Caló is not so much its real usage by Chicano youths and/or by Chicano gangs, and/or by Chicano criminals—granted these uses are empirically resolved—as much as the usage by a lower-class group, distinctly a working class" (Ortega 1991:xiii). In a number of chapters in the present study, contemporary cholo dynamics are mentioned for purposes of comparison with pachuco times to examine continuity and changes in customs, language, and ideology. All but two of the interviewees saw the two cultures (pachuco and cholo) as a continuum, with the cholo phenomenon being a contemporary form that grew out of the pachuco culture. The term *cholo* was adopted in California in the 1960s by youth following the pachuco tradition, as a label for that identity (Cuellar 1982:2).

A Stigmatized Culture

Some of the quasi-official discourse put forth on the origins or causes of *pachuquismo* in both Mexico and the United States are informed by deviance perspectives and contribute to stigmatizing the identity. In the United States, the existence of pachucos and pachucas has been attributed to crowded conditions, language problems, "normal" urban dynamics, and "incomplete acculturation." In Mexico the existence of pachucos has been attributed to cultural contamination (*contaminación cultural*) from the United States, along with other causes such as disintegration of the family, ignorance, lack of respect, and alcoholic, ignorant, or lazy parents (*El Mexicano* 1983 article). The identity is stigmatized in both countries.

To elucidate the origins of forms of stigma encountered by pachucos on both sides of the border, it helps to look at the region and populations in which the culture occurs. In the United States, origins of the stigma can be found in geographical and racial images and meanings. The region where the culture emerged in this country is the Southwest; the west, of course, was considered wild and uncivilized, the home of outlaws and savages. In popular terms, the relevant population is both "racially" and culturally "mixed," the latter being most readily apparent in its cryptic, hybrid language variety, which I refer to as Pachuco/caló, after Galindo (1992). The element of lower socioeconomic class also contributes to the stigma.

In Mexico, geographical images also inform quasi-official characterizations of the culture, lending stigma. The population in which it has developed is in the north, the land of the Chichimecas: the less civilized, nomadic peoples. For Spain, the north was considered the wild, barbarous frontier. Social-class origins occasion much stronger stigma in Mexico than in the United States, and cultural hybridity lends stigma in the sense that Mexican culture has been "contaminated" by elements of Anglo-Saxon origin.

Racial and cultural status, along with social class, are reflected in the term *cholo* itself, which, as we saw, was adopted in California in the 1960s by youth following the pachuco tradition, as a label for their identity (Cuellar 1982:2). In 1571, Fray Alonso de Molina, in his Nahuatl vocabulary (*Vocabulario en lengua castellana y mexicana y mexicana y castellana*), defined the word *xolo* as "slave," "servant," or "waiter." The Porrúa Dictionary defines *cholo*, as used in the Americas, as "a civilized Indian" or "a half-breed or mestizo of a European father and Indian mother." The word has historically been used along the borderland as a derogatory term to mean lower-class Mexican migrants, and in the rest of Latin America to mean an acculturating Indian or peasant (Cuellar 1982:3).

To explain the stigma accruing to the Indian dimension of the term *cholo*, it is useful to examine another word containing assessments of racial and cultural identity: *indio*, the Spanish word for "Indian," which in Mexico conveys two principal images. First, there is the image of Indian identity communicated in nationalist discourse taught to children in elementary school about the brave and noble Indian heritage of Mexicans. However, another definition seemed more pervasive on an everyday basis in popular discourse, at least in Baja California when I lived there in the 1970s and '80s, and that is the use of the term *indio* as a common insult to mean dumb, uncivilized, or unsophisticated. This is also implied in widely used popular phrases in northwest Mexico such as *acaba de bajar del cerro* (he/she just came down out of the hills), or *trae el nopal en la frente* (he/she has the image of a prickly pear cactus on his/her forehead). The cactus, of course, is one of the elements in the symbol of the Aztecs and appears in the national seal on the

Mexican flag. These phrases ostensibly refer to Mexican identity but do not appear to be used to refer to persons of primarily European descent and cultural background. Rather, they refer to the peasant population of the ranchos. Despite, or because of, its long history of denigrating semantics, the term *cholo* was turned on its head and used as a symbol of pride in the context of the ethnic power movements of the 1960s.

But who are the cholos' predecessors, the pachucos, and what are the regional contributions to the twentieth-century hybrid hip culture that has been alternately characterized as degenerate, criminal, ridiculous, or savagely violent? In addition to the peninsular and Gypsy roots often cited briefly in the literature with reference to the culture's language variety, we will see that some regional contributions to the phenomenon can be discerned through an examination of the culture's key words and symbols, some of which contain political commentary and cultural critique.

Analysis

To elucidate aspects of Pachuco culture and interactions recounted by Barker participants and those of this research, I use theoretical tools in linguistic anthropology, especially the concepts of metapragmatics and indexicality (Silverstein 1976, 1985) and dialogicality (Bakhtin [1929] 1984) to explore the interpretive frameworks used by people as they discussed history, culture, language and identity.

To understand how consultants historicize the pachuco youth culture in talk and the terms of their engagement with their social and linguistic traditions, I looked at Pachuco/caló and other metapragmatic framing, together with other methods of discourse analysis. The conversations of the Barker recordings and consultants' commentaries were analyzed using Silverstein's concept of the relationship between metapragmatic usage in the language and "the ideological and cognitive strategies that speakers employ in culturally conceptualized situations of speaking" (1985:138). Silverstein describes metapragmatics as a metalinguistic domain that signals usage in communicative situations. He states that,

> metapragmatic usage in a language frequently centers on seeming $functional_1$ descriptors of what people use the language for, constituting a lexical set of verba of saying or

> communicating (verba dicendi). These can, for example, range from quotation-framing verbs, that can take locutionary complements (He went, "Wo-o-ow!") through those that can take finite, propositional that-clauses (He argued that the earth is flat) or infinitive complements (He asked [for me] to leave) to those that can exhaustively describe an event, usually in "illocutionary"—or even "perlocutionary"—terms (He protested too much). (1985:133)

I have found the examination of such metapragmatic constructions an ideal tool for looking at pachuco-defined situations of speaking: they describe those situations from "a certain privileged perspective" (Silverstein 1985:135). However, whereas Silverstein found primarily quotation-framing verbs as metapragmatic descriptors in Chinook discourse, the descriptors in the conversations of the Barker tape and in the various language varieties used by interviewees are of two types. Quotation-framing verbs and reported speech are important but are combined with something akin to the last, "exhaustive" type of metapragmatic descriptor. These appear primarily as verb phrases describing verbal strategies and modes of interaction. The Pachuco/caló descriptors label interactional strategies that include speech but do not refer to speech exclusively. They appear in the discourse after the recounting of an interactive event through reported speech as a sort of summary encapsulation of aspects of the interaction.

The metapragmatic descriptors in the conversations point out particular *instances* of these Pachuco interactional strategies, which, upon examination, reveal examples of interactors (often culturally labeled) and information about the context of that interaction. This can include details about time, place, surrounding circumstances, and motivations, and even information about interactors' language use in the particular context. This, because pachuco history has been played out in and through these culturally labeled interactions by the culturally defined persons involved in the action. In discussions with interviewees about the descriptors and particular interactions, they were able to make explicit indexical information not apparent to an outside observer.

I have organized interviewees' comments on various topics by generation: participants who were teenagers before or during World War II, those who were teens immediately after the war and through the 1950s, and those who were teenagers in the 1960s and

'70s. In this way I have tried to illustrate the distinct physical and social environments each group experienced as young people. Most participants have been given pseudonyms. The appendix provides a one-page, at-a-glance listing of their pseudonyms and dates and places of birth. When Spanish or code-switching were used during interviews, I have given translations immediately following the quotes in the text.

PACHUCAS AND PACHUCOS IN TUCSON
Situated Border Lives

1

Pre–World War II Teens

In the recollections people of this generation shared of local landmarks and social customs, memory is strongly attached to place, especially to public centers of community social life like *la acequia* (the irrigation canal) and dance and sports venues like El Westside, Soto's Ranch, El Blue Moon, Arviso's, La Alianza, and Los Pinos, places that seemed tied to the community's group identity. The term *barrio* (neighborhood) reflects such a place, with the sense of community it embodies.

Many of the older people fondly recalled the intimacy and sense of community in the residential areas of the old barrios. Louie described Barrio Anita's residents, saying, "Most of the people were . . . living there for years and years and years. . . . Everybody knew everybody else." All of the older folks remembered sleeping outside in the summertime. (Younger generations have childhood memories of older persons continuing to sleep outside or on screened porches even after evaporative coolers came into use.)

Residential neighborhoods were segregated up until the late 1960s. Dora described them as "*americano*, Mexican, [and] black neighborhoods." Martín mentioned different barrios primarily inhabited by Yaqui Indian residents:

> Tuvimos diferentes barrios, pero yo no los miré, los barrios esos. Los conozco ahora porque mi ma me decía, "Mira; aquí estaba el barrio Pascua antes." Estábamos en la Speedway, luego nos fuimos pa'llá pa'l lado dea donde está el overpass ahora, el, ¿qué es? ah, Tierra Floja, le decían. Y luego de allí nos cambiámos otra vez pa'cá. . . . Pues aquí es donde desparramaron toda la gente. Unos se quedaron. Otros se fueron, y así. . . . Y al fin se quedaron aquí. Se'stablecieron aquí pa siempre.
>
> (We had different barrios, but I didn't see them, those barrios. I know about them *now* because my mother used to say to me, "Look, this is where Barrio Pascua was before." We were on Speedway, then we went over there, to where the [freeway] overpass is now . . . Tierra Floja, they called it. And then from there we moved over here again [Old Pascua]. . . . Well, this is where they scattered all the people. Some stayed; others left. . . . And in the end, they stayed here. They established themselves here permanently.)

Martín noted the unique cultural and religious customs of his local community, Old Pascua, especially the Yaqui Easter ceremonies in which he participated for years.

Dora recalled seeing, as a small girl, a Tucson with wooden sidewalks and iron hitching posts for the horses. She had seen the ruins of the walls of *la catedral,*

> Ahí donde está el Community Center. En ruinas eran; ya no estaban altas. Ya eran pedazos, no más. . . . [Y] al pie del "A" Mountain estaba un convento de monjas. Tenían hospital, hospital de caridad. Lo comenzaron unas monjas que vinieron de allá del East.
>
> (There where the Community Center is. . . . They weren't high any more. They were already just pieces, that's all. . . . [And] there was a convent r un by nuns [from back east] at the foot of "A" Mountain. They had a hospital, a charity hospital.[1])

Delia remembered the tree-lined Santa Cruz River running near the base of "A" Mountain in the 1920s, when that area was brush-covered land (*monte*) with no houses.

Figure 2. Fourth Avenue and Ninth Street, Tucson, in 1895. (Arizona Historical Society, AHS Photo Number 47858)

A number of people described downtown Tucson as they remembered it before and during World War II. Dora recalled, "a very small town. [It] was just the downtown area, which was Congress, Meyer, Broadway, and Pennington [streets]; that was all there was. There were no shopping malls or anything. . . . There was no Community Center. Right there where the Community Center is, there was El Charro, a very large restaurant. And the Peking . . . the Ruben [Ruben Gold] furniture store, the Rialto Theater, the Plaza, the Fox, the State, and the Paramount. There were theaters in all of that area. And Jácomes, Sears, Montgomery Ward's, Penny's, all of that." Trolleys on tracks "like the ones in San Francisco" provided public transportation.

Lydia described downtown Tucson by the early 1940s with its business street, Congress. "Everything was really nice. They had Woolworth's, McLellan's, the Kresses; they had the Thrifty, Walgreens. . . . You didn't have to go so far shopping like you do now."

The Social Scene

Many older interviewees recalled family picnics in parks and various places around town as a popular social and recreational activity. Dora recalled, as a child, going on Sundays with her family in a horse-drawn wagon to a small ranch at Tanque Verde (now within Tucson's urban sprawl). It took quite a while to make the trip. The ranch produced vegetables: chiles, onions, tomatoes, melons, and carrots. Her family would picnic, visit with friends that owned the ranch, and pick fresh vegetables from the fields. Usually their friends would kill a calf and have a barbecue. The women would converse and the men would "drink their beer." There were other little ranches in the area, some of which had only three or four cows and small fields. Tanque Verde proper was described as a small barrio where the people that worked on the surrounding ranches lived. Dora's father later bought a Fordito in which they continued to make Sunday trips to Tanque Verde.

La Acequia

Until the early 1950s an irrigation canal (*acequia*) ran through Tucson from near the base of "A" Mountain, north toward Marana. An earthen ditch ten to fifteen feet wide lined with trees, it served primarily to carry water to cotton fields and other agricultural lands, although the water was also used by residents along the canal. Older people often mentioned it in their accounts of social life in Tucson. Martín and Carlos said families would come from church on Sundays, walk along the canal and socialize. Families would pack a lunch and picnic there, especially during the Easter holidays.

Two women happily recalled the yearly "Día de San Juan," a day when young people would go on an outing to the canal.[2] Dora said,

> Así les llamaban, "Las Pompitas," porque todo el tiempo estaba la pompa sacando agua y ahí se iba por una acequia. . . .

Figure 3 (facing page). Tucson woman washing clothes in the Santa Cruz River below the Convent of San Augustín del Pueblito, 1891. (Arizona Historical Society/Tucson, AHS Photo Number 21969)

> Corría pa la Marana, pero corría por aquí por un lado del freeway . . . corría esa acequia. La gente se iba, iba a acampar ahí. Pa'l Día de San Juan todas las muchachas íbamos a la acequia a las cuatro de la manaña. Llevaban música, llevaban sandías, y ¡uuy!, era una fiesta, el Día de San Juan. . . . Yo fui alguna vez con un montón de muchachas, porque sola no me hubieran dejado ir.
>
> (They called it Las Pompitas because the pump was continually drawing water that went off down the canal. . . . It ran toward Marana, but over here to one side of [where] the freeway [is now], that canal did. People would go to picnic there. On San Juan Day all of us girls would go to the canal at four in the morning. They would take music, watermelons, and ooh! it was a fiesta, San Juan Day! . . . I went once with a bunch of girls, because they wouldn't have let me go alone.)

An orchestra of live musicians accompanied the girls on this occasion in the late 1920s or early '30s. The acequia and San Juan Day came up again when Lydia mentioned some old photographs of Tucson.

> Have you ever been to Carrillo School? . . . Inside, they've got [pictures of] the school and the first people who went there and the river that was in the back, la acequia, cuando se bañaban en el Día de San Juan [the irrigation canal, when they would go in the water on San Juan Day]. They used to go over there. . . . They would party. I mean, nobody would bother you, throw you in the water. . . . We'd go early and pass the day there. Take a bath. . . . It wasn't deep. It was about [indicates two to three feet]. . . . The kids would make a tire from one tree and then swing to the other side. When you fell in, you fell in. I remember. What a time it was!

I asked Carlos about the demise of the canal. He remembered that there had been an old man who used to take care of the ditch. He would walk along it and keep it cleaned out. People who lived along the canal gave him food. The ditch fell into disuse, he said, "when the city came in." That was in the 1950s when the city installed pipes to carry the water. There had also been a number of drownings in the canal, over the years. Today, there are still some big, dead trees standing along the route the ditch used to take.

Soto's and Other Dance Places

Most individuals who were teenagers before World War II spoke animatedly of going to family dances as young people. Many of these dances were held outdoors with live music. Dora recalled Arviso's, a place "way out on Benson Highway."

> Arviso's era un baile al aire libre. . . . ¡Uuy! Ese, sí, me encantaba porque a mi papá también le gustaba ir a las carreras de caballo y nos llevaba. Pos, nosotros bailábamos y él allá en las carreras.
>
> ([It] was an open-air dance. . . . Ooh! I really loved it because my father also liked to go to the horse races and he would take us. Well, we would dance and he would be out there at the races.)

This combination of a sporting event and dance held at the same place was popular at a number of Tucson entertainment spots. Louie spoke of his social life as a young man living in Mammoth: "We used to come here [to Tucson] maybe every two, three months . . . to the baseball games or the boxing. . . . [I would come with] guys . . . that used to work up there in Tiger. Where San Manuel is now, there was a mine named Tiger. And there were a lot of people there who used to come down. Baseball games or football and dances and whatever."

Rudy's uncle had been a jockey at local horse races in Tucson. Rudy recalled that "back in those times Rillito was very popular. Rillito, Westside, Soto's Ranch; I remember all that. . . . [Soto's Ranch] was a place where they'd meet and all the best horses would, you know, like a horse show. It was like a, well a horse track and stuff like that, but all the rancheros would bring their best horses and do it like a challenge . . . every other Sunday. And then they had ball games and baseball games. Teams from Mexico would come over. It was like an *outing* on a Sunday. Everybody would head over to Soto's Ranch."

Some folks recalled a place called the Lakeside. It was located in downtown Tucson on Congress, by an artificial lake (*pila*) where there were boats and outdoor dances were held. Martín and Carlos also recalled a large open-air patio where dances were held in Old Pascua when they were young. People came from all around, Mexicanos, Yaquis, and blacks. Young men came to the dances from Fort Lowell, Tanque Verde, and la South Side, among other places. Carlos described the Tanque Verde and Fort Lowell fellows as "puros [just] . . . cowboys and stuff." The dances were held on Saturdays, although Martín said they didn't always attend. "Sometimes we had to pick [cotton] because we didn't make enough money." These men also mentioned dances at the Blue Moon and the Del Río. Lydia described the music at the Blue Moon as a mix of Lalo Robles, jitterbug, and *cumbias.*[3] Dora named many places around town where dances had been held:

> Allá donde está el Desert Inn, allí estaba un salón grandote que se llamaba Riverside. Ahí hacían muy bonitos bailes, tardeadas, y luego el Blue Moon. Ese estaba allá donde está el Tucson House. . . . Allá estaba el Blue Moon. Y luego estaba La Alianza en seguida, enfrente del Plaza, por la Congreso. Ese era otro baile, La Alianza, muy de pipa y pompa. . . . Y luego cuando se quemó el Blue Moon hicieron El Casino. . . . Y luego comenzaron bailecitos para acá, y bailecitos por El Latino, Los Pinos, El Sahuaro. . . . Y luego estaba La Pasadita. Después hicieron La Pasadita aquí en la veintinueve, que todavía está el building y está el corral donde está la plataforma donde hacían los bailes, también al aire libre. Y El Westside, también pa'cá pa por la Doce pero más pa'dentro pa'llá, que ahora está una estación de radio allí. Allí está El Westside, también al aire libre. Muy bonito, ¿no?; sí. Ahora ya no. Ya no está igual como estaba antes.
>
> (Over there where the Desert Inn is, right there was a great big dance hall that was called "Riverside." They had very nice dances there, *tardeadas* [afternoon/tea dances], and then the Blue Moon. That one was over there where the Tucson House is. . . . And then the Alianza was next door to it, across from the Plaza [theater] on Congress. That was another dance [place], the Alianza; [it was] very fancy. . . . Then when the Blue Moon burned down they built El Casino [Ballroom]. . . . And then there began to be little dances here and there . . . The Latin Club, Los Pinos, El

> Saguaro. . . . And then there was La Pasadita. Afterward, they built La Pasadita here on Twenty-ninth Street. The building is still there and the fence where the platform is where they held the dances; they were held outdoors. And the Westside, also over here along Twelfth [Avenue] but set back over there, where there is a radio station now. That is where the Westside was, which was also an outdoor place. Yes, it was really nice. But not any more. It's not the same now as it was before.)

Carlos said the present Del Río Ballroom was called Los Pinos at one time, for some pine trees that were there. Lydia recalled dancing at La Pasadita on Twenty-ninth Street, saying, "they'd have the dance outside. . . . That's when they'd charge ten cents a dance. They'd buy tickets to dance. . . . The Blue Moon was the same thing for a while." When Martín and Carlos recalled dances at La Pasadita and El Westside, they seemed to savor the words as they pronounced them, as if carried back by nostalgia. "El Westside estaba acá en la Veintinueve, pero puros cowboys allí. Puro ranchero." (The Westside was over here on Twenty-ninth Street. They were all cowboys over there. All rancheros.)

Lydia spoke of dances during World War II when she was fifteen or sixteen years old, out of school and working at a soda fountain. She would go with a group of six or seven girlfriends.

> We'd go to the Lakeside. . . . What's that place right up here where they used to have the wrestling matches, near Congress, years ago? . . . Well, in the back they had, they used to call it the Lakeside. They had a lake. Then they had like a bar. But they wouldn't sell to us 'cause, you know, we weren't of age. We'd just go sit there and kick back. We'd go with other people, older guys or girls. They'd drink; we'd drink sodas and potato chips and if you got a chance, we'd sneak a drink.

Lydia and her female friends would walk home at night after a dance. "[It] would be over about 9:30, 10:30. . . . And we walked home from the Blue Moon, from where the Tucson House is on Miracle Mile. And from there we used to walk all the way down Main till we got home." Other women of her generation also spoke of walking to and from social events at night without fearing for their safety.

Social Dynamics and Courtship

Pre–World War II youth lived in an environment of rather strict social customs overseen by parents and the community in general. Chaperones were the rule for girls, and there appears to have been a marked degree of gender segregation at social events. Dora described dances during the 1930s:

> Entonces se usaba que los muchachos no se sentaban con las muchachas en las mesas. No se sentaban. Los muchachos estaban parados, todos allá, y las muchachas sentadas en las mesas. Cuando tocaban una pieza venían y sacaban a la muchacha a bailar, pero no se sentaban con uno.
>
> (Back then it was the custom that boys didn't sit with the girls at the tables. They didn't sit down. The boys were all standing over there, and the girls were sitting at the tables. When they would play a song, they would come and ask the girl to dance, but they didn't sit with you.)

Lydia noted the social necessity of going out with a parent or chaperone. "You know, [back] then we would go to the dance, and we would always have to be accompanied by an adult. It was twenty-one to get in. . . . [My friend's] mother used to take her daughters and me to the dance. I used to spend Saturday night, and Sunday she'd take us to a tardeada (tea dance) to the Blue Moon. Otherwise you couldn't get in."

Dora elaborated on socializing and courting when I mentioned to her that although her family and others allowed their daughters to have a *novio* (boyfriend), some women's fathers had prohibited this.

> Sí, pero todo el tiempo estaba mi madre ahí. Pero no me dejaban salir sola con él. Cuando iba al baile, si mi mamá no me podía llevar, la señora vecina me llevaba. . . . Y luego en ese tiempo los muchachos no eran adelantados. Respetaban a uno; respetaban a uno. No como ahora. Ahora las muchachas ya no más tienen doce años y ya andan con el novio ahí solas. A mí, pos, de la escuela nunca me encaminó un muchacho. Nunca me encaminó un muchacho. Tenía que llegar sola a mi casa y *sola.*
>
> (Yes, that is true, but my mother was always there; they didn't let me go out with him alone. When I went to the dance, if

> my mother couldn't take me, the neighbor lady would take me. . . . And at that time the boys weren't so forward. They would respect you; they respected you.[4] Not like now. Now the girls, they're only twelve and they're already out with their boyfriend alone. Myself, well, no boy ever walked me home from school. No boy ever walked me home. I had to come home by myself, *by myself*.)

Lydia made a related comment about young men's behavior at these community social events. "Of course the guys would drink and all of that, *pero* [but] they weren't as rough as they are now."

Martín and Carlos spoke of dating and what interaction was like with girls' mothers, from a young man's perspective. Martín recalled,

> Antes te ponían cita, las mamases de, "¡A tal hora me la vas a trae!" Y a esa hora tenías que estar allí con ella. . . . ¡Y ojalá y estuvieras!

> (Before, the mothers would set a time. "You bring her back to me at such and such a time!" And you had to be there with her at that time. . . . And you'd better hope you were there!)

He also spoke of a culturally specific experience he had as a young man, when a friend (M3) present at the interview brought up the subject of arranged marriages.

> **M3**: ¿Te acuerdas, Martín? ¿Te acuerdas que en los tiempos de antes los padres a los muchachos los casaban con los que querían, ¿verdad?
>
> **M:** and **C:** Sí.
>
> **M:** Ese era el estilo de los Yaquis, antes. . . . A mí me querían casar asina, sin que yo tuviera nada que ver con la muchacha. Sí, la conocía, ¿no?, porque era de aquí. "Nooo," le dije. "Yo no. Yo voy a buscar la que a *mí* me guste, no la que le guste a *usted*." También el indio, el Apache, e' la misma. . . . Le gusta aquella muchacha, y ellos la piden al papá, y luego cuando ya crecen, entonces se casan. . . . Pero ahora no.
>
> **L:** ¿Eso no le causó problemas a Usted en su familia?, ¿que ellos querían en esa forma y Usted no quería?

M: Sí, también. Pero yo no quise. ¿Cómo van a casarme con una que no andaba yo?

C: Que no la *querías.*

M: No la quería.

C: No, no puede.

M: Y ésa tenián, antes.

(**M3:** Do you remember, Martín? Do you remember that in the old times the parents married their children to the ones they chose for them? Isn't that true?

M and **C:** Yes.

M: That was the Yaquis' way, before. . . . They wanted to marry me that way, and I didn't even have anything to do with the girl.[5] I knew her, of course, because she was from here [his neighborhood, Old Pascua]. "Nooo," I told her [his mother]. "Not me. I'm going to find the one that *I* like, not the one that *you* like." The Apache Indians also had the same custom. . . . They like that girl and they ask the father for her, and then when they are grown up, then they get married. But they don't do that anymore.

L: Didn't that cause problems for you in your family that they wanted to marry you that way and you didn't want to?

M: Yes, it did. But I didn't want to. How can they marry me to someone I wasn't going with?

C: That you didn't *love.*

M: I didn't love her.

C: No, no you can't.

M: And that was the custom before.)

Carlos added that they imposed the girl on the young man. Martín had preferred the girl he finally married to the one his mother recommended.

Such "modern" attitudes can be seen in events in other people's young lives, especially during World War II and immediately thereafter. In a segment from the 1947 Barker recordings a young girl defied her mother's mandate at a dance, not to dance with a particular young man. Finally, the young couple brazenly ran away from the dance. Hearing this story led Carlos to tell how he had gotten together with his wife after being rebuffed by one of her uncles.

> Yo también me llevé a la mujer. . . . Y el tío no me quería y me corría. Yo le dije, "Usted no manda aquí. Mi suegro manda." "Ah, entonces 'stá bueno," dice. "¿Puedo llegar?" le dije. "Seguro," dice. Así no tienes que andar escondiéndote, tu sabes, hiding behind the doors or the whatever. . . . Yo me junté con ella, ¿no?, en la casa. En la cantina le dije a su papá, "Yo me voy a juntar con ella," le dije. "'Stá bueno," me dijo. "No más mantenla, es todo."
>
> (I eloped with my wife, too. . . . Her uncle didn't like me and he used to chase me away. I told him, "You're not in charge here. My father-in-law is in charge." "Oh, all right," he says. "May I come in?" I asked. "Certainly," he says. That way you don't have to go around hiding behind the doors or the whatever. . . . I started living with her at her house. At the bar I told her father, "I am going to start living with her." "All right," he said to me. "Just support her, that's all.")

His wife was fourteen at the time and had their first child at age fifteen. Here we see an example of what began as what Anglo society calls common-law marriage. This mode of marriage was not unusual or necessarily scandalous. In this case the young man followed the prevalent social rules and attempted to visit with the young woman at her home. He did not like the idea of "hiding." Before living with the girl, he consulted with her father and received a tacit blessing for the relationship, at which time he was apprised of his responsibility.

Also after listening to the story about the mother's objections to a dance partner in the Barker recordings, Aurora told of her aunt's elopement. It occurred after the suitor was rejected by her aunt's father.

> My aunt, my *tía* was, like, fifteen when she left with my *tío* [uncle] . . . and he was a pachuco. And my grandparents didn't like him at all. And he went to talk to my grandfather to see if he could go see my tía and visit her and be her boyfriend. And my grandfather said, "No, and stay away from her," you know, "I don't want you around or anything." But she was too young; she was like fourteen, fifteen years old. . . . But my tío didn't stay away from her. So one night he just came and took her! The only one that knew about it was my mom, because my tía told my mom. She told her that she was

> going to leave with my uncle. . . . I just know that my mom was the only one that knew that she had left. And then they had a big commotion about it. My grandfather got his rifle, and then he found them over there in [place-name]. But he [the suitor] was working. . . . Then they brought them over to Tucson and made them get married.

Here again, the suitor made an initial attempt to abide by the rules, going to the home to ask permission to see the girl. Elopement appears as a last resort when good-faith efforts have failed. This particular story also demonstrates other conventions surrounding the traditional elopement process. The aunt tells a female relative that she is going to leave with the young man. This establishes consent on her part so that the young man may not be later accused of abduction, rape, etc. Even so, many women and men of this generation, when telling of such elopements, continue to use phrases like "he came and took her" or "*se la llevó*" (he took her away), which don't foreground consent.

The Early History of Pachuco Youth in Tucson

Unlike many published sources on the pachuco phenomenon that date it to the 1940s, this study's eldest participants dated the youth culture in Tucson to the late 1920s and early 1930s. The earliest description of pachucos in the interviews dates to approximately 1929, precisely the time of the disastrous stock market crash and the beginning of the Great Depression. It was a time of widespread unemployment, but especially for ethnic minorities; a time of increased anti-Mexican sentiment and mass deportations.[6] Louie suggested that for historical purposes, the heyday of the pachuco era could be defined as 1935 to 1945. He described early pachucos as mostly Mexican American. A number of individuals mentioned that Indians were among the early pachucos; some said the Yaqui pachucos of Old Pascua were among the earliest. Martín and Carlos identified themselves as Seris. Louie recalled a few early Yavapai Apache pachucos. Even at the time of the interview in 1985, Bob said he would see older Indian men who still dressed pachuco and had the distinctive walk.

Delia described pachucos she saw in 1929, when she was nine years old. They lived in makeshift camps on the Santa Cruz river at the foot of "A" Mountain, as the homeless do now. She said they would steal chickens from people's yards, take them to their camp, and roast them over an open fire on a rotisserie made of sticks. "They weren't kids; they were big. Eighteen, seventeen, nineteen, twenty." When I asked her opinion on pachucos' reputation, she responded,

> Pues, eran malos porque agarraban, como si tu lavas, ¿no?, tienden la ropa; ellos vienen y agarran. Eso era lo malo, porque, pues, no agarraban dinero ni nada. Pues agarraban un trabajito y no más, y ya. Como barrer yardas de escuelas. . . . Pues ellos iban y agarraban sábanas y agarraban fundas y los trapos más viejos de ellos, los lavaban, ¿no?, en una piedra en el río; corría el río ahí, todavía entonces. Y los lavaban y los secaban en los trees asina. Y luego los cortaban, los Levis, y todos muy viejos, ¿no?, y luego hacían almohadas a mano. . . . Iban mucho a la escuela, ¿no? Hacían lo que tenían que hacer, ¿no? Iban muy serios, muy buenos; parecía que no eran pachucos, pero, sí eran, porque eran pachucos.
>
> (Well, they were bad because, like if you wash [and] hang out the clothes, they come and take them. That was the bad thing, because they didn't take money or anything. They would get a little odd job, that's all, like sweeping school yards. . . . Well, they would go and steal sheets and pillow cases and their oldest rags, they would wash them on a rock in the river; the river was still running there at that time. And they would dry them in the trees. Then they would cut the Levis and all, the old ones and make pillows by hand. . . . They went to the school a lot. They did what they were supposed to do. They were very serious, very good; it didn't seem like they were pachucos, but yes, they were.)

Delia's daughter Aurora asked her how she knew they were pachucos. She replied, "By the way they talked." She also said they wore very baggy pants, and their hair was long in the back.

All the earliest accounts of pachuco males and females given by interviewees foreground use of the language more than a distinctive dress style, suggesting that early pachuco identity was manifested in linguistic practice. Three persons who worked with Barker dated the language in Tucson to at least 1933. Since this predated the apex of the classic dress style, Barker concluded that the language "predates the pachucos themselves" (1950: 21). However, older individuals interviewed in this study consistently referred to people who spoke the language between 1929 and 1935 (before the distinctive dress style became prevalent) as "pachucos" and "pachucas." Louie's older brother, who was about fifteen years old in 1935, spoke the language. However, Louie said that "the guys from the mining towns, they didn't dress like regular pachucos until after that fad got to them." When asked if his older brothers had dressed pachuco-style and influenced his taste in clothes, he responded,

> No, no, because when we, my brothers were growing up, my oldest brother, he wore bell-bottoms. When the bell-bottoms came out the first time, they came out in the '30s, late '20s and early '30s. My brother, he'd be about seventy-five, seventy-six now [in 1990, the year of the interview], so, and he started another style, instead of what we've got. But I think that, like, the style changed; the people that go with the style, they changed with the style, whatever.

I asked Martín, who was fifteen in 1940, if his generation was the first generation of pachucos or if there had been others before.

> **M:** Pues, ya había. Antes, había otros *antes* de nosotros, porque pues, yo los miré a ésos. Ya'staban mayores ya, cuando nosotros oíamos a ellos.
>
> **L:** ¿Y eran ellos gente de acá también, de Tucson?
>
> **M:** Diferentes partes. De Tejas, de California, había. Venían pa'cá a dar la vuelta, también.
>
> (**M:** Well, there already were others *before* us, because I saw them. They were already older when we used to hear them.
>
> **L:** Were they from Tucson, too?
>
> **M:** Different places. There were ones from Texas, from California. They would come here just traveling around.)

During the Depression, many pachucos and a multitude of other young men joined the government-sponsored Civilian Conservation Corps (CCC) to make a living.[7] Lydia's older brother, a sharp, pachuco-style dresser in the late 1930s, went to the Corps camps in the 1930s, as did Louie's older brother. Louie recalled, "When he

Figure 4. CCC (Civilian Conservation Corps) Camp in Southern Arizona, 1933. (Arizona Historical Society, AHS Photo Number 98886)

came to the CCC camps, he never went home again. He stayed in the CCC camps. Then he went to work at Superior [Arizona]; and then when the war broke out he went to live in Oakland, and there was a lot of pachucos in Oakland."

Early Pachucos' Appearance, Demeanor, and Reputation

A number of interviewees said that many early, pre–World War II pachuco males and females tattooed a small cross on the hand, at the juncture of the thumb and forefinger. Some of the earliest tattooed a cross on the forehead and/or chin, just below the lower lip. While living in Tucson, I had noticed that the ceremonial masks of Yaqui *pascola* dancers carry crosses in precisely those positions, crosses that are said to serve as protection for the dancers.[8] A formée cross is also found on the inside of each Yaqui ceremonial *chapayeka* mask "where it touches the forehead" (Painter 1986:213). According to Painter, who wrote extensively on Yaqui culture, pascolas and chapayekas need this protection because they are in an especially liminal, and thus vulnerable, position during ceremonies, being the simultaneous embodiment of two opposing systems (of good and evil; God and Satan). Culturally speaking, pachuco youth found themselves in an analogous situation.

During an interview, I told Martín what I had noticed and wondered aloud whether the early pachucos' forehead and chin tattoos might not have something to do with the crosses on the pascola masks. He nodded and answered, "I think so." I mentioned that Painter said the crosses were believed to protect the bearer and asked, "Did they [the pachucos] believe it was protection? Or what did it represent?" Martín could not resist making a joke:

> **M:** Representaba la "P."
> **L:** ¿La "P"?
> **M:** Sí. "Pendejo." [L laughs] Los que se creían muy chingones traían éso.
>
> (**M:** It represented a "P."
> **L:** A "P"?
> **M:** Yes. "Pendejo" [stupid, lit.: cuckold]. [L laughs] The ones that thought they were real "bad" had that [tattoo].)

Interviewees' comments clearly indicate that the cross tattoos date to the early, pre–World War II pachucos. It is probable that their placement and function, in some cases, were related to syncretic indigenous beliefs and practices.[9]

In addition to the Yaqui religious practice, according to nineteenth-century accounts, some Hermanos Penitentes also tattooed a cross on the forehead (Weigle 1976:91, 257).[10] Commonly called "the Penitentes," La Fraternidad Piadosa de Nuestro Padre Jesus Nazareno (the Pious Fraternity of Our Father Jesus Nazarite) is a lay religious organization related to the Roman Catholic Church in the southwestern United States, principally in northern New Mexico and southern Colorado (Weigle 1976:xvii). The brotherhood's observances involved rituals such as extended rosary services (*rosarios*), Way of the Cross processions (Via Crucis), and penitential devotions, primarily flagellation and cross-bearing. The practices have clear precedents in the history of Spanish Catholicism and its mystical, penitential, and especially Franciscan traditions. Such lay associations of the pious were common in Spain from the twelfth century, and many were established in the New World colonies (Weigle 1976:xviii).

During the second half of the nineteenth century and the early twentieth century under United States political control of New Mexico, as an insignia of membership the Hermanos Penitentes cut a seal (*sello*) or obligation (*obligación*) into the back of initiates with sharp flints (*pedernales*), obsidian, or broken glass. The seal was in the form of a cross (Weigle 1976:156). In some chapters, or *moradas,* the cross was cut between the shoulder blades; in others, a cross was cut under each shoulder blade; and in others, a cross was formed by two long cuts down the length of the back and one horizontal cut across the center (Weigle 1976:268, n. 6).

However, the other custom of tattooing a cross on the brother's chin or forehead (usually the forehead) is occasionally reported as an insignia of membership during this time period. A Mrs. Thomas Harwood reported that some new Hispano Methodist preachers "had the cross tattooed on their foreheads which could never be erased." Early in the twentieth century, Lorenzo de Córdova recalled seeing a herder at Valdez who had "the figure of a cross, light gray in color, imprinted in the middle of his forehead." He notes that "palms or boughs blessed on Palm Sunday were burned and their ashes used as a filler, rubbed into the design of a cross pricked into the skin." Bonney R. Gaastra, describing Chimayo, Cordova, Truchas, and Trampas, New Mexico, had talked to a man with "the faint purple cross tattooed under the skin of his forehead" (Weigle 1976: 257, n. 61).

Weigle, who has done the most thorough research on the Hermanos Penitentes, believed the facial tattoos represented an earlier custom that, because of high visibility, had been discontinued out of expediency after United States acquisition of New Mexico in 1848, due to vehement public opposition to the Brotherhoods on the part of newly arrived Protestant sects. These zealously pursued missionary activities with United States government support. During this time, the Catholic church also made public statements of opposition to the brotherhoods; however, its opposition was not consistently strong and was probably motivated by political expediency (Weigle 1976:910). Further research would be needed to ascertain whether or not there is a relation between the facial cross tattoos and the cross tattoos on the hand.

Pachucas' Appearance and Demeanor. Flor Saiz (1973) and Letticia Galindo (1981) have noted the dearth of information on females in the literature on pachucos. Galindo also points to grossly misrepresentative characterizations of that identity in the social science literature: "Those studies that did indeed mention women as users of caló [the language variety spoken by pachucos] have categorized them as being either prostitutes, barmaids, or mates of gang members" (1981:2). The dearth of information about pachucas is one manifestation of a trend in social science literature noted by Melville (1980:1), the absence of information about Mexican American women in general. Angie Chabram-Dernersesian noted that "Chicano identity is written with linguistic qualifiers—o/os—which subsume the Chicana into a universal ethnic subject that speaks with the masculine instead of the feminine and embodies itself in a Chicano male" (1992:82). For Chabram-Dernersesian, the focus on males in early Chicano literature is a function of the male-centered practices of Mexican and Chicano male academics who produced the early literature that became the canon. Similarly, many social science studies of the pachuco youth culture claim that it was and continues to be a male phenomenon (Barker 1950; Webb 1982; Sanchez 1983; Ortega 1991; Ornstein-Galicia 1995). Other studies make no such claim, yet by focusing solely on males convey the same impression. Nevertheless, many women were among the initial participants in the culture and were early speakers and transmitters of Pachuco/caló. All of the eldest interviewees spoke of the pachucas, the girls of the youth culture.

Participants who were teenagers during the 1930s and '40s consistently described pachucas as wearing their hair in a high roll or "pompadour" in front, with a knife or blade concealed inside. They were most distinguished from other girls by virtue of their reputed armed status and willingness to fight. The eldest women recalled that the earliest pachucas did not wear a dress style different from that of other girls. Dora explained,

> [Vestían] igual que todas las demás. Pero lo que sí, todas las pachucas se pintaban una cruz, una crucecita [en la mano], o se pintaban una cruz [en la frente]. . . . Y casi todas las

pachucas tenían la fama de ser muy pelioneras. Donde quiera armaban pleito. . . . Y luego se peinaban con un rollo aquí, ¿no?, así. Se les miraba muy bonito, pero adentro le metían una *fila*, una navaja. Traiban una navaja.

([They dressed] the same as all the other girls. But what they did, all of the pachucas would tattoo a cross, a little cross [she points to her hand at the base of the thumb and forefinger], or they would tattoo a cross [she touches her forehead]. . . . And almost all of the pachucas had the reputation of getting into fights. They would get into fights anywhere. . . . And then they combed their hair with a roll here [in the front]. It looked very pretty on them, . . . but they would put a *fila* inside, a knife. They carried a knife.)

For the early pachucas who didn't dress much differently than other girls their age, the cross tattoo between the thumb and forefinger on the hand or, for the more daring, between the eyes on the forehead or below the lower lip, was one of the most patent symbols of pachuca identity.

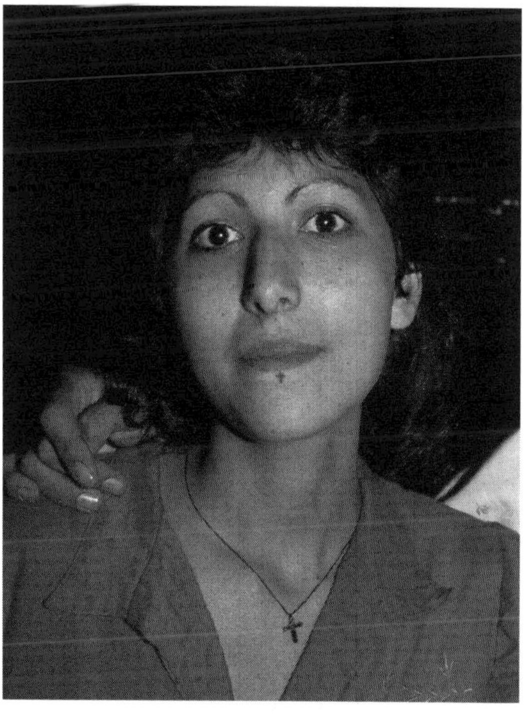

Figure 5. Young woman with cross tattoo below her lower lip, Chihuahua, Chihuahua, Mexico, 1984. Although a rarity today, this tattoo was worn by some early Tucson pachucos in the 1930s. (Photo by the author)

In some female groups the girls had identical tattoos. In 1945, Lydia's group of five or six friends did this. Fifteen years old and still in high school, she put a cross on her left hand at the juncture of the thumb and forefinger.

Later, during the pachuco heyday in the late thirties and early 1940s, women wore a dress style that, while more distinguishable, was close to that of American popular youth culture in general at the time. Louie described this dress code as short skirts, though not as short as the miniskirt, and the pompadour hairstyle. Lydia described her wartime generation's attire as "a skirt and blouse and the oxford shoes, black and white, with the white socks. . . . If you had something nicer, well, you know, you could wear it. But a lot of us couldn't afford it, so we shined our shoes, you know."

Dora said the female groups were gender-segregated, and she called them *gangas.* She had not been a pachuca but had many pachuca friends that she saw at Tucson's family-oriented dances.

Lydia pointed out that *ganga* did not mean "gang," but a group of friends that socialized on a regular basis. Her group consisted of six or seven female friends.

Comments on the intimidating demeanor projected by pachuco youth appeared throughout the interviews. Women described pachucas as *bravas* (fierce), *peleoneras* (fighters), and *chingonas* (powerful/ capable/ "bad"). When asked why she got into fights at school, Delia said, "Pues, no me quería dejar de nadie." (Well, I didn't want to let anyone treat me badly.) The phrase *no dejarse* describes a strategy of not allowing oneself to be treated unfairly or badly and implies a judgment that the interaction instigated by the other person was inappropriate.

Pachucos' Appearance. I asked Delia about the early pachucos that lived by the Santa Cruz River in 1929:

> **L:** ¿Pues, cómo se vestían aquellos pachucos? ¿Cómo les gustaba vestirse?
>
> **D:** Muy feo. Pues, se miraban, parecía que estaban viejos, pero eran jóvenes, muchachos, ¿no? Pero se ponían como viejos; andaban todos aguados, aguados ya, la ropa. . . . Sí, pues, se vestían de a tiro hilachentos, ¿no? [Los pantalones] de aquí así muy bombos y luego muy güilitos aquí [abajo]. Y

luego en veces traiban camiseta no más, no más shirts ansina, pintadas así (**L:** ¡Pintadas!); sí. Pues, yo creo que con color soaking, I don't know. Muy, muy pobres se veían. Y luego en veces traiban tupé y luego pelo largo, así; así agarrado.

L: Pulled like in a pony, almost a ponytail?

F: Ajá.

(**L:** How did those pachucos dress? How did they like to dress?

D: Very badly [lit. ugly]. They looked like they were old, but they were young, boys, you know? But they dressed like old men; they were all baggy; their clothes were already all baggy. . . . Their clothes were completely tattered. Their pants were baggy up here and then very narrow here [at the bottom/cuff]. And then at times they would have on only an undershirt, just shirts like that, and dyed. (**L:** Dyed!) Yes, well I think with color soaking; I don't know. They looked very, very poor. And then sometimes they had bangs(?) and then long hair pulled back like this [she gestures].

L: Pulled like in a pony, almost a ponytail?

F: Ahuh.)

Rudy attributed early pachucos' long hair to the fact that they didn't go to barbers. It was just combed back and often left long and curly in the back. Some wore a *trenza,* or braid, in the back.

Martín and Carlos said pachucos' hair had big pompadours in front and a *cola,* or tail, in the back. Bob remarked, "You could tell that he was a pachuco by just looking from the back." Louie said pachucos "wouldn't wear a [head] band like the cholos do now. It took him too long a time just to comb his hair. Everything came out right . . . and you wouldn't put something there to mess it up. . . . He wouldn't even let you *touch* his hair. If . . . you touched his hair, he would get up and tell you off. . . . See, it took him too long a time to put everything in place [laughs softly]."

Rudy recalled that in the late 1930s his older brother wore his dress shirts (*camisola*) buttoned only at the top button with the shirt tail out. More than seventy years later, the style is still popular with many contemporary *cholitos* and *chucos* on both sides of the U.S.-Mexico border.

Figure 6. Cotton harvesters near Gila Bend, Arizona, in 1934. (Arizona Historical Society, AHS Photo Number 3-2353)

For at least the pre–World War II generation of pachucos, dressing up well was mostly reserved for weekend dances and special events. Martín had spent most of his time picking cotton. He said, "Tenía uno que vestirse pobremente. ¿Pues, cómo vamos a poner la ropa buena pa salir a trabajar? Si no había. Si no pagaban nada." (You had to dress humbly. Well, how are we going to wear our good clothes to go out and work? We didn't have any. They didn't pay anything.)

The classic dress most often associated with the image of the pachuco was the *tacuche* or zoot suit. Males in full array were called *tipos,* translated by Rudy as "all dressed up." A tipo, he said, "probably had on a three-piece suit." Tucson pachucos of the late '30s called this being '*tacuchado* (dressed in a *tacuche*). Tipos were so fancy as to wear silk shirts or dress shirts with ruffles in front and on the cuffs with their tacuches. Many wore suspenders. The suits Louie's brother favored were tailored grey sharkskin and occasioned heavy dry-cleaning and pressing bills. They were worn with brown or black wing-tip shoes, the best being black and white or brown and white, and highly polished.

Tacuche, an early word for "zoot suit," is a Tarascan/Pure'pecha term that Santamaría (1974) defines as (1) "a bundle/wrapping of rags" or "trouble," (2) students' slang for suit, (3) adj. despicable, worthless. Said of a person of low status/class (1974:994). Cobos gives New Mexico and southern Colorado usage as (1) a kind of prisoners' uniform or (2) slang for a man's suit (1983:159–60); and Aguilar Melantzón (1981) gives "lawsuit" as one meaning for the Ciudad Juarez area.

Figure 7. Frank Allison, wearing a zoot suit, with a friend in Tucson, 1942. (Photos courtesy of Warren Allison)

After the war, Dora said pachucos wore wide pants with pleats,

> y huilitos de abajo. La chaqueta hasta abajo, luego la cadena, una leontina que les colgaba aquí en el pantalón. Pero *larga.* La chaqueta, los coats, eran *largos* (**L:** ¿Hasta la rodilla?) ¡Uuuy, sí!
>
> (And skinny at the bottom [narrow at the cuff]. The long jacket, and then the chain, a watch chain that hung here on the pants. It was *long.* The jacket, the coats, were *long.* (**L:** To the knee?) Ohhh, yes!)

Whether relating fact or fantasy, one of the vatos of the Barker recordings described meeting a very rich girl (una chavala bute rica), who once lent him a zoot suit when he hopped a freight to Los Angeles.

> Me dice la chavala, "Yo sé que tu vienes de trampulín," dice, "pero aquí tengo bastante garra yo de chavalo, ¿ve?" Pues, abrió el ropero, ese, buti garras, ese . . . Y me dice, "Órale pues, ese, guy; ¿cuál quiere, pues? ¿Cuál quiere? Escoga ahí." Pues sí, ese, yo escogí un tacuchi muy de aquellas. Muy, muy de aquellas, ese.
>
> (The girl says to me, "I know that you are bumming around/ riding the rails," she says, "but I have a lot of guys' drapes here, see?" Well, she opened the closet, guy, lots of drapes, guy. . . . And she says to me, "Go ahead, guy; well, which one do you want? Which one? Choose one." Well, yes, guy, I chose a real sharp zoot suit. A very, very sharp zoot suit, guy.)

Carlos recalled how Yaqui pachucos dressed in Old Pascua: "The ones before, from the barrio here, used to wear black Levis and shirts and a tweed hat." Those that wore a chain didn't use the extra-long ones; some wore no chain at all.

Pachucos' Demeanor. Pachucos were known for their unique demeanor. A number of men stressed that snappy clothes alone did not make a pachuco; it was also necessary to have a particular comportment, the "ways" to accompany the '*stilo* (style). This could not be acquired through superficial means but required sustained socialization. Rudy explained, "You'd have to grow with the 'stilo."

A number of men said pachucos were "tough." Ida found pachuco and contemporary cholo demeanor intimidating. "They've got such a cocky look, you know, like they're trying to tell you, 'Hey, I'm not afraid of anything!'"

Rudy recalled, "Those pachucos, they were really pretty tough, you know. [chuckles] It'd cost you a buck to go around their corner, you know? It was that way. And if they didn't want you around the neighborhood, they'd let you know. You know, get hurt, or become one of them, you know."

Symbols on pachuco males might be seen as analogous to the females' hairstyle. One was the long, elegant watch chain. Aurora's mother, Delia, told her she could always tell when there was going to be a fight because the pachucos would twirl the long chain. "Then everybody would just scatter." Aurora asked her, "Did they really used to fight with the chains?" "Sometimes they did," she answered, "but most of the time mostly to scare somebody." Carlos also alluded to the message conveyed by chains—chain = pachuco = possible confrontation—when he described them and added: "But in motion, you know; '¿Quehúbole?' [What's up?] So, 'I'm a pachuco, too.'"

Thus, both young men and women are characterized as being prepared to fight. Women carried a blade in their hair, "just to protect themselves," and pachuco males twirled the chain "mostly to scare somebody." Pachucos and pachucas conveyed a "make my day" demeanor: the message that, if messed with, they would respond in kind. Perhaps their greatest offense, in the eyes of both Anglo society and elite sectors of Mexican American and Mexican society, was that they did not assume a servile demeanor. Rudy had stressed the deterrence value that can accompany intimidation. He described one way of getting "respect" as being able to "kick some you-know-what."

In addition to an (apparently) intimidating demeanor and reputation, these youth found security in numbers when attending social events outside their segregated neighborhoods.[11] Referring to his year-long stay in Los Angeles as a young man in 1947, Louie said,

> when they went out, they went out in force. . . . In Los Angeles, there was this dance hall in the *other* part of town; right there on Main [Street]. So when those pachucos hit Main . . . there was mostly pachucos in different styles of dress, and

> I think that when the people or the cops or whatever, they saw all the bunch of pachucos, they would be intimidated or [thought] maybe that something was going on. There was *not.* Everybody was going to the dance hall.

Pachucos' Reputation. In my conversations with older individuals in Tucson about pachucos and their times, I cannot help but note the often stark contrast between what they have to say about their experiences and the images of pachuco youth presented by deviance-influenced approaches in both academic literature and popular discourse. Stereotypes of pachucas and pachucos are so pervasive that individuals' remarks about them were almost invariably accompanied by hedges. And what people repeatedly said that pachucos *were not* may be indicative of what the stereotype said they *were.* Louie's comments imply that stereotype-pachucos were "messing with" people: "The pachuco, he liked his dress style and he wasn't messing with nobody else." And "There were . . . good pachucos and bad pachucos. But they see a bad pachuco, they think that everybody is going to be the same." Ida said of husband, Louie: "He was a pachuco, although he wasn't a *bad* pachuco; he wasn't a mean person. They never were." Lydia said, "We would hang around, you know, like maybe six or seven girls and we would all have the same thing [tattoo]. . . . But we didn't used to get into trouble."

Both the English- and Spanish-language national press largely vilified pachucos. One older woman who had learned details about the males from a local newspaper, *El Tucsonense,* gave the following description: "Todo el mundo les huía. Eran muy atrevidos. Agarraban a la cadena y le daban al que le dieran." (Everyone would flee from them. They were very, very *bold.* They would grab that chain and hit anyone.)

The other interviewees' perspectives, however, diverged markedly from the stereotype. Bob said, "I've just seen 'em; it's not true . . . you break a bottle and go nuts." Louie made a comparison: "Nowadays you got the lowriders. You're gonna say they're bad people. . . . They got the dress code almost like the pachucos, same thing. They drive their cars down [lowered]; that's *all.* They don't go around looking for problems. . . . Like the pachuco; he liked his dress style and he wasn't messing with nobody else."

Louie spoke about how pachucos were portrayed in the press, recalling that his mother was frightened by what she read in the paper.

> She used to say about the pachucos, and we used to tell her, "That's just a dress code. Don't get your theory because you read in the paper in Phoenix that they had a gang fight in Phoenix." Because she used to read *La Opinión*, a Mexican paper . . . read all over the United States. . . . I think people had in mind that the pachuco was something they're not supposed to be, like she read. And *no*. . . . Newspapers can get a story and stretch it out till you believe anything you read, and it's not that *way*.

Lydia and a number of others did not agree with the characterization of pachuco youth as "gangs." "I don't think it was gangs. I think it is the group that you hang around with. They were just friends." Dora commented on the criminal image of the pachucos presented in the national press at the time of the zoot-suit riots.

> Pues, te decía, pero, pues, no todos. No. No todos deben de ser. Como ahora, pasa alguna cosa y luego, luego les echan la culpa a los trampas, a los transients, a los homeless. Luego, luego les echan la culpa a ellos. Y tu sabes bien que no todos son malos.
>
> (Well, that's what they told you, but not all of them can be. Like now, something happens and right away they blame the homeless; and you know very well that not all of them are bad.)

She foregrounded a priori blame by analogy with the plight of the homeless today. Louie noted that pachuco-dressing young men were regarded as "bad guys." However, he said, "We were just in the wrong place at the wrong time." Demeanor notwithstanding, Louie and others emphasized that interacting appropriately would keep one from incurring harsh treatment from pachuco youth. "It's like in any place you go. If you know how to treat the people you're with . . . they'll treat you the same and you're accepted. But if you go in there and you say, 'Hey! I'm the king here,' no; they'll put you down right away. . . . Treat people like they're supposed to be treated and they'll treat you *right*."

These sentiments were borne out by interviewees' statements about public safety in Tucson prior to World War II. Many spoke of sleeping outside in the summertime, walking distances at night, and leaving their homes unlocked without incident.

Pachucos and the Meaning of Clothes

The classic clothing style identified with pachucos began to be worn in Tucson in about 1935, during the Great Depression. Society was still openly segregated in residence and social life, and Mexicanos and Indians were relegated to the lowest rungs of the economic ladder. Interestingly, in interviewees' remarks pachucos' clothes appear as a symbol of the work ethic and pride (precisely self-esteem, which "ethnic minority" youth are said to lack). People spoke of pachucos' clothes with special attention and emotional attachment. When asked if pachucos had jobs, Dora responded,

> Pues, sí. ¿Cómo se iban a vestir? Pues, sí, muchos tenían trabajo. Mi viejo cuando vino del servicio luego, luego comenzó a trabajar en el Southern Pacific. Y antes trabajaba en la Marana, antes de irse al servicio; trabajaba en la Marana en los algodonales.
>
> (Of course. How [else] could they buy their clothes? A lot of them had jobs. When he got out of the service, right away my husband started working for the Southern Pacific. And before going into the service, he worked in Marana in the cotton fields.)

Louie echoed this. "I liked the style of the pachuco. It's a very good style. . . . And there's a lot of people that wear a jacket because that's the style; . . . there was nothing *wrong* with the style. The *real pachuco*, they wore that thing with pride. . . . They worked for their clothing. That was the main thing."

To many members of the dominant society, however, and elite Mexicanos, too, the pachucos' clothes, together with a nonservile demeanor, signaled danger. They signaled that some previously fixed boundary had moved, that something was wrong and out of place. The pachucos were, to use Louie's words, "something that they're not supposed to be." Indeed, boundaries had shifted, and as Sanchez Tranquilino and Tagg note, pachucos had "negotiated changing conditions of urban working-class life, family structure, and employment, and had found their opportunity in the emerging patterns of a new cross-national and intercultural economy as war work brought a relative affluence and changed patterns of labor and consumption" (1992:561).

Pachucos That Didn't Work, and "Trampolinazos"

In spite of the predominating respect for the work ethic, a few people said there were some pachucos, not representative of the majority, who were "guys that didn't like to work." It appears that these young men actively rejected the work ethic under the circumstances of the time: occupational segregation, forced assimilation, ubiquitous vilification, and police harassment. Others got the most mileage they could under the circumstances in which they found themselves. In a segment of the Barker recordings, one young man describes himself to another *vato* (guy) as follows:

M1: No me gusta jalar. A mí no me gustan los jales, por decir.
M2: ¡Usted le gusta andar al talón, eh!
M1: Puro talón, oiga, pidiendo un nicle aquí, un daime allá.
M2: ¡Simón que sí!
M1: Pa ir al borlote no más a . . .
M2: Simón.
M1: Usted se da cuenta, oiga. Usted no es bruto.

(**M1:** I don't like to work. I mean, I don't like jobs.
M2: You like to hustle, huh!
M1: Just hustling [*puro talón*], you know, asking for a nickel here, a dime there.
M2: Of course!
M1: In order to go to the dance and just . . .
M2: Yes.
M1: Hey, you understand. You're not stupid [*bruto*].)

Bruto carries the connotation "complete idiot" and could be taken as this young man's label for those who perform wage labor. When

Barker made his recordings in 1947, Mexican Americans and Indians faced a limited range of employment opportunities and thus a limited wage level. In this context, Bob's comments about "job" dynamics at about the time the recordings were made are revealing and illustrate the double bind in which many intelligent males found themselves: "See, if I was down, or no good . . . then I'd have somebody like me, you know, because that way they knew that they were smarter than I was. But I'm thinking all the time how to go up, how to get up there instead of being at the bottom. . . . I'd meet a lot of people at work. When I can go ask for a job if I know more than the foreman, he won't hire me. You know? And if I'm dumber, then I haven't got a chance either. 'Cause I'm too dumb; I don't know nothing. It's, ah . . . challenging . . . for me."

Dora defined *puro talón* as finding someone to tag along with who will treat you or to find some other way not to pay. Rudy said such fellows "wouldn't work or nothing," but "they got money; they got *beer* and stuff." Lydia defined *andar de talón* as to "mess around and get easy money." That included making money playing pool. Other words and phrases were synonymous with or related to *talón.* A vato in the Barker recordings mentioned traveling *de trampolín* (as a tramp or bum), which another speaker humorously modifies to *trompulín* (something like: a tramp/bum with a long snout or big mouth), defining that as, "nunca pago" (I never pay). One woman defined traveling *de trampolín* as hopping freight trains. Another man labeled getting something for free a *trampolinazo.* For Art, a pachuco of the 1960s, *talonear* means "partying and being irresponsible." However, Rudy pointed out that *talonear* is not necessarily used in a negative sense but can convey going after something with one's best effort.

The following descriptions of activities carried out by some pachucos could be considered examples of *talonear* or of *trampolinazos.* Recall that Delia said that the early pachucos camped on the Santa Cruz River stole chickens from people's yards and clothes from clotheslines, for their own use. Martín and Carlos recalled stealing unattended beer at some of the neighborhood dances when they were young.

> **C:** Venían de, you know, from different parts, ¿no? . . . ¿Ya ve?; Llegaban allá al baile, y todos traían su , su beer. Y que llegamos nosotros y sssw (ja, ja, ja) [He makes motion with his hand of swiping one.]

L: ¡A sacar beer!

C: Seguro.

C: "¡Órale, vato! ¡Vámonos!" you know? "¡Wáchale! ¡Haga esto, pero de volada!" Eso era lo que era decirles "clavarles," you know, steal from them. ¿Verdad, Martín?

M: Pues, simón. Pues no más andaban luciéndola allí. [L laughs] ¿Cómo la ves?

(**C:** They would come from, you know, different parts, you know? . . . You see?; they would arrive at the dance, and they would all bring their, their beer. And we would come along and sssw (ha, ha, ha) [Makes motion with his hand of swiping one.]

L: Getting beer!

C: Of course. "Come on, dude! Let's go!" you know? "Watch this! Do this, but do it fast!" That was saying "clavarles" to him, you know, to steal from them. Right, Martín?

M: Well, yes. Well, they were just showing it off there.[12])

In another trampolinazo, Carlos and his brother had hopped a freight to California as teenagers, feeding themselves from agricultural fields along the tracks.

Another woman's account of a trampolinazo illustrates social class antagonisms among Mexicanos, and the political and economic realities they experienced in the United States immediately following the Mexican Revolution of 1910.[13] The segregated, racist environment lumped displaced Mexican elites (businesspeople, *hacendados* [hacienda owners], and professionals) together with displaced former (and quite possibly revolutionary) peons and working-class groups (Gonzáles 1967). The following account of things that took place at the interviewee's sister-in-law's restaurant is telling:

L: ¿Qué cosas hacían los pachucos en el restaurán?

F: Le daban café y no lo querían pagar. O ordenaban una cena y no querían pagar. Teníamos que hablar a la policía.

L: ¿Trataban de salir?

F: Ah, no, eran muy, muy—¿cómo te diré?—muy calmados. "¿Cómo le va a hacer falta la comida que no pagamos?" decían; "¿Una taza de café, qué le damos? ¿Qué vale?" Y mi

> cuñada les decía, "No señores. *Pagan,* o se les lleva la policía." (**L:** ¡Se les ponía!) Luego ponía la llave a la puerta, y yo tenía miedo a que la golpearan. (**L:** Muy valiente, la señora.) Muy valiente es.
>
> (**L:** What kinds of things would the pachucos do at the restaurant?
>
> **F:** They would give them coffee, and they wouldn't want to pay for it. Or they would order a dinner and not want to pay. We would have to call the police.
>
> **L:** Would they try to leave?
>
> **F:** Ah, no, they were very, very—how can I say it?—very calm. They would say, "She won't even miss the food we didn't pay for; the cup of coffee. How much is it worth?" And my sister-in-law would say to them, "No, señores. *Pay,* or the police will take you away." (**L:** She would stand up to them!) Then she would lock the door, and I was afraid that they would beat her up. (**L:** The woman was very brave.) She is very brave.)

The pachucos here appear to be playing on class antagonisms, almost saying, "Do you really need the money? Are you that needy?" They seem to taunt the elites about their plight in the United States.

Conflicts and Confrontations

The stereotype of uncontrolled, random violence and bloodletting on the part of pachucos contrasts sharply with the ways in which fights were actually socially organized within the youth culture of the pre–World War II teens.[14] Most interviewees of that generation said physical confrontations were relatively infrequent. The prevailing custom was that only two men fought, with fists. Others present formed a circle around them. It appears that fights could be expected to occur under predictable circumstances. There were (largely) respected social conventions about how they should proceed, and measures for mitigation and containment.

> **C:** Habían unos que se agarraban, y luego se ponía toda tu raza como en un ring.

M: Una rueda.
L: ¿Y cuántos se peleaban?
C: Los dos. Dos, no más.
L: ¿No en bola, todos contra todos?
M: Oh, no.
C: Aquí, después comenzó eso.

(**C:** There were some guys that would start fighting, and then all of your people would get like in a ring.
M: A circle.
L: And how many would fight?
C: The two of them. Only two.
L: Not in a group, like that, everyone against everyone?
M: Oh, no.
C: Here, that started later.)

Reasons given for fights among males of this age group had to do with control of females and related interbarrio frictions, interbarrio frictions due to breach of social etiquette, and male group dominance–hierarchy dynamics. For example, Martín said, "No le podían ganar a uno con la novia. Antes no te podían llegar a; te gustaba la novia de aquel otro, acá . . . y a ganarla; no. Te ponían una serenata. (They couldn't take your girlfriend away. Before, they couldn't; if you liked that other guy's girlfriend here, and to take her away; you couldn't. They would beat you up.)

Interbarrio frictions related to gender dynamics might surface at dances attended by young people of different neighborhoods. Louie witnessed an interbarrio fight occasioned by breach of social etiquette in Los Angeles in 1947. His group of male friends were socializing one evening with vatos from another barrio, drinking, playing guitar, and singing. When the guests took a turn on the guitar and improvised song verses portraying their hosts in a negative light, a fight ensued in which a knife was pulled. That was the only time Louie recalled seeing a knife drawn during an altercation.

Martín and Carlos alluded to male group dominance–hierarchy dynamics when they said a leader might batter group members who did not obey his orders (an enforcement practice).

Carlos told how the local sheriffs handled fights in the old days at dances in Old Pascua. "Si se agarraron a pleito, ''Pérate. Párate.

Stand up again! Start all over. No más no saquen cuchillo.'" (If they started duking it out, "Wait! Stand up! Start all over. Just don't pull any knives.") During all those years, Carlos could recall only one fatal stabbing, which occurred at a card game in his neighborhood when a man was caught cheating. It was unclear whether this incident involved pachucos.

Louie compared fights in the early days with the use of guns now in Los Angeles: "The pachuco didn't use a gun at that time, that I know of. . . . It was a fight between two men; they would let them fight. And they had switchblades and the filas (knives) . . . but they used to pull them out only like a last resort. . . . But it was mostly an unarmed fight. . . . Guys from nowadays, they don't *fight*; they pull out *guns* and everything. They should have been there. . . . If maybe [it would] get out of hand, then you really either run, or stay in and fight." Referring to gang vs. gang fights, Louie explained, "But, I mean, there were no killings, nothing like that."

Dora said pachucos weren't bad. "Yes, they got into fights, but amongst themselves."

In a conversation with another vato, a pachuco in the Barker recordings related the story of a Tucson *chavala*'s (girl's) role in a fight in El Paso, Texas. He and a young woman friend were approached on the street in El Paso by a *norteño*-speaking man who tried to engage the couple in conversation using a smattering of Pachuco/caló vocabulary.[15] The pachuco replied in a more standard border Spanish, but the man kept trying to converse in Pachuco. When the pachuco finally spoke to him in caló, the man did not understand him. At this point the pachuco handed him a blatant insult, "Bueno, ese, usted parece guacho por derecho." (Well, guy, you seem like a genuine wetback.) The man responded by physically attacking the pair. The pachuco related,

> **M1:** Se nos viene encima, ese. Pues, fíjate, qué abusada la chavala, ese. Se pone abusada y a darle un pierdón, y se lo deja ir, ese, y pobre del cácaro sufriendo.
>
> **M2:** ¿En la chompa?
>
> **M1:** Órale pues; le da en la chompa y lo tumba, ese, con un pie, con una roca en el coco, ese.
>
> **M2:** ¡Eeee, esta chavala no se pone trucha!
>
> **M1:** ¡Simón que sí! Truchona, ese.

(**M1:** He attacked us, guy. Well get this, the girl was really on her toes, guy. She reacted quickly and threw a rock at him; she threw it and the poor guy was suffering.

M2: She hit him in the head?

M1: That's right; she hit him in the head and knocked him down, guy, in the head with a rock, guy.

M2: Oooh, isn't she smart!

M1: You bet! Super smart, guy.)

Speaking of fights between pachucas, Lydia had said that fights between girls sometimes occurred, infrequently, in the restroom at a dance. She said the principal motive for such fights was jealousy over a young man.

World War II

A number of men said that their prewar generation's style, ways, and some aspects of the language ended abruptly with the events surrounding World War II. Martín said, "Pues, a nosotros nos llevaron en cuarenta y uno, y ya de ahí pa'cá era otro, diferente." (Well, they took us away [drafted us] in '41, and then after that it was something else, different.) Louie said the younger men that didn't go to the war "still kept the dress code, but they were different from us." Rudy's uncles were drafted during the war years. He related,

> When they first came from Texas, they passed through Texas and went to California when the *draft* got 'em. You know, they put 'em in the service. Like,"All the pachucos, let's go." Vinieron como vacas; se los llevaron. [They came like cattle; they took them away]. . . . Picked 'em up and put 'em in the army. . . . I think the draft went and made a big, big *haul.* Guys that they needed for the service. So the guys that weren't working or nothing kept, like, bumming around the street. Those are the ones they got. My uncles were in that bunch. So they took 'em to L.A., and that's where they put 'em in the service; like, you know, you got no *choice*; this is the *draft.*

Barker mentioned one traveling bunch of pachucos during the war, a migration of boys who hopped freights from El Paso to Los

Angeles in 1942. This was "instigated by a 'floater' or '*flora*' from the El Paso police department, which placed suspended sentences on a number of the boys. Under the terms of the floater, these pachucos were to receive prison sentences if they ever returned to El Paso" (1950:22). The comments of an elderly Tucson woman, born in 1910, may refer to that event: "Casi todos los pachucos de El Paso se vinieron para acá, a Arizona, porque en Arizona no les hacían nada, mi'ija. En parvadas se venían. . . . Les pusieron penas que siguieran aquí en este pueblo. (Well, almost all of the pachucos from El Paso came here to Arizona, because in Arizona they would leave them alone, *mi'ija.* They came in droves. . . . They gave them sentences to serve out here in this town.) She added, "En el Paso les perseguían mucho." (In El Paso they harassed them a lot.)

A number of men said that servicemen returning from the war were greatly changed. Louie observed that "most of the guys . . . that they were chucos, most of them went to the *service* and they came out; they got tired of fighting, so there . . . I think that they mellowed out and something happened." Rudy and Martín had made similar comments. Louie continued, "I couldn't tell you about the fights that the navy guys had with the pachucos, but most of the pachucos that went into the service traded their pachuco style for bell-bottoms. They liked the dress of the sailor and the marine and the army and they were not fighting each *other* then; they were fighting *together.*" Louie gave three factors responsible for changes in pachucos of the World War II generation and for postwar change in the culture (I have numbered them): "I think that (1) putting them together and (2) they mellowed out, that (3) all the criticism that they had before . . . that came out."

The third factor is probably a reference to the stigmatization of pachucos proceeding from events in Los Angeles, California, in 1942 and '43—the trials related to the "Sleepy Lagoon" murder case of 1942–44 (Mazón 1984:20–27) and the so-called zoot-suit riots of June 1943, which received extensive, sensationalized national and international press at the time. Louie's previous mention of "the fights that the navy guys had with the pachucos" is surely a reference to the "riots." Mauricio Mazón's study of those events finds that the press predominantly "focused on zoot-suiter culpability" (1984:80). However, facsimiles of military documents (many once classified), that Mazón reproduces from the Federal Archives and Records Center in Laguna Niguel, California, "reveal a tale that is radically different from popular assumptions about the riots" (1984:xiii). For example, a report to the district patrol officer from the senior patrol officer of downtown Los Angeles dated June 8, 1943, begins, "continued disorder. Hundreds of service men prowling downtown Los Angeles mostly on foot—disorderly—apparently on prowl for Mexicans. Have by joint agreement with Army Provost Marshall declared following Los Angeles city territory out of bounds to all Navy-Marines, Coast Guard, and Army personnel. Main Street east to Los Angeles city limits" (cited in Mazón 1984:123). Captain Heim speaks of the restriction of servicemen from that area in a transcript of a telephone conversation with Admiral Bagley dated June 11, 1943:

> It has been a good thing in two ways—it was good for the city and our men need discipline. We find that there are no old timers but that they are the young reservists just caught and they are egged on by civilians telling them what [a] fine job they are doing and by the press. Yesterday Fogg tells me, just to show you how they get worked up, a draft of men came through the station and read about this in the papers and 8 men got out and left; they were supposed to wait at the station for their train, but they started a band and looked for zoot-suiters and started some trouble. The Patrol round [*sic*] them up and locked them up but it just shows how excited they get about it from just reading the papers. (cited in Mazón 1984:123)

The measures restricting the servicemen weren't conceived at the local level; Mexican diplomacy played an important role in stemming the "riots." According to McWilliams, "the Mexican ambassador in Washington . . . addressed a formal inquiry to Secretary of State Hull." It was after this that official Washington advised Los Angeles leaders "of the utterly disastrous international effects of the riots" ([1948] 1968:226).

Marilyn Domer, who carefully studied official records of the "riots," says that police officials were near the truth when they described the events as a series of isolated fights, noting that zoot-suiters were never the principals in the confrontations (cited in Domer 1955:119). Indeed Marcos Sanchez-Tranquilino feels the events should rightfully be called the "Servicemen Riots" (1987:35). Barker says of the fights, "Most of them seem to have originated with the dating of pachuco girls by servicemen" (1950:23).

One man I interviewed spoke of such altercations as occurring throughout the duration of the war and mentioned them without making reference to the "riots." He said many women's preference for men in uniform caused resentment on the part of all civilian males, both Hispanic and non-Hispanic. Indeed, these dynamics are also important to an analysis of the hostilities. There is a pressing need to carry out oral history of the wartime clashes, their contexts, nature, and causes, and for descriptions of situations and fights, while there are still living informants.

One Tucson Mexican American man I spoke with had been stationed in San Diego in the navy at the time of the "zoot-suit riots." When they heard of the events in L.A., his company commander and the company prepared to go out looking for "zoot-suiters" one night. They invited the Tucson man to go along, but he told the group, "I joined the service to fight the Japanese, not Mexicans." The company commander excused him from participating.

Navy records demonstrate that the national public at large was introduced to pachucos through sensationalized newspaper accounts, now known to be false, of zoot-suiter culpability in these events. Arturo Madrid-Barela wrote of the "riots,"

> Already conditioned by the centuries-old heritage of anti-Spanish, anti-Catholic sentiment, by the century long campaign of vilification and violence against Mexicans, and enmeshed in the xenophobic and racist atmosphere of World War II Anglo America easily accepted as justifiable the most recent of attacks on its Mexicans. Whatever the Pachucos may have been historically and despite the efforts of an objective portion of the press and populace to place them in a proper historical context as the alienated and brutalized products of a racist and exploitative society, the vision that Anglo America and many of America's Mexicans came to have of the Pachucos was that provided by the press and the police: Namely that they were biologically inferior, culturally degenerate, criminally inclined, sexually promiscuous, bloodthirsty, drug-addicted, etc. (1973:34–35)

Nationally, the public climate toward pachucos was most certainly more hostile after the war, because of that press.

2

POST–WORLD WAR II TEENS

World War II brought many changes in social, economic, and political life. Older people recalled marked changes in social contexts and their age, racial/ethnic, and gender composition both during the war and after. Dora spoke of changes in the way parents raised their children and alluded to changes in social contexts when she said:

> Después del cuarenta cuando la guerra, no me lo vas a creer, yo anduve de novia con un soldado *americano*. . . . Pero era de Wyoming; era de Wyoming. Sus padres eran ganaderos. Cattle ranchers. En ese tiempo había los USOs donde se juntaban todos los soldados y podíamos ir a bailar y platicar. Ahí lo conocí.
>
> (After 1940 when the war [began], you're not going to believe this, I was going with an *americano* soldier. . . . He was from Wyoming; his parents were cattle ranchers. At that time there were the USOs where the soldiers would gather and we could go and dance and chat. That's where I met him.)

After World War II there was a major change in the size and origins of Tucson's population. Dora had described war-related dynamics, saying,

> Venían y los estacionaban aquí en Davis Monthon a los soldados. Y a muchos les gustó y se quedaron. Muchos fueron a la guerra y cuando volvieron, los tenían que volver al base donde los habían mandado, ¿no?, para que los hicieran discharge. Y muchos ya se quedaron y mandaban traer la familia y ya comenzó a venir la gente.
>
> ([The soldiers] came and they would station them here at Davis Monthon [Air Force Base]. And a lot of them liked it here. Many of them went to the war and when they came back, they had to bring them back to the base they had been sent from so that they could discharge them. Many of them stayed and sent for their families and then the people started coming.)

Tucson's long-time residents of Indian and Mexican origins were increasingly affected by the influx of a large, foreign population. More and more, the original Tucson and its residents became a segregated enclave, as evidenced in Rudy's description of the town in the late 1940s and early 1950s. "Right there—where the Community Center is now?—was [Barrio] Hoyo. That used to be the main street. The majority was Mexican and black in that area right there. They used to have all kinds of nightclubs, pool halls, everything. Well, it was just a little town built itself right there, for the black and Mexicans." Art explained, "The Anglos would live in the other part of the city. Just lately, and probably in the late '50s, they started moving to the west. But all the West and South Side were all Mexicans and Indians and blacks."

In the years 1954–64, the first wave of small commercial shopping centers was constructed to serve new suburbs. Thus the 1950s and '60s brought new and different patterns of business and residence, culminating in an "urban renewal" project. A number of older people mentioned shopping malls as a novelty. Dora recalled, "Los shopping malls vinieron después de la guerra. Fue cuando comenzaron con los shopping malls y comenzó a morirse downtown, por los shopping malls." (The shopping malls came after the war. That was when they started with the shopping malls and downtown began to die, because of the shopping malls.)

Aurora remembered seeing the first drive-in movie theater: "You know where Rodeo Park is? Rodeo Park is way at the end of 6th [Avenue] on Irvington, where they have the rodeo. Then on the other side of the park there was a drive-in, Rodeo Drive-in. It was one of the first drive-ins that they had here."

Social Life

Family-oriented cross-generational social events continued in popularity in the postwar 1940s and 1950s. Rudy told of horse racing in Tucson at Rillito, the Westside, and Soto's Ranch where they also held dances. His uncle had been one of the jockeys. Aurora met her future husband while out with her family at such a dance:

> In Soto's Place right on Old Nogales Highway. . . . In those years there was this building. I think it's still a bar but they had like a . . . ramada outside, and the outside dances in the summertime were real popular at that time. And—what was the name of the *conjunto* [musical group]—it was Chuyito Garcia and his . . . you know, the guys that played with him. And they had dances Friday, Saturday, and Sunday, and on Sunday they started early, in the evening, before sundown. After the ballgame. Cause they always had a baseball game. And then after that they would make a *dance.* And so *mostly* they were always playing Nogales. The people from Soto's were playing Nogales.

After the war, the automobile took on increasing importance in young people's social lives, although by no means did most young people own cars or have access to one. One young man in the 1947 Barker recordings spoke of being out riding in a car as if it were something he didn't do all the time: L'otra noche también anduve en una ranfla. Me gusta andar mucho en las ranflas a mí, ¿ve? (The other night I was out riding in a car, too. I really like to go around in cars, see?)

A number of men who were teens immediately after the war alluded to the importance of having a car, or access to one, as a means of impressing young women. Access to a car might allow a young man to offer a young woman a ride or a ride home, or to take her parking, as was the case in an ill-fated incident involving

"A" Mountain recounted on the Barker recordings. In that case, a couple's getaway from a dance and the girl's disapproving mother was facilitated by a car. The young man involved recounted his conversation with the girl:

> "Si quiere salir a raitear ahorita, ando en el carro con un vato que se llama David," le digo. "Si quiere salir, salga conmigo. ¿No quiere, oiga?" dije yo, ¿ve? "¿Sabe qué? Yo me voy pa'l chante aunque mi jefita no quiera," ¿ve? Entonces bailé con ella, y su jefita le agarra del brazo y me la quita, ¿ve? 'Tonces yo le digo a la chavala, "¿Sabes qué? 'rránquese de su jefa, y nos borramos pa'l "A" Mountain, oiga, y allá nos quedamos un raitón," ¿ve?
>
> ("If you want to go for a ride right now, I'm in the car with a guy named David. If you want to go, come with me. Wouldn't you like to?" "You know what? I'll let you give me a ride home even though my mother said no," see? Then I danced with her, and her mom grabs her by the arm and yanks her away from me, see? Then I say to the girl, "You know what? Tear yourself away from your mother, and we'll split for "A" Mountain, see, and we'll stay up there for a while," see?)

In contrast to the Barker tape account in which a car appears as a desirable novelty, descriptions of social life in the 1950s take the automobile's presence for granted. Desert and house parties were favorite activities and were attended by unchaperoned individuals of both sexes. For young men, the automobile continued to be important for obtaining dates and impressing girls. Armando recalled, "One of my biggest *dreams* was to have a hot-rod. . . . And so I used to fool around with cars a lot. . . . I used to love cars. It'd . . . get you to parties, get you here, there, the best wheels possible." Lydia recalled, "We'd go out in the desert. . . . We used to get together, make bonfires and drink beer till maybe three, four in the morning. And the police wouldn't bother us 'cause we wouldn't bother nobody. They'd just say, 'Don't throw the bottles or cans on the highways,' you know. 'Be sure to put out your fire.' But now you can't do that because then they [the police] chase you." Both Art and Lydia were in their late teens and early twenties when they attended such parties.

One reason for the desert parties is suggested in Lydia's statement "And the police wouldn't bother us," and also in the following account by Rudy:

> Back in the fifties you couldn't drink a beer on the street. They'd arrest you so quick. . . . Now you can have beer in your trunk . . . ice chests in your trunk, anyway. Sit out in the parking lot down south Sixth [Avenue], drink beer . . . 's long as you're not doing nothing. . . . We had to go out in the *desert.* We'd go out in the desert, and the only time we went into them bars was when we were *old* enough. Other than that, you got caught drinking, it was wrong. Could be a real severe punishment. Mother Higgins, or what used to be a detention center.

Armando described house parties:

> I never saw any chaperones at the parties. Once in a while there'd be a fight, but not too many fights. Mostly really calm and stuff. . . . You better respect everybody . . . and everybody respects you. It's very clean. I never saw any heavy drinking. I used to drink, but it wasn't out in the open. It was *a escondiditas* [on the sly/hidden]. And forget it; marijuana, forget it. . . . I'll tell you the truth; I never saw marijuana in high school.

Although people spoke of unchaperoned house parties, some women were not able to attend, because of strict parents. For example, Bob's experience differed from that of his wife, Aurora. He said, "We had a good time back in the old days." Aurora responded, "I'm glad he can say that, but I can't, because like I said, my dad didn't let me do nothing. . . . People used to go to the drive-ins and all that, and my dad didn't let me go. I never went out to a drive-in with a guy, never. Until I married him. He was the one who took me to a drive-in the first time. . . . I already had [name of her first child]."

Controlled Substances

Most interviewees said that marijuana use by young people at this time was unknown or very rare. Only one person said they had smoked it, and that appears to have been in the early 1960s. Bob said of his group, "We used to sing and drink and smoke. There was no pot, just alcohol. We used to play the guitar, you know, sing." One man compared substance use in the 1950s to cocaine and substances available now:

> **M:** It [cocaine] wasn't even around. The only thing that was around when I was at that age, well, let's say sixteen to nineteen, between there, was, ah, marijuana. And the guy that had it would be very rare you know, 'cause at that time, if one guy would have it they'd call them a *marijuano.* The whole *family.* You know? "Ahi viven los marijuanos," you know? And yet there's always somebody that'd say, "Hey, shove us a *leño* [joint]," you know?
>
> **L:** Well, what do you think was the average young person's level of marijuana use, for example, in your generation?
>
> **M:** Most of the older guys used to. The older guys, talking 'bout guys from twenty-five to thirty five, between that age category. 'Cause you would *see* those guys. "Ahi viene el loco" [Here comes the dude], you know, and I don't know before that if it was around or if it was well *hidden.*

He added, "In the '50s it was very rare for somebody to have weed."

When I asked Armando when marijuana had come along, he answered, "During the '60s, the hippie *chingadera* [thing]." Penalties for marijuana use during the 1950s were harsh. One man recalled, "If you would get caught, it was worse than getting caught with alcohol. Even with alcohol it was a hard penalty."

Post–World War II Pachucos' Appearance and Demeanor

The post–World War II generation of the early 1950s instituted some changes in dress style. Rudy and Bob recalled straight-legged pants, sometimes pegged at the bottom. White T-shirts were popular, although Rudy remembered that some fellows dyed them another color, black being the most popular. Some groups of males might all wear the same color shirt. They did the dying themselves, boiling the water and dye mixture, then soaking the T-shirts. Tucson's South

Side preferred khaki pants, combining these with khaki shirts, white T-shirts, or a dress shirt (*lisa*). Barrio Hollywood preferred Levis, white T-shirts, and sunglasses.

Rudy described a popular haircut called a "teddy bear," which was a bit curly or fuzzy, and combed upward. Another cut was called *cuadrado*. It was shorter than the early pachuco hairstyle. Long on the top, the sides and back were trimmed in a square cut "like Bill Haley."[1]

Bob wore "sleeper-type" jackets when in the service at Fort Ord in California. He ironed his own starched shirts, making three creases down the back and "fancy deals with the iron. All kind of marks." He wore the shirts with the collar up. (Jose Cuellar [1982:9] attributes pachucos' taste for creases on shirts to the influence of the military.) Bob and his friends wore loafers or black boots; never shoes with laces. "That was sissy with us guys." Dress pants (slicks) matching the shirt completed the ensemble. Pants were "straight-cut at the bottom but loose;" tight cuffs were out of style at the time. "The pachuco," Bob said . . . "had to be dressed neat. . . . Style. . . . And be tough. . . . The clothes mean a lot to you." Bob stressed that they were a means of gaining respect.

Art, a South Side resident during his teens in the late 1950s and early 1960s, wore the going dress style for young men of his time, "khakis and french toast." The latter were "pointed, double-soled shoes with horseshoes" and "taps all over the place." Shirts were "*lisas* [dress shirts], baggy ones. . . . Probably either my brother-in-law's, my father's, you know; something to look cool."

Alineado was the word used by pachucos of the 1950s to refer to a sharply dressed vato. In Tucson at that time, the differences in male dress style preference followed a socioeconomic dynamic: Barrio Hollywood, sporting Levis, was better off economically than the South Side, which wore khakis. Upon saying that he thought of himself as a pachuco, Armando added, "but then I'd notice *que* [that] there was this *other* segment of society. A lot of Chicanos que didn't dress the way I did and stuff, you know, they were into a lot of sports; they were into becoming very *americanados* [Americanized]."

Ducktail hair enjoyed continued popularity. Julie and Armando recalled boys' hair during their 1950s and early '60s school days. Referring to boys in their early teens, Julie said, "The hair had to be just right. I remember I used to see these guys in front of *store* windows, man just [gestures combing hair]. All they *cared about* was that. And then they'd pack it down like this, a waterfall [in front]. Then they had a ducktail back here with grease on it." Armando added, "vaselina, también. [Vaseline, too.] . . . Every hair had to be *just exactly flat*, with a ducktail. . . . I had wings *en el lado* [on the side]. I had to comb it *todo el tiempo* [all the time]; I'd *never* go without a comb in my back pocket." He recalled running the comb vertically down the center of the back to put the final touch on the ducktail. Julie remembered, "when I used to see a guy with a comb in his pocket, I used to always think he was a pachuco. . . . They would take care of their hair. Their shoes were always spit-shined." Armando added, "Well, see, the other pocket, I used to have my rag for my shoes. That was a must. All through junior high, high school."

Pachucos' Demeanor

Pachucos continued to be known for their unique demeanor. Speaking of his military service in California in the early 1950s, Bob recalled, "there were some guys there that even if they dress right, they still didn't look right. The clothes didn't fit them. They wanted to dress like us but they looked more like a nut. . . . They didn't go together, your personality and your dress. . . . You get a guy, any guy, and dress him the way we used to dress . . . you can't buy it."

Bob mentioned safety as a feature of the male cohorts. "You'd feel *safe* with them around. . . . You'd call somebody for help; you'd ask them and they'd be there." The members of his own post–World War II group became "meaner and meaner" as they moved into manhood from adolescence. They went from carrying slingshots, as boys, to knives and chains after about age eighteen. This was around 1946 and Bob stressed that they were trying to protect themselves.

After World War II, in the 1950s and '60s, a number of male groups gave themselves names, apart from their barrio designation. Art belonged to such a gang in the late 1950s and early '60s. "We had about 350 members. We called ourselves 'The Drifters of Tucson.' . . . We had people from all over. Old Myers, Downtown, Pascua, South Side, North Side. . . . We were a big gang."[2] Other groups mentioned were the Red Devils, a South Side group that probably dated from the late 1940s; a '50s and '60s group called the Rebels, from the Meyer and Convent area of Barrio Libre; the Moonlight Drifters, bounded by Thirty-sixth St. and Ajo Blvd. and Fourth Ave. and Park (an area that is now Barrio Centro); and the "Gaylords," which organized as a quasi car club, though many members could not afford cars. This last group organized more formally, had representatives, and used lawyers to defend themselves against police harassment.[3]

Conflicts among Males

Reasons for fights mentioned by males of this post–World War II generation included friction between individuals over something that happened in the past; gender dynamics, including control of females; alcohol; blatant insults; and someone starting a fight and then leaving another person holding the bag. Rudy gave one example: "Let's say there's ten guys in our group and we're drinking. There's two of 'em that we know that had a run-in back, long time ago. That's where the fight's gonna start. . . . It's already in the back of their head." Like several others, he described fights as being relatively infrequent:

> Maybe fights once in a while, *pero* [but], you know, if there's guys that don't like each other, they settle it right there. Nobody gets in, you know. There might be something like that happened when they were little kids, you know, and it seems like it's stupid, but they still bring it up. They say, "Well, I've been wanting to kick your so-and-so for *years*." And, "Remember, you threw that rock and hit me in the head," and all that stuff, "when we were in junior high?" . . . That's the way it starts. And there's always somebody say, "Hey, don't you get in. No te metas." And they say, "Tu no te metas; solamente yo [just me]." And that's the way it goes. So then they let each other just hook it out for a while, and that's it. They get it out of their system. You know, it's better, 'cause when, like that, one of 'em might get a gun later, or somewhere else, you know; cause a lot of *more* severe damage than what it is, you know. So, and it's happened. Guys have just duked it out, and that's it. They're friends. . . . They say, "We were kids at that time; now we're grown men, so . . ."

Bob gave the reasons for some specific fights he recalled, like, "You married my girlfriend." He added that beer and alcohol precipitated some fights. "It was *stupid*; that's no place [laughs]. You know? But, ah [sighs], that's the way it *was*." Bob also gave other examples of fights over gender dynamics: "If you didn't like a guy with that girl, you'd tell him to respect the girl, you know. . . . They were jealous of other gangs, so there'd be fights" [laughs].

Immediately after the war, the conventions of fighting continued to be largely those practiced by pre–World War II pachucos, the one-on-one fistfight supported by an ostensibly amicable gentlemen's ideology. Others were not supposed to jump into the confrontation. Fights were mitigated and kept from escalating through mechanisms of social control. As Bob said, "It's not true you break a bottle and go nuts." Rudy spoke of how group members would practice conflict mitigation when an intragroup fight was brewing between two members. "The friends that know each other *that* well, they know. 'Watch out, man; you keep him over there. Don't let him mention nothing about . . .' Or if a fight was about to erupt: 'Hey, don't you get in; just me.'" Rudy's comments illustrate the amicable gentlemen's ideology, conflict conventions, limits, and closure: "I remember we young guys would say, 'Hey, me and you, let's have it out. You beat me; you're a better man.' Whoever won shook his hand and that was *it.* You don't *see* that anymore. . . . 'Just me and you.' 'Where?' 'Anywhere.' Or 'Me and you go down to the river, and whoever comes back,' or let's say I had enough, 'That's it.' Shake your hand; 'You're a better man.' But now you don't. They pull a *gun* or something."

The ideology and conventions surrounding fights seem to have been a central part of the prevailing definition of honorable manhood at the time. Rudy and others stressed this, especially when making comparisons between early, original pachucos and conflict dynamics observed today. Rudy said, "'Ese es *hombre.*' He's a man. He'll fight you and get over it. You beat him, he respects you; that's *it.*"

Bob described fights as face-to-face and fair.

M: Fair fights. Fair fights.

L: Like how?

M: Face to face. And if there wasn't just one man, you know, who had to fight, the other one had to go around [take their turn].

L: The other guys, wouldn't they jump into the fight?

M: No. No, that's not fair. Unless somebody jumped him.

Son: Now they do that [jump people].

D2: Um-hum . . .

L: And the pachucos didn't used to do that?

Bob: Very, very seldom. Except when they were drunk, you know. Fistfights. Only one-on-one.

D1: Sure; they couldn't get away. They surrounded them.

Bob described the way that friends would look after friends, to even a score, for example, in the case of a person who is jumped. "Usually you get beat up, you know? But then if you get beat up, some more of your friends come over, you know, and they'll go find him out. They'll go looking for them. But then they say, 'You know, I found out who it was, and . . . ' 'Did you beat him up?' 'Oh, yeah, I beat him up, took care of him.' [chuckles] 'O.K.' (**L:** That's it?) That's it. So everybody's happy."

Free-for-alls were rare and appear as undesirable, chaotic phenomena. One free-for-all recounted began when a person who was not a direct party to the dispute egged a foe into a fight, promising assistance to the offended individual. When the fight began, the instigator disappeared, and the offended person was left fighting two men. That prompted others to jump into the fight, which quickly escalated. Such dynamics suggest a loss of social control and a breakdown of adherence to the rules. Instead of acting as a referee or mitigator of a direct one-on-one dispute, the third party here instigated a larger conflict.

Post–World War II Pachucas

Flor Saiz described the pachuca style of the 1940s and '50s as "white bobby socks rolled in wide, thick cuffs . . . jeans . . . or tight calflength skirts with tight sweaters or long sleeve blouses. Uniform differed some, depending on area and gang" (1973:47).

Aurora called pachucas "the girls that hang around with [the pachucos]. Las rucas [the chicks]." Art remembered that most of the girlfriends of boys in his gang, The Drifters, belonged to one particular girls' group. He described the groups of pachucas as "a bunch of girls hanging around each other." Patty characterized her group as "the neighborhood girls," and she had one principal friend she hung around with.

From the 1950s on, some of the girls' groups gave themselves names. Although Patty's group had no name, her sister and friends called themselves The Rockin Teens. The sister called this group a gang but then immediately qualified that, adding, "It wasn't a *gang*. It was sort of a club." The girls wore blue jackets with the words "Rockin Teens" and met every Saturday at a different girl's house for a members-only party.

The postwar pachucas instituted some changes in appearance. The rolled pompadour hairstyle was replaced by others. One of Veronica's friends recalled some of the hairdos worn by her generation of pachucas in the late 1950s. "They used to *tease*, and *tease*, *tease* it all *up*."

Veronica spoke of the hairstyle popular in the early 1960s:

> I used to wear that stupid beehive. The higher the better, you know? [Other, younger women present exclaim, "Beehive!" and laugh.] And, boy, toilet paper was as expensive then as it is now and my mother wanted to *kill* me, 'cause I remember I used to do it and wrap my hair up in toilet paper [laughing]. [The other women laugh uncontrollably.] And I thought it looked *cool*, too! [laughter] . . . And we used to wear *bell*-bottoms. . . . And hip-huggers. The bigger the bell, the better.

She also mentioned the heavy makeup worn at that time: black eyeliner, mascara, and blush. Many of the fashions and hairstyles point to the American popular-culture dimensions of pachuco and cholo youth cultures.

Veronica, like Patty, had one main friend, although she said that in the early 1960s, there was strong social pressure to affiliate with larger groups. She described the cohorts of her times as "just a *group* of people. It wasn't gangs. . . . Mostly it was the clique, and it was girls you were just chumming around with at school, you know, and talk and put your eyeliner way out to here."

In the early 1960s, Julie's group of friends consisted of six girls who called themselves Las Black Widows. They had met at school and got together at girlfriends' houses. She described her activities on a typical weekday when she was fifteen or sixteen years old: "I'd come home from school and change into my jeans and a sweater top, and then I'd get on my bike . . . and ride on over to my girlfriend's house. And she used to live in an alley, so we used to hang out in the alley, which was really fun, 'cause all different kinds of kids used to go by the alley, so we were right in the right place. And then I'd go home, and then I'd do my homework and stuff."

Alluding to the inability of many Mexican American families of the time to compete in the conspicuous consumption that marked upward mobility, Veronica said, "You didn't hang out with a more elite crowd. You didn't *have* the stuff that went with the more elite crowd, you know? You couldn't wear Capezios and all that other stuff, and you lived in the *South Side.*" Her comments and those of others suggested that even during the upbeat consumer economy of the 1950s and early 1960s, many working-class Mexicanos continued to occupy a less-than-affluent socioeconomic position.

Females continued the tradition of pachuca tattoos. Aurora attempted to do a cross on her hand with washable ink. "I remember that I did that when I was a young girl, and my father almost hit me on the hand. He said, 'I don't want to see you doing that, writing on yourself.'" Patty was about fifteen years old and drinking with a group of high-school girlfriends when she did a tattoo on her hand: "Ohhhh! My mother! Ohhh, when my mother saw me with a tattoo, I almost got it cut *off.* She had a heart attack, man." Her sister explained, "She never saw that in a girl, you know. It was something new." Patty interjected, "New to *her.*"

In the early '60s, Julie's group of six friends also had identical tattoos. "We had a tattoo, with my pachuca friends, you know. [She had said, "It was just a dot."] . . . And you know what? For three years I wore a tape over this so my father would never see it. And finally one day I got so tired of wearing this tape that I took it off, and nobody ever asked me anything about it." She continued, "Some [girls] used to put a tattoo on their face, and I thought that was pretty cool, but I wouldn't dare try that 'cause my father. How could I wear a tape on my face for three *years*, you know?! So I never was brave enough to try that."

She told about when her group did their tattoos:

> We all did it at once. One girlfriend that we were hanging around with at the time, she was from Good Shepherd's. She had come from . . . those homes where they keep girls. It's like a jail. . . . She had been there for maybe about a year, year and a half, 'cause apparently she was running away from home. . . . Pero she was real pachuca-like and I met her at [high school]. And when I met her, I thought that she was *so cool* and *so nice*, and she had this dot on her arm. . . . She had told me about that she was with a gang of girls and she

> said, "Yeah; this is our trademark." . . . And anyway, we were all at my girlfriend's house, and [the Good Shepherd girl] was there, and she'd shown us this tattoo and about how her and her friends had done this. So we said, "Hey, let's *us* do it! Let's all of us have a little mark, you know, and only *us* will *have* it. And someday we'll grow up and stuff, and we'll all have this mark." Menos la [name]. La [name] era muy culona. [But not (name). (Name) was really a coward.] She wouldn't dare try it. She's the only one that wouldn't jab her arm. . . . There was four of us that put the mark on, and [the Good Shepherd girl]. She already had the mark.

The naming of girls' groups continued well beyond the 1950s and '60s. A woman who graduated in the early 1980s spoke of her high-school group, consisting of eighteen girls, all schoolmates: "My gang was called The Copper Queens. . . . We loved to all hang on the lockers . . . and our clothes'd be gold and black. Black pants. And then on the back [of the jacket] we used to have 'Queens.' . . . It was like a cholo type, then." The girls attended school sports events together. She added, "It wasn't like a *gang*."

In the early 1980s, two of Aurora's daughters were in a school-based club composed of four girls who went by the name, Las Rucas Unidas ("L.R.U.") (The United Women/Fine Old Ladies/Chicks). The club's emblem, drawn by one of the girls, was a large cross with a sacred heart at the base. A flowing ribbon across the top read, "Las Rucas Unidas." The emblem was posted on one of the members' lockers. Leadership in the club took the form of an elected president. The girls planned to get matching jackets, but the group ceased to exist when a key member dropped out of high school.

Pachucas' Demeanor. The post–World War II pachucas continued to project the tough demeanor. Patty said, "I used to think I was bad," using "bad" the way it is used in inner-city black teenage English. She defined that attitude as, "nobody messes with me," a phrase which, like *no dejarse*, implies defending oneself in the face of unfair or inappropriate interaction.

The pachucas' hairstyle continued to communicate the aura of possible armed status and perhaps served as a warning or deterrent. The feared image of the pachuca with a razor blade in her hair has endured for more than a few decades. However, some of the comments from Patty (a pachuca in the late '50s and early '60s) elucidate at least one function of the hairstyle: "The cholas . . . they'd put the razor-blades in their hair . . . before you got into a *fight*, just to protect themselves. [She and her sister laugh.] But, you know how women, girls, the first thing they'd go for is to the hair. . . . [When] I used to get into a fight I used to get a couple cuts on my *hands*." Her comments suggest that the blade in the hair was not necessarily an offensive measure but served as a defense and deterrent to aggressors.

Dating and Courting. Aurora's father was very strict with her, and she was not allowed to go to dances until she was eighteen. At that time she began attending dances with the family. However, when she began dancing a lot with a boy her father didn't like, she was forbidden to go to more dances. She and the young man wrote letters to each other for two years before giving up hope that the father would accept a relationship. They finally eloped.

Veronica's mother had been born and raised in Mexico and felt that unchaperoned dating was quite improper, even in the 1960s. Her brothers also kept a close watch on her. This put Veronica in a cultural bind vis-à-vis other young people's patterns of dating at the time. (Some other women of this age group also mentioned strict home environments that attempted to uphold what they felt were outdated norms of gender relations.) At one point in high school in the late 1960s, Veronica was asked on a date by a pachuco young man whom she liked very much. However, her mother would give permission only if she could accompany them as a chaperone. Veronica informed the young man, and although she thought her mother's presence was inappropriate, they decided to go on the date with the mother along. The attempt was ill-fated, for while the three of them ate at a hamburger place, some young men (rivals of the boy on the date) picked a fight with him in the restaurant. The situation came to blows, and the mother forbade Veronica to see him again. Nevertheless, the account demonstrates the young couple's efforts to compromise and prove their good intentions to the mother. Veronica said,

> I think to this day, if my mother would have let me go out with him, or talk to him on the telephone, or . . . The first time he brought me home, you know, he brought me home

> from school; we'd gotten home from school, and I was sittin' in his car, and he was askin' me, "Do you think that I can come over and visit you later?" He was pretty nice. And I said, "Well, I don't know. I'll, I'll, I'll *ask* and see what *she* says about you." And the next thing I know, my mom comes home from work, and she rammed right up to the back of his car, and she pushed it up to the end of the block in her car and dragged me by my hair *all* the way up, smacking me and everything. My books and papers flying all over the place, and that's when I thought, "Well, I'm going to go ahead and *marry* the guy," right?

Veronica commented on her mother's upbringing saying, "They couldn't go to the dance unless her mother went." She also labeled as "stupid" the strategy of marriage as a solution to the situation: "We were so stupid then."

Postwar Reflections

For postwar generation males, the military continued to be an important source of employment for young men. A number of interviewees spoke of making friends from other states in the service who were also into the pachuco style. Bob had met some chucos from New Mexico at Fort Ord, California, in the early 1950s. However, training that would be useful to these men after military service was limited, due to occupational segregation within the military. Most Mexican American working-class men were limited to the bottom rungs in low-skilled jobs; for example, in the army most were riflemen, infantrymen, or in artillery and armor. Few ever made it into communications, engineering, electrical, secretarial, or administrative positions, or jobs such as supply or inventory. This was true even during the Korean conflict. So although World War II had brought some changes for this group, occupational segregation continued to limit prospects for these men.

In the 1950s postwar environment of altered social, interethnic, economic, and gender boundaries, the youth culture continued to project the distinctive demeanor. Females wore "big old hairdos" that still reputedly hid weapons, and males partially conveyed the demeanor by accessories added to their shoes and boots. Bob described pointed shoes worn at the time:

> **B:** Some used to have taps, for kicking.
>
> **Daughters:** For kicking. [They laugh]
>
> **B:** But you never kicked anybody, you know. They're nice shoes. You just carried them, you know, like for fancy. . . . Taps on the toes and horseshoe taps on the heels.
>
> **L:** I bet you could hear the guys coming.
>
> **B:** Yes, you could hear 'em coming! Damn right. And so you had time to prepare yourself, you know. [His son chuckles and his two daughters laugh.]

Aurora remembered her mother Delia and her aunt's apprehension upon hearing the sound of approaching taps in the night. "I remember that. We used to stay right there on 18th Street, and there was a house, it's torn down now, and we used to come and sleep there, and I remember that my mom and my tía used to say [she whispers], 'Shh, shh. Be quiet! ¡Por ahí viene un pachuco!' [There comes a pachuco!] [She and Bob chuckle.] Because they could hear 'em, you know."

Bob stressed about the pachucos, "They didn't bother nobody . . . unless they were *bothered*," adding, "[People] think they were robbers or something like that." Julie recalled, "My friends' mothers used to think I was real wild . . . pero . . . it was just *puro* [nothing but] an *act.* I wanted to be cool." When Aurora drew a temporary tattoo on her hand with washable ink, her father had scolded her saying, "Only p—— . . . bad girls do that."

Aurora recalled parents' attitudes toward the young men. "I remember everyone telling their girls, 'Stay away from those guys, because they're no good.' [laughs] . . . They're not so bad."

Bob said, "They didn't want to be the bad guys. They wanted to be out having fun." His comments reflected those of others when he said, "Before, you could leave that [front] door open at night and go out to the store. [Pachucos] could walk by and they wouldn't come in."

3

Family Histories

Pre–World War II Teens

Dora

Dora was born in Tucson in 1920 in her parents' home "in the railroad section" (*la sección del ferrocarril*) (now Armory Park). Her parents were born on a hacienda in the state of Michoacán, Mexico. Her father, a traveling merchant (*fayuquero*), sold goods in Nuevo León, Guadalajara, and Monterrey. When her parents were only recently married, a brother-in-law came one night to tell her father that Villista forces were approaching the hacienda, forcibly conscripting young men. "They were going to take him away, and my mother would be left alone." The brother-in-law helped the couple flee, and they entered the United States through El Paso, Texas, around 1912. Her parents were the only ones in their families to come to the United States. (Her father left behind a sister and stepmother; he tried to contact the sister later but was unable to find her.) Dora still has relatives in Michoacán that she has never met. At one time she and other relatives contacted cousins there but did not continue to communicate with them because the cousins always asked for money; Dora said, "as if we had a lot here" (como si nosotros tuviéramos mucho aquí).

Upon crossing the border, her parents went first to Louisiana, where her father worked as a lumberjack. However, her mother felt this occupation was too dangerous, so they went to Phoenix, Arizona, and then on to Indio, California, where her father got a job with the Southern Pacific railroad. He was soon transferred to Tucson, where he worked in the yard; he worked for the railroad for thirty-eight years before retiring.

Dora's father was literate in Spanish, having been to school in Mexico. In Tucson he subscribed to the Spanish-language newspaper *El Tucsonense* and was a faithful reader. He had no schooling in English but was able to communicate functionally in that language. Dora's mother knew no English and only occasionally worked outside the home, when she did domestic work for other families.

Dora herself completed the ninth grade in Tucson before leaving school to work during the Depression. Her first job was working for an Anglo-American woman (*una americana*), doing housework and child care. With her earnings, she bought clothes for her brother and herself and remembers taking her mother to see Spanish-language movies twice a week.

Dora married three times. She met her first husband at a dance. He went into the service during World War II, was sent overseas, and was hit by ordnance exploding nearby. Left in a vegetative state, he later died in a hospital. She had a son by this husband. Her second husband drank a lot, so she opted for a divorce. He had not been violent with her but spent all his money on binges and even borrowed to continue these. On payday he would pay back the loans, and the family would be left with nothing. She met her third husband, who dressed pachuco style, when he returned from the service. Before going into the service, he had worked in the cotton fields in Marana, just north of Tucson. Upon returning from the war, he got a job with the Southern Pacific railroad on the Pacific Crew Express. They had been married for eight years when this husband was hit and killed by a drunk driver. She did not marry again.

During this third marriage, Dora worked only when holidays such as Christmas, Easter, or the Fourth of July were approaching, "to buy what we needed, because a lot of times the man's money alone isn't enough." (Pa' comprar lo que necesitábamos, porque también muchas veces el dinero del hombre solo no alcanza.)

During World War II she had worked briefly for the railroad and also for Consolidated Air. She left both jobs because she did not like to wear pants. "I had to wear pants to be climbing around on the airplanes" (Tenía que usar pantalones pa' andarme trepando en los aeroplanos). Later in life her daughter-in-law gave her a pair of pants, and at some point she began to wear pants exclusively.

After being widowed, Dora always worked and held a variety of jobs, at a dry cleaning business, a curtain factory, and in restaurants. Now retired, she lives on a small Social Security income. She is a homeowner. Her son is a broadcaster in the T.V. news industry in a large southwest city.

Martín

Martín was born in Tucson in 1925 in Old Pascua, a Yaqui Indian neighborhood, and lived there all his life. He was of Seri ancestry. His maternal grandparents were born in Ímuris, Sonora, Mexico. Martín assumed that they worked in *labor* (subsistence agriculture). They came to Arizona fleeing *la guerra,* the war against the Indians that lasted for fifty years at the end of the nineteenth and beginning of the twentieth century. His mother was born in Phoenix, Arizona, where her parents had gone to work; she was brought to Tucson as a baby. Martín's paternal grandparents were from Batuc, Sonora, Mexico.[1] They had also worked *milpa* (subsistence agriculture) and came to Arizona fleeing the war. They died before Martín was born. He described his father, who was born in Tucson, as Indian but not Yaqui, although his father had self-identified as Mexican. His father had some schooling in Tucson and spoke English well.

> No sabía hablar la lengua; no sabía porque era un poquito de a medio gabacho, mejor.
>
> (He didn't know how to speak the [Indian] language; he didn't because he was sort of more Americanized.)

His mother spoke only Spanish and could neither read nor write. She cared for the children at home while his father worked in agriculture. As a young boy, Martín scoured the dump near his home for items the family could use. He attended school only to the third grade. When he was about fifteen years old, the whole family worked together picking cotton. He recounted that it was,

M: Puro enganche. De aquí del barrio iban muchos. Piscar.
L: ¿Cómo pa cuál lado iban?
M: Coolidge, Eloy, Marana. Se desparramaba toda la gente. (Se nos enganchaban y luego los enganches lo llevan.) Se quedaba todo triste, aquí el barrio, porque todas las muchachas se iban [laughs]. De manera que nosotros 'tábamos por allá también; les seguíamos también, a ver qué había pa'llá. En ese tiempo parece daban cinco centavos la libra de algodón. Veces subía; en veces bajaba. Noooo. Pero sí, salía, porque era muy piscador. El que sabía piscar se rayaba allí con la feria, pero él que era muy plomo, pues no.

(**M:** [It was] all contract work. A lot of people from the barrio here would go to pick.
L: Where would they go?
M: Coolidge, Eloy, Marana. The people would all spread out. They would contract us and the contractors take you. The barrio here would get lonely, because all the girls would leave [laughs]. So we would go out there, too; we would follow them to see what was out there. At that time I think they paid cotton at five cents a pound. Sometimes it would go up; sometimes it went down. Noooo. But yes, it paid off, because I was good at picking. If you knew how to pick you could earn money out there, but if you were very lazy/slow/heavy [lit. lead] you wouldn't.)

Martín's father worked on the railroad during World War II, in the WPA.[2] After that he worked wherever he could. Before being drafted in 1941 Martín had worked on the railroad with him. He described that time:

A mí me tocó estar en el ferrocarril con él. Y luego pues de ahí ya me agarró el servicio y me fui. Allá me levantaron donde estaba trabajando, cerca 'e Yuma. Un campo d'esos de unos ferrocarrileros. Traiban todo. Traiban un trailer. Nosotros traíbamos un tren grande de puros trabajadores. Ahí nos daban comida; traíamos cocina, todo el material. Extra gang, les decían; number one. [Trabajábamos] 'onde quiera. Acabábamos una parte, luego nos mandaban pa otra parte; diferentes partes, así. La vía. Poniendo riel nuevo. Y luego no había lo que hay ahora. Ahora, pues, puro, pura máquina, cranes y todo. Antes no. Nosotros éramos los cranes. Tu tienes que agarrar troncos a levantar la riel hasta arriba y ponerlo, clavarlo, y todo eso. Ahora, pues, no. La llevan suave ahora [laughing]. Eh. Y luego no ganabas nada.

(I worked on the railroad with him. And then after that the service drafted me and I went. They picked me up where I was working near Yuma. One of those camps some railroad workers had. They had everything. They had a trailer. We had a big train full of workers. That's where they would feed us; we had a kitchen, all the construction materials. They called them the "extra gang;" number one. [We worked] wherever they needed us. We would finish one place, then they would send us to another; different places on the line. Putting in new tracks. And back then they didn't have what they have now. Now, it's all done with machinery, cranes and all. But not back then. We were the cranes. You have to grab logs to lift the rail up and put it in place, drive the spikes in, and all that. Now, it's not that way. They have it easy now [laughing]. And then you didn't earn anything.)

Martín earned eighty-five dollars bimonthly on that job. He reflected:

En ese tiempo estaban baratas las cosas, no como ahora. Una camisa d'esas de trabajo valía, creo que dolar fifty. (**L:** ¿Y ahora?) ¡Y ahora como fifteen, eighteen dolars! [both laugh] Noooo. Verás, todo subió y 'stá subiendo todavía. Todo 'stá caro. Oh, con diez dolars, diez dolars de dinero comprabas todo lo que tu querías: azucar, harina, frijol, y todavía alcanzaba. Y ahora vas pa la tienda, al mercado ahí con cien, doscientos dolar; te dan una cachetada y te quitan todo el dinero [laughs].

(At that time things were inexpensive, not like now. One of those work shirts cost, I think, a dollar fifty. (**L:** And now?) Now, about fifteen, eighteen dollars! [both laugh] Noooo. You see, everything went up and it's still going up. Everything is expensive. Oh, with ten dollars, ten dollars in money you could buy everything, whatever you wanted: sugar, flour, beans, and you still had enough. And now you go to the store, to the market there with a hundred, two hundred dollars; they give you a slap in the face and take all your money [laughs].)

After coming home from the service, Martín worked in the cotton fields again, but automation soon changed the employment picture for many people who had earned their livelihoods in cotton. He explained,

M: Ya no usan la gente, pues. Pura maquinaria.
L: ¿Cuándo entraría esa maquinaria a la pisca?
M: Cuarenta y nueve, cincuenta, por ahí, había máquinas.
L: ¿No se quedó mucha gente sin trabajo?
M: Pues, nos quedábamos sin trabajo, porque no había nada. No más en las puntas de los files, o piscábamos pa que diera vuelta la máquina y se arriendara pa trás, y así. Nosotros agarrábamos no más las puntas, de pisca.

(**M:** They don't use people anymore. Just machinery.
L: When was it that they started using machinery for picking?
M: Forty-nine, fifty, around there, there were machines.
L: Weren't a lot of people left without work?
M: Well, we were left without work, because there was none. Only the ends of the rows, or we would pick so that the machine could turn around and go back the other way, like that. We would pick only the ends of the rows.)

Martín was able to get a job with a private sanitation company as a *tirabiche,* or garbage man.

Y luego de los veintidos [años], me salí pa fuera. Ya no quise trabajar porque estaba cansado. Pues, en ese tiempo trabajaba uno, ¡qué bárbaro!, eeee. Levantar la basura con pura fuerza. Y luego los troques 'staban muy altotes. Ooooh, los de ahora, ahí se la llevan suave, ahí corriendo parejito en el piso, pues. Chaparritos, los carritos que traen. Ahora creo que traen esa cosa que no más abraza el tambo y lo dompéa. Antes no. Antes tenía uno que subirse pa'rriba, y luego unos

> rielitos había nada más que tenían donde pisaba uno pa tirar la basura pa'dentro. Uuuuu, yo me enfadé. Me salí. Me metí al demolition. Allí fue donde me caí pa'bajo.
>
> (And then after twenty-two [years], I left that job. I didn't want to work anymore because I was tired. Well, at that time you worked, yikes! . . . Pick up the trash with nothing but your strength. And then the trucks were really high. Ooooh, the guys now, they have it easy now, running along level on the ground. The little trucks they have [are] low to the ground. Now, I think they have that thing that just clamps around the trash can and dumps it. It wasn't like that before. Before, you had to climb up to the top, and then there were just some little rails that they had where you stood to throw the trash inside. Ohhhh, I got sick of it; I left. I went into demolition. That was where I took a fall.)

Here, Martín speaks of a serious accident he had at work in 1966 in which he suffered broken bones and serious injuries. A wall he was standing on was hit by the skid bucket, and both he and the wall crashed to the ground. Afterward, he couldn't move his fingers. He had surgery on his arm and hand, but the results were not very good. His arm and hand were impaired, and after this he could not return to work; he received a small disability pension.

Throughout his life, Martín participated in the ceremonial activities of his community, Old Pascua. He has twenty-seven godchildren. He retired from these activities only a few years before the interviews, when he suffered complications from diabetes.

Carlos

Carlos, a lifelong friend and neighbor of Martín, was born in "South town" in Tucson in 1931. His parents moved to Old Pascua when he was five years old, and he attended school in that neighborhood. His great-great-grandparents were from Mexico, and one of his great-great-grandmothers was from Spain. His family ancestry is Spanish and Seri Indian. Carlos's mother and father were both born in Tucson. Their parents were from Mexico, from the area of Vicam, Sonora. His father died when Carlos was young. Like Martín, Carlos scavenged at the dump as a child for materials his family needed.

C: We used to go to the dump. Íbamos al dompe, chavalos, pa ir a trae' leña. That was the old shacks. They had the old stoves. Mesquite and everything you can find, bring it over to the house. And I used to live close to the dump, 'cause at that time they used to burn the stuff. . . . Es lo que hacíamos nosotros, también. Ir al dompe a buscar. It was . . .

Martín: . . . pobre. Nos llevamos aluminio, ropa vieja, de todo. No comprábamos.

C: It was a store. Ahorita los chavalos no quieren nada. "¡Ay, mom! I wanna buy new shoes!" Cuando estaba yo en la escuela they bought me a pair of shoes, and I couldn't wear 'em. [Carlos was used to going barefoot, even in the icy weather.] . . . You get used to it.

(**C:** We would go to the dump as boys, to go and get firewood. That was the old shacks; they had the old stoves. Mesquite and everything you can find, bring it over to the house. . . . That is what we used to do, too. Go to the dump to look for things. It was . . .

Martín: . . . poor. We would get aluminum, old clothes, all kinds of things. We didn't buy things.

C: It was a store. Nowadays the kids want everything. "Mom! I wanna buy new shoes!" When I was in school they bought me a pair of shoes, and I couldn't wear 'em. [Carlos was used to going barefoot, even in icy weather.] . . . You get used to it.)

Like his friend Martín, Carlos worked in the cotton fields in his youth.

L: ¿Con azadón?

C: Yeah. Y luego después, o sea cuando crecía el algodón, a pizcar. Unos sacos laaargos, twelve feet. Están grandes. You had to put your feet in and tie it up, so it'd weigh more. Sacar más fería. Pero no pagaban nada, ¿no, Martín?

M: Hu-um. Cincuenta centavos.

C: Treinta y cinco. La hora.

M: Y ahora no, tienen siete, ocho, nueve, diez dólares la hora.

C: In loading work?

M: Ajá.

(**L:** With a hoe?

C: Yeah. And then afterward, or when the cotton grew, pick it. Looong sacks, twelve feet. They are big. You had to put your feet in and tie it up, so it'd weigh more. Get more money. But they didn't pay anything, right, Martín?

M: Huh-uh. Fifty cents.

C: Thirty-five. An hour.

M: Not now. Now, they have seven, eight, nine dollars an hour.

C: In loading work?

M: Ahuh.)

Carlos and his wife eloped when they were teenagers. They first lived together at her parents' house before getting their own place. The couple was married for twenty-five years and had twelve children. When Carlos's wife left him, the children remained with him.

Carlos worked for a private sanitation company with Martín, where they earned about thirty-five dollars a week for a seven-day workweek, picking up trash. He had worked since he was fourteen years old, working a total of forty-two years.

Retired at the time of the interview, Carlos received Social Security.

Lydia

Lydia was born in Tucson's old barrio in 1930. Her mother and maternal grandmother were born in Santa Ana, Sonora, Mexico, where her maternal grandparents lived on a small ranch. She doesn't know if they owned the ranch but assumes they were involved in subsistence agriculture. Because of hard times in Mexico, Lydia's mother went to Nogales, Sonora, and worked as a waitress there to help her family. She met her future husband while working at the restaurant, where he used to eat. At the time, he was driving a taxi on the Tucson-Nogales route. "And what she told me, 'se la robó,' you know, he stole her [they eloped] and brought her over here, and they got married." Her mother was sixteen or seventeen at the time. They had nine children, five girls and four boys.

Her father (and she thinks her paternal grandfather, also) was born in Florence, Arizona. She doesn't know what work her father did before driving the taxi. She knows little about the life of her paternal grandfather, but her brothers have an oval picture of him in which he looks "like a nice-looking German man with a mustache."

Her parents lived at three different central addresses in Tucson. Lydia left high school at age sixteen in 1946 and worked seven nights a week as a waitress at a downtown soda fountain. She still found time to go to the dances on Saturday night with girlfriends after she got off work.

Lydia had nine children, four boys and five girls. Now a grandmother, she is an active older adult and holds a part-time job.

Louie

Louie Rivera was born in 1927 in the large mining town of Jerome, Arizona, where his father was a miner. His father, who he thinks was born in Arizona, died in 1934 when Louie was a young boy. His mother was born in the northern part of the state of Jalisco in Mexico. Louie was the youngest of six children, four boys and two girls. Spanish was spoken in the home. His mother was literate in Spanish and used to read the Spanish-language newspaper *La Opinión.*

After his father's death, his mother remarried and when Louie was thirteen, the stepfather moved the family to Mammoth (Copper Creek). During the 1930s, an older brother went to the CCC (Civilian Conservation Corps) camps and did not return to live with the family after that. After the camps, the brother worked in Superior, Arizona, and subsequently went to work in Oakland, California, after World War II broke out. The brother remained in California for the rest of his life.

The stepfather and the rest of the family moved to Tucson in 1939 but returned to Jerome in 1940, where Louie attended high school to the tenth grade. In 1942, at fifteen years of age, Louie began working in the large underground mine. Workers in the mine were "Austrians, Germans, Englishmen from England, and a few Spanish. And Mexicans and maybe a couple of Indians. Yavapai Apaches."

In 1944 Louie enlisted in the Navy and did basic training in San Diego, California. He was subsequently sent to Pearl Harbor and then to Midway Island in the Pacific, where he had shore duty. Upon returning from the service, Louie worked about four months in the mine. He said, "One day I got tired and got my paycheck and went to Los Angeles; went to work in Los Angeles. I worked for Hunts in Fullerton for about a year, and then I moved to Los Angeles, and I was there for another year. And then I got a vacation, and I came back to Arizona, and then I went back [to work in the mine]."

Louie married Ida, the cousin of a close friend, in 1950 after returning to Arizona. His mother, who had been living in northern Arizona, had passed away. In 1954 the couple moved to the West Side neighborhood where they resided at the time of the interview.

Louie retired in 1976 and suffered from painful arthritis. He and Ida felt the condition resulted from his years of work in the mine. However, the company doctors diagnosed the arthritis as non-work-related. Ida said, "He was a full-fledged miner. . . . The doctors won't admit, but you are not going to tell me that it wouldn't affect him, that he's in that temperature underground, an even temperature all the time, and he comes out and it's cold up there; the warm body hits the cold air; then he gets into the hot shower before coming home. And then in the summer time, it's the same thing, because it's cool down there; he walks out into the heat and then into a cold shower."

At the time of the interview, Louie was receiving Social Security and a small pension from the mine. Ida was working occasionally as a housekeeper in a hotel.

Ida

Ida was born on a ranch in Redington, Arizona, in 1934, where her father worked as a ranch hand. Paulina Moreno Montoya, born in Redington in 1905, describes Redington as an isolated community where people were largely self-sufficient, small farmers (Martin 1992). Ida described the place where she was born:

> We went, I don't know how many years ago, and the walls of that old house where I was born are still standing, just the walls, just the adobes. . . . But it was so isolated, and the reason we moved out, my dad was a rancher but they lost two sons

> within a week. One was six and the other was seven. I guess they began to worry and worry about us kids. . . . So they got away. [They moved to Tucson when Ida was one year old.] And so then my dad had to switch from being a rancher to . . . going to construction or whatever. But the cowboys would [still] bring their horses to my dad, bring them to shoe the horse. (L: Down here [in Tucson]?) Yes! I would see my dad; I loved to see my dad shoe the horses. And he would make the adobes to make the houses.

They lived on Anita Street for awhile, and when Ida was five years old her parents bought a lot on Speedway Boulevard near the railroad tracks close to Barrio Anita, where they built their first house. It was the first home they owned. Ida said, "We didn't move too much. We were pretty stable."

Ida's older brother died of polio at age eighteen. The family was quarantined for a while, but no other family member came down with the illness. He had been a good student in high school, holding an after-school job at a fish market: "He wanted to help my dad." One day at age sixteen he came down with a fever and became paralyzed. (The family feels he contracted polio at work.) For two years his parents desperately sought a cure. Ida's mother went to work outside the home, and Ida and her sister dropped out of school to stay home and care for the brother while both parents worked. Ida related, "There was a plant. . . . They would get it, I don't know . . . by the pound; they would go out in the desert and bring it, and they would boil it. And in that water they would bathe him. And see, they had to do it . . . because they tried everything. . . . Home remedies; he was in the hospital, in and out of the hospital. So my dad and my mother would go out to work and they would give instructions. And they bought a real long and kind of narrow tub, aluminum tub, and I had to bathe him. And pour that water on him." Despite the family's efforts, the brother passed away after two years. Ida had left school in the ninth grade and returned to get her GED only as an older adult. "There was no money, see. Everything went towards my brother's illness. So any money that mom or dad might get, it was all invested in that cure. And then my dad, by that time, he wasn't an old man, but in a sense he was, because he worked so hard all his life. So we had to drop out, my sister and I." Ida feels that more education would have helped her get better jobs, because at the time of the interview she was working due to her husband's disabling arthritis. They were living on Louie's Social Security and a small pension from the mine. Ida said, "When I was growing up, if the woman of the house worked, it was because she wanted a little extra, or luxuries, or whatever. Now, it's got to be. The woman has to work, too, to help the husband; otherwise it's hard."

Delia

Delia was born at home in Tucson, in 1921, in the old barrio. Her mother was born in the Río Yaqui area of Sonora, Mexico, and died in childbirth when Delia was a young child. Delia's biological father was a Spanish hacienda owner in Mexico. Her daughter, Aurora, explained,

> My mom's mother used to be a servant to a Spanish guy; a Spaniard . . . on the other side [Mexico]. . . . This Spaniard was a real rich guy, and he had servants. My mom's mother was like, a little Yaqui girl, you know, like a Indian. And she was a servant to them. The Spanish guy, this rich guy, got her pregnant. . . . Well, he had people working for him. My [later-to-be-step-]grandfather worked in the fields in the ranch right there. He was like . . . oh, I guess they're also like servants, but they're working outside with the horses and the fields and everything. He worked there. Now he was married and he had a family. Or he was living with this lady. But he had a family. And so he was like the, you know, the rich people have somebody that are really confident to them; they tell 'em everything. So he got my [step-]grandfather on the side, and he said, "Take this lady to the other side [the United States]. She's going to have my baby. Take her over there; I'm giving you money. . . . [So] the Spaniard told his worker to take my grandmother. . . . And he gave him a *carreta*, you know, those old-fashioned *carretas* [wagons], and horses. And money. "Go buy a ranch, okay? And you set her up." But he wanted him to go back, you know, but my [step-]grandfather *stayed* with my grandmother. He stayed with her. He fell in love with her and stayed with her, and he abandoned his family over there.

Delia's stepfather was also Yaqui. The ranch they bought (evidently in the Spaniard's name), was southeast of Tucson and had horses and cattle. The stepfather worked the cattle, fenced, and did ranch work. The union produced three children.

After Delia's mother's untimely death in childbirth, the Spaniard sold the ranch to an Anglo man, and Delia was raised for a time by a woman married to her maternal grandmother's brother, a woman she called "aunt." This couple was originally from Chihuahua and lived in the old barrio in Tucson at the time. While Delia was small, the hacienda owner occasionally sent money, food, and clothing for her, both before and after her mother's death. Delia remembers seeing him a couple of times. She recalled, "He was like an *americano.* He had eyes like the *americanos,* very green. And he was very light-complected with curly black hair." Of her life during this time, Delia said,

> Aquí con mi tía no más vivía unos días, ansina, porque me pedían pa' que les cuidara los babies a mujeres, asina. Y cuando estaba aquí con mi tía, me fui con los Moreno, con la Sra. Moreno [pseudonym], allá a su casa. Allá me estuve. Me estuve un tiempo porque mi pa' trabajaba ahí en la casa de ella, ¿no? . . . They were rich people. . . . Yo vivía con ella para que barriera afuera, y le diera comida a las gallinas; tenía muchas gallinas, huíjolos; y que le tirara l'agua a las canoas para que los patos se bañaran en agua limpia, y clean the, afuera, ¿no?, y luego adentro de la casa también.
>
> (I'd only live with my aunt for a few days because people would ask for me to take care of babies for women; things like that. And when I was living with my aunt, I went to live with the Moreno family [pseudonym], with Señora Moreno, there at her house. I stayed there. I stayed a while because my [step-]father was working at her house. . . . They were rich people. . . . I lived with her to sweep outside and feed the chickens; she had a lot of chickens, turkeys . . . and to put water in the troughs so that the ducks could bathe in the clean water; and clean the yard, and then inside the house, too.)

She lived in Tucson until the age of eight, when she was involved in an altercation with a boy at school and was about to be sent to reform school. To avoid this, her stepfather sent her to a ranch southeast of Tucson to live with her confirmation godmother. Her uncle also got a job working on that ranch. Aurora said,

> My [step]grandfather worked also as a cowboy. . . . That's what he was doing at [the ranch] over there. He ran a ranch. . . . You know, in those days people were very poor . . . but they had it kinda good because the man that he worked for had a lot of cattle and every month he would tell him to kill a cow. They had meat . . . a lot of meat, and then my grandmother learned to plant vegetables and fruits and everything, and she would can, and then she would make cheeses and milk the cows and everything, and she had to learn all that stuff . . . to survive, you know. They just came to town in a carreta . . . a wagon, to pick up stuff that they didn't . . . they couldn't *raise* over there . . . or have over there. He would only get paid very little . . . money you know, for doing that; taking care of the ranch; but they didn't need anything, 'cause they had everything over there. My grandmother *did* everything. And so it was nice, you know . . . in that way. I remember that my aunts and my uncles, they used to say that they were poor all the time; they didn't have the things that almost everybody took for granted later on. They had a real . . . rough time. My grandmother used to make dresses for the girls from the flour sacks. And underwear and all that; the same color . . . or she would buy some coloring for the fabric . . . to put different colors.

Delia's godmother spoke Yaqui and Spanish in the home. Delia attended school with her godmother's children near the ranch. Later, when her aunt in Tucson was sick again, her uncle took her back to the city to help the aunt. However, the uncle died—not the aunt, as people had expected. Delia described her circumstances later after her aunt had passed away: "Cuantas veces se movía mi pá [padrastro] pa' los ranchos, él me llevaba, porque no me quería dejar porque mi tía ya se había muerto." (Every time my dad [stepfather] went out to the ranchos, he would take me with him, because he didn't want to leave me [behind] because my aunt had already died.)

After she worked for the Spanish-surnamed family in Tucson as a servant, she returned to the ranch again with her godmother.

To her godmother's displeasure, Delia and one of the godmother's sons eloped to Tucson when Delia was fifteen. Aurora said, "My mom says that she [the godmother] used to tell her that she hadn't raised her for him. Or him to be with her." Delia and her husband had four children, three girls and one boy. A fifth child died as a baby. Delia had attended school to the second grade, and her husband had attended to sixth grade.

Aurora gave the following account of her paternal grandparents' background (Delia's confirmation godmother and husband, mentioned above):

> **A:** They both came from over there [Mexico], too. And they were from the area of El Río Yaqui, and my grandmother used to tell me . . . that she used to live on Madera Canyon, over there, in her childhood. But then when she went with my grandfather, they came over here [to Tucson].
>
> **L:** But what were they doing in Madera Canyon?
>
> **A:** When they came from the other side [Mexico], they ended up on a camp on top of Madera Canyon. I guess it was a mine or something, probably, 'cause my grandmother said that they used to live in *tents.*[3] [She had met Aurora's grandfather there.] She has a real interesting story on her side, too, because my grandmother had two little girls before she went with my grandfather. And they say that (**L:** She was very young? **A:** Very.) the oldest [child] was [because she was] raped; some man had raped her, and she had a baby [in the camp]. And then she had another baby; . . . I don't know if she had from the same man or what; I don't know what happened; anyway, she had two kids already when she ended up with my grandfather. And she was, like, fifteen when she left that place to come to my grandfather.

Aurora continued, "And you know it's weird that those two kids died later in the years . . . that she just ended up having my grandfather's kids. One died of chicken pox, I think, and the other one, she was little when she died. They went on to have, like, thirteen, twelve kids."

Delia's husband (her godmother's son) was born in Tucson in 1918 and was taken to the ranch southeast of Tucson as a small child. As a young girl, his mother had lived in Eloy and Casa Grande; her

Figure 8. Helvetia mining camp in the mountains southeast of Tucson, 1901. Helvetia is an example of the camps that existed in the Santa Rita Mountains at the time. (Arizona Historical Society, AHS Photo Number 24320)

family worked in agriculture. They had also lived and worked in Sahuarita. The family moved between cash-crop wage labor, subsistence agriculture, and ranching. The godmother and her husband also picked cotton in Continental, where now there are pecan orchards. Later, their granddaughter Aurora picked cotton there, too. After her parents eloped, Aurora said, "they were living in [the ranch]. Then they came to Tucson. And from Tucson they went . . . around on that side [gestures north], on Coolidge and Eloy for some time. And then they ended up in Continental." Delia worked "in the field" before Aurora was born. "Somewhere they used to grow potatoes over here, on this area. And she was packing them and something happened that she broke her arm. Those *bandas* [conveyor belts] that they call them [broke her arm]." They worked picking cotton; "at that time it was mostly cotton." Delia's husband worked on ranches mostly in Continental and Coolidge. The family later moved to Tucson, where he held various jobs, cleaning up at a drive-in, picking cotton, and then working in an ice plant. He did custodial work at stores, held a job with the newspaper, and then went back to the ranches. At age forty-eight he suffered a heart attack and was unable to work after that. His health failed rapidly and he passed away in the 1950s. At the time of the interview, Delia lived with her daughter Aurora and family.

4

FAMILY HISTORIES
POST–WORLD WAR II TEENS

Aurora

Aurora is Delia's daughter. She was born at home in Tucson in 1942 in the barrio, "where the Community Center is now. There's a little back street, close to the freeway. The street is still there. Some of the houses are still there. The house I was born in is still there. They haven't torn it down. My dad left for the service; they drafted him in '42. He left in January, and I was born in February, two months after he left. And I remember that my mom says that they didn't let him come, you know. But see, he was trained and then he was taken overseas." Her father's wartime task was gathering the dead after the battles. She was three years old when he returned. Aurora's home birth had been attended by a midwife. "But a doctor was there, Dr. Allen, and the midwife, 'cause the Red Cross at that time, with the soldiers, they helped them a lot. So they had a doctor sit there in case something went wrong."

As a child, Aurora recalled gathering firewood and wild plants with her grandmother in the hills behind what is now the retirement community of Green Valley. That was when her parents were picking cotton in Continental.

Aurora's father was very strict with her. She was not allowed to go to dances until she was eighteen, and soon even that was forbidden. Her father would make disparaging remarks about women, comments that today would be called verbal abuse. Aurora and her future husband, Bob, eloped after trying to win her father's approval for two years, during which time they sustained their relationship through letter writing. After eloping in 1963, they first lived in Washington Camp in the mountains behind Patagonia. Aurora said, "I went over there with him. He was a miner. He was mining, but not the right kind of mining. A mine that didn't pay. [laughs softly] They were getting some kind of ore from there. I think it was *cobre*, copper and some black rocks; I don't know what it was. And they would load up some train things, and the train would take them out of there." Her husband described this work during one of his interviews:

> The one I was working in was a small mine. I was bringing the ore out with a machine, a hoist. I was pulling it out and dumping it. Sometimes I worked inside [the mine]; drill, blast. (**L:** Was it straight down or were there tunnels going . . .?) Straight down and then tunnels. About 100 ft. deep. It was a big pot that could carry about a ton of ore. I would dump it on a pile. I used to do that, and I used to go inside, and I'd help them out; get it ready till you can pull it out. And then when it was ready to pull it out, I used to go up there and start hauling it up.

Aurora had said, "So anyway, he worked there. And I didn't like it because they only paid him $22 a week. I told him 'I don't want to stay here. I want to go down.' I call it down, because it was up on the *cerro* [hill]. I said, 'I'm not staying here.' And he didn't believe me at first." The two of them went to Tucson at Aurora's insistence, and her aunt was able to direct them to other employment.

> **A:** My aunt said, "Go to Marana. There's jobs over there." And we didn't have to look hard; he got a job right away. He used to work for Mr. Smith [pseudonym]. He had fields, cotton fields. And he had some cattle fields that they grow for the cattle; he had cattle, too. And he hired Bob to take care of everything: to irrigate, plant, get the soils ready for planting again, and picking everything up and everything. He would pick up the cotton with the machine, the cotton

> pickers. And he would take care of the cattle. Feed the cattle in the morning and then go out in the fields and work in the cotton. Have you ever seen when they hire people to take care of a place?
>
> **L:** Did you folks live there, then?
>
> **A:** Yeah. It was an old house. . . . It was three rooms. Two rooms were connected. The other room was not connected; that's the one that was the kitchen. And they were old. We painted them and cleaned them up so we could live there.

Her husband earned $200 every two weeks at this job, a better salary than at the mine. They stayed there about two years. Aurora became pregnant while they were in Marana and began to have her children. After that, she didn't work outside the home until the children were older. Bob subsequently worked many jobs, driving a tractor in Marana, working on farms and ranches in Rillito, Chandler, Eloy, Phoenix, and Parker, and working in a number of places in California, including Brawley, San Jacinto, San Bernardino, Riverside, and Oceanside.

One winter, in about 1979, when they were living in San Jacinto, the whole family got very sick with flulike symptoms. They were all ill, it rained for days, and they couldn't get out with the car. No one went by to see if they were all right. Aurora felt isolated and thought they should return to Tucson. "If we had lived in Tucson, maybe my dad would've gone to see us. And he would've seen that we were sick, and then he probably would've brought my mom and somebody to take care of us. We packed everything and just came." Aurora also thought her children should have the opportunity to know their maternal grandmother. They never left Tucson again. "It was horrible over there, not having anybody else around." In Tucson, Bob worked as a painter and also sprayed fields and orchards with chemicals.

Bob

Aurora's husband, Bob, was born in Tucson in 1937 at Los Reales (now called Midvale Park). Aurora described the agricultural workers' quarters where he was born. They have since been torn down and replaced with an upscale apartment complex:

> In the old days they used to just make one long building with lots of rooms, and they would put up the workers in there, you know, like, not bunk houses, because families used to live there, the whole family. . . . In the old days, the kids, they could sleep in one room with the parents and everything; there was nothing to it, you know? It was that way. So they just had a couple of rooms, I guess, in that big, long building, the kitchen and one room, and they all lived there. I remember that when the midwives would go over for the ladies when they were pregnant and gonna have babies, they would put, like, sheets all around the bed so the rest of the family wouldn't see anything.

Bob's mother died in childbirth when he was a year and a half old. Aurora said, "In the old days they had midwives, and they never went to the hospital, so this had to do with that. They just didn't get taken care of."

Bob said his father was a miner, "like the old-time miners. The same thing I used to work. Go into the holes. Big mines. . . . At least I could go out and see the sun once in a while. But my dad never did. . . . He went in; never came out of the mine. All the time. That's why he got sick and died." Bob was nine years old when his father died of "lung sickness, from working in the mines." Aurora said that "from then on he was from one sister or the other. He had three sisters and one brother and went back and forth between them until he was, like, seventeen; he enlisted. He took off."

Bob said that after being orphaned, he lived with "everybody. I was all over the place. With different people. Some treated me nice and some treated me bad." Some were not relatives, but family friends. He stayed with a sister in Washington Camp and went to the seventh grade in junior high school in Patagonia. He left school at that time and started doing farm work. He recalled, "I was twelve. That's when I started working. [I worked] down here by Rillito farms [north of Tucson] and then at Three Points; I worked nights irrigating and stomping the cotton crates. (**L:** What is that?) The machine. You pick up the cotton with a machine, and they pick it up and go dump it in the crate. But you gotta be there ready when they dump it, so you can stomp it down, so it fits; so they can do some more, and it'll fit." Afterward, Bob lived with his brother in Tucson, who worked in masonry, building houses. At age fourteen, he returned to Washington Camp and worked on the small farms there that grew wheat, corn, and alfalfa. In 1950 he moved north and worked as an errand boy at the store in Winkelman, Arizona, and subsequently as a musician in Superior, where he played guitar in a group called *Trio Superior* that played parties in 1952. He also worked at an auto sales lot in that town. He said, "I didn't stay on one job too long."

Bob had gone to Winkelman and Superior because his stepmother, with whom he was on good terms, lived in Hayden, and a sister was in Superior. His brother-in-law was a miner there.

Before enlisting in the army, Bob worked for about a year at the mine back in Washington Camp. "In Washington Camp, there's mines; they all mine the same thing. Copper and zinc; ore. Ore means a lot of stuff; all kinds of minerals. But the main thing is copper. The one I was working in was a small mine." He enlisted in the army at age twenty, in 1957, and trained at Ft. Ord, California. From there he went to Ft. Riley, Kansas, and on to Germany. He did his two-year tour of duty and was discharged in 1959. While in the service he completed a tenth-grade education. "You didn't stay in the army?" I asked. "No. I didn't like it. It gets boring. Same job every day. Same hours." He had only liked being out in the field in boot camp. "That's what I'm used to, you know, having fresh air and elbow room in the wild that's way out there. And if we came back to the barracks, same thing all over again. Get up same time . . ."

Upon returning from the military at age twenty-three, he went to Santa Rosa, California, to work in the apple orchards. He caught a bus from Nogales, Arizona, that was taking workers there on a six-month contract. After that, he returned to southern Arizona but did not live with any of his relatives. Aurora said, "From then on he boarded with families he would live with. He would work in the fields. He did a *lot* of work in the field in California. Cotton." He returned to the mines at Washington Camp again and married Aurora during that time. They eloped because her father had not approved of the relationship.

After their marriage, Bob began working on ranches and in cotton fields north of Tucson. The couple traveled a lot, with Bob working in the fields and on ranches in Arizona and California. He worked steady jobs in agriculture if he wanted, or seasonal work if he chose. He saw his mobility and flexibility in employment as a strength and as conducive to independence and self-esteem. At the end of his interview, he made the following statement: "I'll tell you one thing.

I had a good life. I did what I wanted to do, went where I wanted to go, and I've still got things, more things to do. I've been a farmer, a miner, a painter, a mechanic, chemicals, cowboy, a musician. And I wish my sons would do that, but nowadays it's too hard. I did that before because of, times were good. And now . . ."

Rudy

Rudy was born in Tucson in 1933 and lived in the old barrio known as El Hoyo. His maternal grandparents and mother were born in Tucson. His maternal grandfather worked primarily on cotton fields and cattle ranches in the Eloy and Red Rock areas. His father's parents were from Caborca, Sonora, Mexico. They had six children, three sons and three daughters. When his father was twelve years old, the family went to Texas and stayed a while near Houston and San Antonio doing agricultural and ranch-hand work. As a young man, Rudy's father visited cousins in Tucson while on his way to California to pick peaches. He never reached California, because he found employment in Tucson, met Rudy's mother, and married. (They had five boys and three girls.) Rudy's cousins worked for many years for a large construction company in Tucson. His father worked as a lineman with the railroad.

When Rudy was about thirteen years old, his parents separated for approximately three years. During that time his mother and the children lived with one of his uncles in Tucson, and his father returned to Caborca. The father later returned to Tucson, went back to work, and the family was reunited.

Rudy recalled that in 1945 or '46 his father's male cousins left Tucson for California and never returned. They had previously gone there to work seasonal crops but always returned. However, at the end of the war they moved there permanently. Their sisters remained in Tucson.

When Rudy graduated from high school he got a job in Tucson as a gas lineman for a private company. He enlisted in the army in 1950 and served two tours of duty in Korea during the Korean War. Upon return to Tucson he worked as a machinist for a newspaper company, then worked for fifteen years as a groundskeeper at an institution of higher education. He subsequently went to work for the city of Tucson in various sports activities and programs for youth.

Rudy reminisced about the extended family's activities when he was a child and his cousins were still in Tucson (a pattern that many families maintain today): "It was a pretty big family with *todos* [everyone], grandchildren and all. . . . But they're all scattered now. I'm about the only one that's in Tucson . . . that I know of. I have some cousins, but we don't associate or nothin'; just 'Hi, primo [cousin],' that's it." He added that this is also because he is older than they are. Sometimes they see each other at a store and exchange questions about the respective families.

> But we never say, "Let's go get together sometime." But I remember my dad and his brothers and them would always get together. Fridays and Saturdays they would *all* get together at the house . . . all the time. They were always having like a party, but it wasn't actually a party, just to get together. But always the family was there. More of a family-oriented stuff. But then it started fading out. One died, and his family wasn't around. Just moved away, I guess. Scattered. But that's quite a while back. Sometimes I sit back and I, when my mind's at ease, I remember all that stuff. But it's not gone with the wind, either. You still remember it. So when I see somebody's name in the paper, [his surname], I say, "I wonder who he is." Probably my cousin. You never know.

Rudy has been married for thirty years. His wife is from California. Her parents were from the state of Sinaloa, Mexico. Rudy still has uncles in Texas and a brother, sister, uncles, and cousins in California. He also has cousins in the state of Sonora, Mexico. Rudy recently retired but continued to work part-time.

Art

Art was born in 1944 in Tucson's Barrio Anita, a neighborhood he described as located "in between the Mexican, the blacks, and north of the Indian . . . the Yaquis." His mother, of Apache and Mexican ancestry, was born around 1912 in the copper mining town of Mammoth. He added, "But they used to call it El Tigre. Old Tiger."

Art's maternal grandmother was Apache. He didn't know her, because she died young, when his mother was thirty-six. Art also hadn't known his biological maternal grandfather. When asked if he knew anything about him, he answered in the negative, saying, "They used to get mad when I used to search. The old people didn't like, well, my mother and my aunt didn't like looking into the family history." His maternal grandmother had remarried to a German miner in Mammoth who replaced his mother's Spanish-language name with a German one. He sent her to a private school in Oracle. She also attended a boarding school in Benson, Arizona, through the ninth grade. Art said, "My mother was a miner too. My aunt was a miner; my uncle [mother's brother] was a miner. My uncle used to sell uranium. That's how he eventually died of cancer." He said his mother and aunt worked "mining, digging. . . . I've seen some pictures, my mother, man, coming out of like a hole in the ground. A shaft. They used to work like men. Wear overalls." Art thinks that mine belonged to his uncle or his grandfather. "When my mother and my aunt and my uncle moved from Mammoth in 1933 with my grandmother and my great-grandmother, they all came down here [Tucson] 'cause . . . my mother's father had died. . . . Where the San Manuel pit is, the shafts were, that's where my mother and my grandmother used to live. But I think that these people bought the land; I don't know who it was. Eventually, he told everybody to move." Art felt that this move had been occasioned by discrimination.

> **A:** She [his mother] would never say it. I think most people around Mammoth, for some reason, discriminated against. And my mother never, never admitted anything. But that's my theory. She's of Mexican descent and Indian, Arivaipa Apache.
>
> **L:** Did she speak any Apache?
>
> **A:** No. I think a long time ago the Mexicans were ashamed to be Indians. 'Cause the Anglo was always looking down at the Indian. So the Mexicans didn't want to be categorized as an Indian. So he thought he would be . . . Caucasian.

Art's mother and father met as neighbors in Tucson after her family made the move from Mammoth. His father was about thirty years old, and his mother almost ten years his junior, when they married in 1936. They had three boys and six girls, of whom Art was the youngest.

Before marrying Art's mother in Tucson, his father had lived in San Diego. Art said, "I think he used to work for the steel mills up there or the shipyards. National Steel Shipyard, I think they called it on the old 101. I think I have brothers up in San Diego. I just got a feeling. [He hasn't met them.] My father was a pretty sharp guy; had his ways, I think, with women. I'm not sure, but that's what I hear."

Art's father was born in Tucson in 1906, "just right downtown where Main and Sixth Street comes together." His paternal grandfather, "was like an orphan. His mother died sort of young, too. My aunt raised him; his sister. I think their mother was from Patagonia; around that area. And his father was from Mexico. Hermosillo or somewhere down there."

His paternal grandmother's family was described as light-complected and more Spanish than Indian. Art speculated that they must have worked as miners, ranchers, or housekeepers.

In Tucson, his father worked at the old Southern Pacific roundhouse. He and many others were laid off when diesel engines came into use.

Art's mother did housekeeping before she married. He added, "My mother was pretty well educated. For most, in those years, I don't think people would go further than the fifth grade. My mother had nine years of school."

Art described life in Barrio Anita when he was a child: "We were raised in a two-room house. I remember when my mother heated water outside; she broke wood, *leña* [firewood]. Our bathroom was a hole in the ground. Then the sewer came in; the gas came in. [The sewer was installed in the 1950s.] I was probably six. I remember when the gas came in. [Before that] she had a wood stove inside the house. She did everything . . . in those days. . . . My mom was tough. . . . She made tortillas three times a day. She broke wood, washed outside in *bandejas* [galvanized washtubs]. . . . We used to take a bath in there." When I asked about their source of water, he answered, "We had a *tripa* [lit. intestine] outside." I asked if he meant a hose. He answered, "No, a *fierro*; *una pipa* [a pipe]. *Tripa*, we used to call it. And during winter it used to freeze. Then we had to wait. My mother'd put water inside in the night. Then we used to use a *bacín* [chamber pot] in the nighttime or go outside to urinate or whatever. We used to plant our own vegetables in the yard. They had a pretty big yard." His mother also raised chickens, turkeys, and ducks.

Art's father passed away of stomach cancer in 1962, at the age of fifty-six. Art thought the cancer was probably caused by his heavy drinking. His mother and father had stayed married in spite of the drinking. Art said, "I don't think women are made anymore like my mother and the old people. Women can't take mental cruelty or physical cruelty. But my father, when he was drunk, he was mean. . . . I have to ask people; my wife and my new wife says probably the reason my mother stayed so long with my father till his death, 'cause they had nine children. But he was uneducated. He only had . . . three years of school. So he was actually a general laborer." When his father died he left some money to Art's mother. Art recalled, "My mom bought a house right in the middle of Anglo society." By this time, Art had dropped out of high school, in the ninth grade, and was later sent to the reform school at Fort Grant (Arizona State Industrial School) in the early 1960s.

As a teenager and young man in Tucson, Art folded and delivered newspapers, did maintenance work, and drove a truck. He also "spent a lot of time in jail" for drinking and fighting. Art added, "But from those years to this present time I've really changed. I don't think it pays to be bad." He said, "I still have a lot of hate. I don't know [if it's] this society [Anglo society]; I'm trying to figure out what made me this way. Was it my father beating me so much that caused me to be this way? . . . He used to crack my bones with sticks and brooms and fists. The old people used to really beat you up. Now they have got this law against brutality."

When Art got out of reform school he became an alcoholic and drug addict "for many years." One of his brothers also followed this path.

Art was drafted by the army during the Vietnam War at age twenty-three and was sent to Fort Bliss, Texas. He had married a short time before being drafted. His wife was from a Sonora, Mexico, border town and had become a United States citizen. Art's experience in the army was not a good one. He said, "They started stealing my money from the company. They lied. I got more pissed off by the day and [learned], I guess, to not trust Anglos; in those days my best trust for Anglos got worse."

After returning from the army, Art's marriage lasted only a little over a year. His wife left him, divorcing him a few years later. (They had one child.) After that, he stayed single for a long time, although he had a number of girlfriends. "I think I had to find myself, or else I didn't trust myself." He had not treated his wife well and would get drunk and hit her. He described his life after the divorce: "So here

I am back in the streets, fighting. Get drunk in bars. . . . I would wreck a lot of heads in bars. They'd throw me out because I was such a mean guy, I guess."

At this angry stage in his life at age twenty-four, one day in a bar he met an Apache man who became a father figure to him. In conversation he told the older man that his mother was Apache and mentioned her place of birth. The man directed a tribal program and put him to work. Art went to live on one of Arizona's Apache reservations. "So I spent ten beautiful years over there. Ten glorious years up there in the reservation, in paradise. Ahh, I loved it. . . . People would tell me that I got like culture shock . . . going from the Chicano barrio, the Anglo barrio of this world and then back; going to nowhere; just camps. *Campos.* A group of houses here, a group of houses there. Ahh, I loved it; just peace and quiet. [The father figure] taught me a lot of stuff in life. How to camp. How to make a fire; how to break wood without using an axe." (The man had passed away five years before the interview.) Art stayed on the reservation until 1982 when he got sick "from drinking so much." He began hemorrhaging and was hospitalized in Tucson. He recalled, "And I found myself in this society and, 'When?' 'Who am I?' 'What?' So I decided then and there that I was going to change. I didn't drink for almost eight years, nine years. I got re-educated; I have a GED and I got about three years of college."

Looking back on his life, Art said he spent "many a year bumming around." When not on the reservation, he had stayed "here and there." For two years in San Diego he worked intermittently in lumberyards, restaurants, and as a groundskeeper. At the time of the interview he was doing yard work. He said, "I'm good at what I'm doing, but it's hard labor." He also drives a truck and moves furniture.

Art had remarried to a much younger Anglo woman with two children from a previous marriage. He expressed ambivalent feelings about supporting her children, even though he felt affection for them. He noted, however, that he had never given anything to his own child from his first marriage. Of his previous defiant attitude and ways, he said, "I really have changed my way of thinking now. I guess because I'm older, more softer. I think more now. I think twice."

Art drives a lowrider-type, classic car, which he referred to as *mi carrucha,* and was wearing a *tando* (pachuco-style hat) and khaki pants the day of the interview. His mother had passed away in the late 1980s of complications from diabetes. Two of his sisters also died from diabetes-related causes. He added, "And if I drink another drop, that's what is going to happen to me, too. [He also has diabetes.] I had a second chance to live, so I'm trying to take advantage of the situation, to better my life slowly."

He recapped stages in his life by recalling the teen years, the pachucos, then the Beatles and his transition into "Beatle shoes, long hair and tight pants." He recalled the years as a tattered alcoholic and then his college studies. He said, "Now I'm a house owner, married; I got two children. I have done a lot. But my best life was living in the reservation. Not paying for nothing. Planting corn, going acorn hunting, game hunting, hearing the old people talking Apache, singing, going to the [girls' puberty] dances. I think those were my most exciting days of my life. I learned a lot. I think that's when I sort of opened my eyes and said, 'Now I'm ready,' and it happened that I got sick and I came back to reality." Art said, "people tell me, you know, that I was born a hundred years too early or late, the way I was against the Anglos. But I've learned; I lived; I changed; I've accepted. And here I am. I mean, it's pretty hard to change the world, now."

Patty and Sister

Patty was born in Tucson in 1946. An older sister, born in Tucson in 1942, also participated in her interview. Their mother, an orphan, was from Mexico City. Their maternal grandmother died giving birth to the mother, who was raised by an aunt. However, the mother felt unwelcome and ran away at age fourteen. She was apprehended and the aunt placed her in a convent. Their mother ran away from the convent at age sixteen and met her first husband, an Anglo-American man who was part French, the father of Patty's oldest brother. Although that marriage didn't work out, she obtained immigration papers during that time. She had divorced the man, not wishing to tolerate his drinking and womanizing.

In the United States, she tried to make it on her own with the baby. Her daughter explained, "She did a lot herself, 'cause she had to work to support my brother after she got a divorce. He was a year old. My mother told me she used to live in those little houses, but not like this kind of house, cardboard houses. It's just something to keep my brother and feed and support him. At the time they didn't have no welfare." She also explained, "My mother never had any childhood of her own. She was always on the go, working. She worked all her life. Scrubbing floors, washing, maid work."

The mother had gone to California and worked packing pickles before meeting her second husband in Tucson, father of Patty and her sister. (She met him when she would go dancing with a friend and her sisters. He was the friend of a brother-in-law.) Born in Glendale, Arizona, he had come to Tucson to work as a carpenter with the railroad. He raised the son by her first marriage; however, he drank a lot and the marriage was troubled. Patty related, "My father had his own room, and my mom had to sleep in the living room. Ever since I can remember; she still sleeps in the living room." Her sister added, "From the day it happened. It happened on the day a baby was born to them. And my mother caught my father with another woman. And then my mother told my dad, 'Yo no soy plato de segunda mesa' [I'm not the dessert]."

Although this husband turned out to be much like the first, Patty's mother opted to remain in the bad marriage rather than strike out on her own again or try another marriage. The sisters had been told that their parents stayed together for the children's sake. Patty added, "My dad never left her 'cause my mother was, to be truthful, she was a very good cook. That's why my dad never left her. He knew he did wrong, but it was way too late."

Patty is the youngest of five children, three brothers and two sisters. Spanish was the language spoken at home while they were growing up. The family has Yaqui heritage on the father's side. When they were small, the family first lived in the old barrio. They subsequently moved to Barrio Anita, where some of the children were born, including Patty's sister, who was born at home. Patty and her younger brother were born in St. Mary's Hospital. In 1946 the family moved to an adobe house on the South Side that their father bought for $1,500. The house is still in the family.

Their mother was employed outside the home intermittently while they were growing up, doing housekeeping. She was very strict with the children and used liberal doses of corporal punishment. Patty's sister remarked, "It was like child abuse." Patty ran away as a child to avoid such punishments at home and at school, while her sister "just took it."

Patty left high school in the mid-1960s and went to work without attending college. She obtained her first job through the Neighborhood Youth Corps. At age twenty she moved to California because of the situation at home. She explained, "I was so frustrated. I didn't want to hear cussing and yelling, every day, the same routine. One time I had to get in the middle of it. And I told my dad, 'Don't hit her,' because I didn't want my dad to hit my mother." In California, Patty came to realize that her sexual orientation was lesbian. She said, "I'm tired of hiding. You know, people don't understand why the reason is; why a person, not because, hey, you go ahead. People don't understand that. People think that being a lesbian is ugly-feeling. When I saw people letting out what they are, what they feel, that's when I did it." Patty and her sister felt this orientation was already apparent when she was a child. Her sister described her as *marimacha* (a tomboy). As a girl she would play with her brother and break her sister's dolls. Patty also mentioned that she was molested by a man when she was a teenager and had been afraid to tell her mother. Later, as a young adult, she had boyfriends but was not sincerely involved.

In California, Patty lived a freewheeling lifestyle, drank heavily, and used pills. A female partner urged her to free herself of substance abuse and successfully saw her through a long rehabilitation process. The partner later died, and that woman's mother took everything the couple had accumulated together. Patty lost everything.

After being away for many years, Patty returned to Tucson when her father was diagnosed with cancer. She cared for him for a few months until he passed away.

Patty has a small son. At the time of the interview, she was living with a female partner and received public assistance.

Julie

Julie was born in St. Mary's Hospital in Tucson in 1947 and grew up in a neighborhood located midway between Barrio Hollywood and the South Side. Her father was born in Tucson and worked as a union electrician. Her mother, born in Nogales, Arizona, worked for Consolidated Aircraft in Tucson when single but no longer worked outside the home after marrying Julie's father.

Julie's maternal grandparents were from Caborca, Sonora, Mexico, where her grandfather was a bricklayer. The grandparents came to Tucson in a wagon train in search of work. Julie said the wagon train navigated a hazardous crossing of desert areas where the Indians were at war at the time. In Tucson, the maternal grandfather's sons followed their father's trade, as did the grandsons, Julie's male cousins, some of whom now own construction companies. One of Julie's uncles and his son worked on the restoration of the San Xavier del Bac Mission (1992–97).

Julie's paternal grandfather was born in Argentina. His parents brought him to Tucson as a boy when they came, she assumes, in search of work. He married Julie's grandmother, a Mexicana residing in Tucson. It is not clear whether she was born in Tucson, but she was living there when he met her.

Julie described her upbringing as very strict. She attended public school for two years and then Immaculate Heart Academy, a Catholic school for girls located near downtown Tucson, until the tenth grade. Julie recalled the academy, saying, "It was haunted. They used to see nuns floating in the halls. *Flotaban* [They floated]. There were s'posed to be spirits. And then a couple times I heard that they had seen this other man roaming in the hall, holding his head [in his hands]. A lot of nuns have died there, too, and some priests."

In tenth grade she entered a public high school and recalled the relief she felt at not having to genuflect "every time you walked by the statue" (a statue of Mary that stood in a hallway at the Catholic school). She graduated in the mid-1960s. Her older brother, who had been into pachuco-style clothes, was killed in Vietnam at age nineteen, soon after her graduation.

As an adult, Julie, along with her husband Armando, has been active in a number of community activities and in political causes. They have two children. At the time of the interview she was not working outside the home.

Armando

Julie's husband, Armando, was born in Douglas, Arizona, in 1941, one of eleven siblings. His mother was born in a small town in Sonora, Mexico, that no longer exists. (He doesn't know its name.) Her lack of a birth certificate proved troublesome when she applied for Social Security retirement benefits. "She had to prove her age . . . and her birth certificate, they could never find it. So anyway, she knew where she was baptized at, what church, but the pueblo does not exist anymore, so they found out they should've. . . . In fact she got retroactive pay because she was really older than what she thought she was."

Armando's father was born in Mexico and is of Mayo Indian ancestry. His father and mother settled in the border town of Agua Prieta, Sonora, Mexico. Armando does not know how or why his parents went to Agua Prieta. (It is not clear whether they went there together or met once there.) He described his father as a jack-of-all-trades who took all kinds of jobs to make a living, working as a laborer for different construction companies, doing yard work and odd jobs. He also worked as a laborer in the Phelps-Dodge smelter in Douglas, Arizona; however, this job was sporadic due to company layoffs. When these would occur, he would live just across the border in Agua Prieta. It was a subsistence-level existence. When the job was terminated altogether, he moved the family to Tucson to a neighborhood on the South Side. At the time, Armando was eight years old.

Armando was the third-youngest of eleven children. He recalled an impoverished childhood: "Me acuerdo que nos bañábamos (I remember that we bathed) when we were kids *en* [in] Douglas, even *aquí en* [here in] Tucson . . . en una tina, you know, galvanized tub, two at a time! So my familia has known *pobreza* [poverty]." When asked how they dressed, he said, "any which way possible. *Una camisola* [a dress shirt], usually buy the cheapest and the ones on sale. So we really couldn't choose styles and all that." Armando recalled that the Anglo principal of his Douglas elementary school had taken him by the hand one day, walked him down to the Phelps Dodge Mercantile store, and bought him some *cachoronas* (long johns), because it was so cold.

Only four of the eleven siblings graduated from high school; Armando counts himself among the fortunate ones who did. There had been no lack of hopes and dreams among the brothers and sisters, but many were not realized. No one in the family has ever graduated from a university.

Armando recalled a sacrifice his mother made during his high school days: "When I was 16. My mother, I don't know *how, pobrecita mi ma* [my poor mother], I don't know how; for thirty dollars . . . *how* in the *world* she could ever buy me this junk car that was a '38 Ford, just so that I could stay home and I could tinker with the car.

We were on welfare. We were on everything. There were a lot of times *que no teníamos ni papas para comer* [that we didn't even have anything (lit. potatoes) to eat]." He described his mother as a strong woman who's "gone through hell and back."

Armando worked for the railroad for a number of years. Julie is his second wife. They have two children. His first wife was Anglo. Fairly recently, Armando and Julie moved from the South Side neighborhood where they had resided for years, to a West Side subdivision. Armando explained that they moved there for the schools, even though he thought that "culture-wise" the children would have more Chicano influence on the South Side. However, it was important to him that in the new school, "they really expect those kids to learn." He and Julie felt that families in this West Side area were more active in the educational process. Armando also described the current high population turnover on the South Side. "You don't have that stability. I don't think *que la escuela* (that the school) can maybe keep up with it. Not only that but nearby neighbors are dealing. I wanted to get from that whole scene." Nonetheless, Julie, Armando, and the children recently moved back to the South Side, having experienced an uncomfortable, isolated feeling in the West Side subdivision, where interaction patterns were quite different.

Veronica

Veronica was born in Douglas, Arizona, in 1951. Her mother was born in 1933 in a small town in Sonora, Mexico; however, she grew up in one of Baja California's border cities and had other relatives in a Sonoran border town.

Veronica's father was a miner born in Douglas, Arizona. Her father and mother met in a Douglas nightclub. The couple had six children, four boys and two girls. Veronica described her father as a macho heavy drinker who had not been supportive of the family and had not been a good husband. He left her mother when Veronica was in the third grade. She said, "Back in those days it was hard. Usually the father was the main provider, right? The father left; the mother was S.O.L. [shit-outta-luck]." Her mother, who had a fourth-grade education and didn't speak English, was left with six children. (Two others had died.) She divorced and moved back to the border city in Baja California, where Veronica began attending

Spanish-language elementary school. When she was seven and still a monolingual Spanish speaker, her mother moved the family to Tucson. The mother never remarried and always worked; however, this meant that Veronica, the oldest daughter, carried heavy child-care responsibilities from a very early age. She began working at age twelve and contributed to the household economy.

Veronica dropped out of high school in eleventh grade and married to escape pressures at home, but the marriage was short-lived. She was able to get her GED and subsequently worked for a time in Los Angeles, starting at seventy-five cents an hour. She went to that city because her father was living there. Veronica observed, "You know how you always wanna find out who your dad is, and I don't know why." The experience was disappointing, and today she has little respect for her father.

While in Los Angeles, Veronica married again. She and the young man drove to Las Vegas on the spur of the moment and married at a wedding chapel. However, that marriage also ended in divorce. She has since remarried in Tucson. Veronica is a cosmetologist and owns a home in a suburban South Side neighborhood. She has three children.

5

The Pachuco Language Variety in Tucson

When a member of a speaking collective comes upon a word, it is not as a neutral word of language, not as a word free from the aspirations and evaluations of others, uninhabited by others' voices. No, he receives the word from another's voice and filled with that other voice. The word enters his context from another context, permeated with the interpretations of others. His own thought finds the word already inhabited. Therefore, the orientation of a word among words, the varying perception of another's word, and the various means for reacting to it, are perhaps the most fundamental problems for the metalinguistic study of any kind of discourse. (Bakhtin [1929] 1984:202–3)

Ornstein-Galicia has summarized the historical trajectory of the language variety spoken by the pachucos:

> Chicano Caló may be traced, although remotely, to Romani or Romany, an Indo-Aryan language spoken by a possibly pariah group in Central India, which migrated to Europe by way of Persia (Iran) in the fifteenth century (Common Era). The Romanies or Gypsies, contrary to common practice, settled on the edges of Spanish cities, particularly in

> Andalucía. Gradually their speech shifted from the ancestral tongue to Spanish, although the Romanies did retain a Gitano Caló which had developed on the Iberian peninsula. Carlos Clavería points out in his seminal *Estudios sobre los Gitanismos del Español* (1951) how both the Gitano Flamenco culture and its Caló became a veritable vogue in Spain, influencing the popular arts and music as well as Spanish language. Immigrants and settlers from Spain, especially Andalucía, brought elements of the Caló to the New World and of course Mexico City. In turn it was carried from there to El Paso and other border points, diffusing throughout the Southwest where it developed with its own norms, accepting loans and calques from English and other sources. (Ornstein-Galicia 1995:114)

Bakhtin has observed that, "especially in epochs dominated by conventionalized discourse, the direct, unconditional, unrefracted word appears barbaric, raw, wild. Cultured discourse is discourse refracted through an authoritative and stabilized medium" ([1929] 1984:202–3). Certainly Pachuco/caló has been seen as "barbaric" and "raw" and can be characterized as often direct and unconditional. Art referred to the directness of the language during one of the interviews, saying, "You talked the way you seen things." That directness had caused him a lot of grief when he used it with members of the dominant ethnic group. It had not been conducive to his survival, and he had curbed the practice. Being frank redounded in a loss of what Kochman has called "social warrants," the entitlements to which individuals can lay claim in social interaction, since these entitlements bear directly upon the degree of leverage that individuals can hope to muster in establishing parity for their point of view or, more generally still, in influencing the course and outcome of encounters and transactions in which they are participants (1984:202)." Kochman also finds that social warrants are culture-specific: "Rarely do people see social warrants or entitlements in terms of the cultural norms that society has set to regulate social interaction. Yet, social warrants do have a cultural basis" (1984:202).

Some aspects of warrants are based on conventions of appropriateness for the organization of discourse, while others involve content, mannerisms, and even conversational rhythms. Kochman has concluded that there is a political dimension to mainstream

American public protocols, explaining that "mainstream American social etiquette . . . acts as a principal socializing agent: it promotes mainstream American communication and discredits that of other social or cultural groups (e.g., the lower classes or ethnic minorities), at least insofar as their patterns of behavior are incompatible with the way power is promoted and exercised in mainstream social life" (1984:203). Kochman adds that "this political character is often lost on mainstream Americans who tend to see the standard they set for social interaction as impartial, that is, serving the political interest of all participants equally" (1984:200).

Just as Bakhtin found words to be "already inhabited," Voloshinov stressed the need to see utterances as the product of interaction between speakers and "the broader context of the whole complex social situation in which the utterance emerges" ([1927] 1973:78). "Social" here must be seen to include political and economic relations, including imposed or established patterns of deference between ethnic groups, nationalities, classes, and genders.

Academic Approaches to Language Contact

Sapir pointed to the importance of examining processes of language contact in 1931, noting that language use can embody 'social attitudes' and express positive resistance to something perceived as 'hostile' during periods of cultural change (Hill 1988). Early on, Dozier (1964) addressed the manifestations of interethnic politics and attitudes in linguistic processes in his article, "Two Examples of Linguistic Acculturation: The Yaqui of Sonora and Arizona and the Tewa of New Mexico," giving attention to regional varieties of standard languages and the effects of politics and the quality of interethnic relations on attitudes about linguistic borrowing. He also pointed to differing mechanisms of linguistic elaboration available to or favored by a people's cultural and linguistic system.

Continuing this tradition, Hill and Coombs (1982) and Hill and Hill (1987) have described in detail dynamics of the political economy of language use by Indian groups in the Americas. Urciouli (1991) has also made detailed observations and analyses of the political dynamics of language use in her study of Puerto Rican language use in New York City. She has observed that "the topography of English and Spanish is shaped by the equality or inequality of relation.

When class and race are unequal, language boundaries are clear and distinct. When class and race are equal, language boundaries are negotiable. Gender creates subtle distinctions in the language landscape" (1991:295–96). Bakhtin had noted in 1929 that use of particular language varieties can be taken as semantic positions: "Dialogic relationships are also possible between language styles, social dialects, and so forth, insofar as they are perceived as semantic positions, as language worldview of a sort, that is, as something no longer strictly within the realm of linguistic investigation" ([1929] 1984: 184). Importantly, though, Urciouli (1991) has pointed out that varieties do not inherently carry a semantic position in the usage of the bilinguals she observed. Her work distinguishes between "code neutral" and "code relevant" moments.

Hill and Hill (1987) note that scholars of language have focused overwhelmingly on linguistic divergence and that relentless focus has precluded an understanding of the extent and mechanisms of linguistic convergence.

Anthropologists Hill and Hill (1987), Hill and Coombs (1982), and a number of creolist scholars have written about the stigmatization of "mixed" linguistic forms such as Pachuco/caló in both academic and popular discourse. Academic work in linguistics has traditionally been concerned with "standard" languages (those called "authoritative and stabilized media" by Bakhtin), a concern probably derived from attitudes that stigmatized oral varieties, let alone those considered "mixed" or even "mongrelized." The stigmatization of these varieties carried over to the scholars who studied them. Baugh (1983) has noted that because their work concerned an unwritten and "mixed" tradition, creolist scholars were not taken too seriously by other linguists working with more "classic" languages.

Urciouli has expressed the opinion that "what actually come into contact are not codes per se, but speakers whose linguistic practices and identities vary. Nevertheless, the terminology of language contact—borrowing, interference, assimilation—metaphorically implies the existence of a monolithic, pure and separable entity called code" (1985:363).

Hill and Hill, and Hill and Coombs, have called code-switching, creoles, and creole-like languages such as Pachuco/caló "the great syncretic systems of the New World" (Hill and Coombs 1982:226). Hill and Coombs and other creole scholars have noted the "symbolic ambiguity" that is central to such linguistic systems. Their complex processes of generation of meaning cannot be approached without examining the interethnic political and economic relations involved. The centrality of "symbolic ambiguity" reflects what the Hills call "the struggle to control . . . the symbolic universe" (1987:53).

The Emergence of Pachuco in the U.S.–Mexico Borderlands

The places where Pachuco/caló emerged in the United States are places where populations converged and speakers of a number of languages were brought together as a result of Spanish colonial and Anglo-American expansion into, and economic exploitation of, what is now called the Southwest in the United States and the Northwest in Mexico.

Pachuco/caló emerged along the U.S.–Mexico border in the early part of the twentieth century. El Paso, Texas, a key geographical location on the border, was the place of the language's emergence in the present United States. It is said to have been spoken in the El Paso area in the 1920s (Armando Trujillo, personal communication, 1985). There is some evidence of vocabulary and perhaps the caló itself being brought into the area from Mexico at least by 1916, if not earlier.[1] The violence, upheaval, and famine in the wake of the Mexican Revolution of 1910 had occasioned large population displacements and migrations to the U.S.–Mexico border area, especially through El Paso, which at that time was a center of labor contracting for the western United States. It appears that caló came with this migration.

A few words and phrases from the caló spoken previously in Mexico's Distrito Federal during the first decade of the twentieth century are documented in a brief article by Eugenio Gómez Maillefert (1920). He lists words and phrases still used in contemporary Pachuco/caló in the United States; however, semantic shifts have taken place.[2] That caló shares mechanisms of lexical formation and masking with Pachuco/caló,[3] as seen in the following example sentence given by Gómez Maillefert: "¿No querétaro tomatlán un tequesquite chicorro? ¿No quieres tomar un tequila, chico?" (Do you want to drink a tequila, guy?) (1920:30).

Possible semantic angles contained in the word *pachuco* itself are provocative. Images and forms originating in different cultural and linguistic systems produce layers of meaning through their juxtapositions and intersections. Barker (1950) defined the word *pachuco* as "a fellow from El Paso," adding that, "many of the writer's informants have pointed out that the word *pachuco* is a colloquial way of saying El Paso" (1950:21).

My research has located a Kiowa term in use at least by the mid-nineteenth century that most likely predates Anglo-American occupation and political control of the area. It appears in James Mooney's 1898 *Calendar History of the Kiowa Indians*, first published in the *Seventeenth Annual Report of the Bureau of American Ethnology, 1895–96*. Mooney lists the following term in the Kiowa-English glossary: "Pä'sûñko or Pasun-T'a'ka'-i: Mexicans about El Paso on the Rio Grande: from the Spanish *Paseños*" ([1898] 1979:417). The Kiowa word appears in a historical narrative in the section of the calendar entitled, "Summer 1857" when, after a Sun Dance, "two war parties started out, one against the Pä'sûñko (Paseños, Mexicans of El Paso), and another, consisting principally of Comanche under the chief Mawi, against the Sauk and Fox tribes, who had so badly punished them three years before" ([1898] 1979:302). The account illustrates some of the region's linguistic and ethnic diversity, and interaction between groups at the time. It also tells about the origin, in 1839, of the *a'poto* staff of the Sun Dance. In that year, twenty Kiowa warriors had started against the Pä'sûñko. While resting one day, they were surrounded by a large force of Mexican soldiers and had to take refuge in a cave.[4] As Mooney relates the story, "the Mexicans had with them several Mescalero Indians (*E'sikwita*), who, however, were rather doubtful allies, as one of them who spoke Comanche shouted to the Kiowa in that language, encouraging them to hold out" ([1898] 1979:302–3).[5]

In the word *Pä'sûñko* /p^{h}á:sę̀gɔ̀/, the Kiowa suffix *-go* (pronounced "ko") means "people" or "ones," so one meaning is "Paso people" or "Paso ones." However, a second reading is possible: "musty-smelling ones." The reference is to body odor and generally an unpleasant one.[6] This double, superimposed meaning is characteristic of one of the ways meaning is generated in many Pachuco/caló words (Cummings 1994:163). The second term given by Mooney, *Pasun-T'a'ka'-I* /p^{h}á:sę̀-t'ɔ̀k^{h} ɔ̀y/, is defined as "musty-smelling Caucasians," suggesting cultural critique of and political commentary about the Mexican people of El Paso.

Another possible intersection of form and meaning for the word *pachuco* present in the region at the turn of the twentieth century can be suggested in a term recorded by Peveril Meigs, in his book *The Kiliwa Indians of Lower California*: "*pachugós*, the dreaded robes of human hair used in the *niwey*, ghost-calling ceremony" (1939:112). (Such rituals have also been characterized as memorial ceremonies for the dead.) The robes covered the shamans completely, from head to foot (1939:54). Anita Alvarez de Williams (1975) lists a number of historical accounts of such robes of human hair recorded in Spanish colonial documents from the early eighteenth century on. Geographically, these describe practices extending from mid-peninsula Baja California, Mexico, north to the Kiliwa, who are located to the southwest of Mexicali, Baja California. From the various accounts, the robes appear to have functioned as symbols of the life, death, and healing of the corporate people in a sense that transcends the Western past/present dichotomy. The robes themselves were an important link in communication with the dead. According to Meigs's informant, the last niwey ceremony was given by Jose Luciano Espinosa, a shaman who was then captain, in about 1893 (1939:50).[7]

Mauricio Mixco's contemporary work on Kiliwa language adds interesting semantic dimensions for the word *pachugó*, which has been borrowed into local Spanish to mean "pachuco," but only in the sense of *ladino* (Spanish-speaking Indian) or "town dweller." A number of implied meanings converge in the term, including "clothed person" (the connotation of having an outer wrapping or of being clothed, derived from the shaman's cape); "person of power and wealth" (because of the shaman's status); and "townsperson" (because townspeople both were clothed and had de facto power over rural Indians) (Mixco, personal communication, 1993).

Another key symbol of the incipient culture, *tacuche*, an early word for zoot suit, is a Tarascan/Pure'pecha term that Santamaría defines as "a bundle/wrapping of rags" or "trouble" (1974:994). Cobos (1983:159–60) gives New Mexico and southern Colorado usage for *tacuche* as (1) a kind of prisoner's uniform or (2) slang for a man's suit. Aguilar Melantzón (1981) gives "lawsuit" as one meaning of the term in the Ciudad Juarez area. A common semantic thread runs through these key terms, Kiowa *pä'sûñko*, Kiliwa *pachugó*, and Tarascan/Pure'pecha *tacuche*; all refer to cloth-wrapped town dwellers, pernicious relations of power, and trouble. The semantic content of the Tarascan word *tacuche* was preserved when it was brought into Spanish and Pachuco slang as *garras* (rags).

The line drawn in 1848 representing the U.S.–Mexico border cut through the traditional territories of a number of Indian groups. It divided some, came between closely allied groups, and affected seasonal migratory patterns and trade networks. The Kiliwa were one such group, being closely allied and intermarried with the Cocopah people to the north, some of whom are now in Baja California just below the border near Mexicali in the areas of El Mayor Indígena, Río Hardy, and the Sierra de los Cucapá. Many more are in the area of Yuma, Arizona (Ochoa Zazueta 1978:167; Sanchez Otamendi, personal communication 1997). Cocopah workmen were among those of the area's earliest labor force, working on the steamboats on the Colorado River that supplied Fort Yuma and the town that grew up there from the 1850s on, and which were a vital link in both east–west and north–south travel, making this area an important regional crossroads for miners, merchants, and agriculturalists. Cocopah also worked in support tasks for the boats, such as woodcutting, and in the harbor and shipyard where they were built, which was established by the Colorado Steam Navigation Company in 1865 at Port Isabel, below the border from Yuma at the upper end of the Gulf of California. It was in that port that cargos and personal effects were transferred from seagoing vessels to the riverboats, and vice versa. Port Isabel was second in activity only to San Francisco in the waters of the Pacific (Iglesias Serafín 1992:4, 24). (When Dora's father was transferred by the railroad company from San Francisco to Tucson [before her birth], the family took a ship from San Francisco around the southern tip of Baja California and up to Port Isabel. Their effects were then transferred to a riverboat that took them up the Colorado to Yuma, where they caught a stagecoach to Tucson.) Riverboats continued to navigate the Colorado until 1916 (Lingenfelter 1978:xiv). It is quite conceivable that Kiliwa individuals might also have been in the workforce or would have at least been familiar with the language use of in-laws and allies, and vice versa.

The yearly reports of the region's Indian agencies to the commissioner of Indian Affairs between 1905 and 1920 contain statistics on the employment of Indians, by tribe, in work on the railroads along the border. Kiowa and Cocopah workers were among those listed,

Figure 9. The Colorado No. 2 *in dry dock in Port Isabel, 1868. Note Cocopah Indian man standing on bow. (Arizona Historical Society, AHS Photo Number L)*

Figure 10. Riverboat on the Colorado River at Yuma, Arizona, date unspecified. Riverboats traveled the Colorado from 1852 to 1916. (Arizona Historical Society, AHS Photo Number 40722)

along with Indians from groups in California, Arizona, New Mexico, and Texas. Indeed, Mixco's eldest Kiliwa informants, now deceased, had worked as cowboys and participated in many cattle drives to Mexicali and were familiar with that urban, border area (personal communication, 1993). Mexicali was a railhead that connected to the east–west Southern Pacific line in California's newly developing Imperial Valley, the line that ran between Los Angeles and El Paso, passing through Yuma (Walther Meade 1983:183).

Barker mentioned the role of the railroad in the dissemination of Pachuco language along the border but did not mention the Indians working on the lines from at least the turn of the twentieth century or their possible role in the process. In the research on Pachuco, there is a general lack of attention in the literature to the region's Indian-language varieties and cultures, and to intertribal and Indian–Mexican relations. That Indian languages are known to have influenced the region's Spanish varieties is evident in many of the dictionaries of regional Spanish that give Indian-language derivations for words. However, this influence is not taken into account in most discussions of Pachuco/caló lexicon or conversational and other sociolinguistic dynamics.

Even during the period of Spanish exploration and settlement of New Mexico, many Nahuatl-speaking individuals were listed as *españoles* in the rosters of the expeditions to the region and in the settlements. Historian Antonio Ríos Bustamante has pointed this out, noting that the Spanish racial classification system (which was tied to a hierarchy of salaries) was more flexible than has been previously assumed, especially if one had connections (Ríos-Bustamante, personal communication, 1993).

Ruben Cobos (1983) discusses words of Nahuatl, Rio Grande Pueblo Indian, and Navajo derivation in his *A Dictionary of New Mexico and Southern Colorado Spanish.* Santamaría's *Diccionario de mejicanismos* (1974) would be one place to begin searching for Indian and Indian-language-derived words; he lists words of Aztec, Cahita, Mixtec, Otomi, Tarascan, and Zapotec origin. Regional Indian-language dictionaries and vocabularies would yield additional words that came into Pachuco/caló.

The convergence of populations and interethnic, multilingual environment in the region point to a juxtaposition of discourses and semantic systems within a given power field, providing a context in which the possibility exists for diverse forms and meanings to be played off one another. The meanings of the multivocal key terms are precisely those generated by such juxtapositions.

Barker, Ortega (1977, 1991), Sanchez (1983) and most others have characterized Pachuco as a bilingual, Spanish–English phenomenon. There is a need for attention to the region's Indian-language varieties, cultures, and intertribal and Indian–Mexican relations in the research on Pachuco.

The lack of systematic inquiry into the role of Indian languages and cultures in the shaping of the pachuco phenomenon in the greater Southwest may perhaps best be understood in light of the stigma attached to Indian identity and the violation of their human and civil rights, especially after the United States acquired the Southwest in 1848, after the Mexican–American War. Menchaca (1993) calls this phenomenon "racial repression" (but it was both racial and cultural). As a result of the hostile environment, many people represented their identities in such a way as to be exposed to the least possible hostility, danger, and trouble, and to maximize consideration for their persons under the new U.S. system. Under that system, persons of Indian ancestry faced extermination, enslavement, segregation, and prohibition of citizenship and voting rights. In the legal domain, the federal government did not acknowledge the existence of people who practiced *both* Mexican and Native American traditions; these experienced greater racial discrimination than the rest of the Mexican population (Menchaca 1993: 599–600). While Native Americans were being condemned to these fates, a more viable option of racial and cultural identity, when possible, was the assumption of Mexican identity as a means of survival and a ticket to more freedom than Indians could hope for. The legacy of "racial (and cultural) repression" may well explain why the Indian influences have not been more specifically addressed in the literature on pachuco, even in Chicano scholarship of the 1960s and '70s.

Language Dynamics in Southern Arizona

Language varieties used in southern Arizona that were mentioned by participants in this study (using their labels) were Apache, Seri, Yaqui, and many kinds of Spanish: *el lenguaje común* (the common language), ordinary language, real Spanish, Mexican, *español chafa* (poor Spanish), Pachuco, real Pachuco, real Mexican Spanish, Chicano or Mexican American Spanish, Yaqui Spanish, half-Spanish, *mezclado* or "mixed," going bilingual[8]; broken-down Spanish, and street language; English ("American") and German were also mentioned. Add to this complex linguistic web: variation by nationality, region, socioeconomic class, ethnic group, village, and other subgroupings.

Economic and political changes in the region since the nineteenth century have driven radical changes in the socialization contexts of language varieties, in their domains and contexts of use, in relations between languages, and in cultural and linguistic viability itself. Speakers of Indian languages were especially caught in the politicoeconomic crunch. Families of some interviewees had experienced very rapid linguistic change, moving through a number of language varieties over two or three generations. Aurora spoke of her own situation: "My *grandmother* tried to teach me [Yaqui]; she used to tell me to learn. . . . And I remember that when we used to take long walks she used to try to teach me but I never could learn. I had a hard time learning English; how was I gonna learn something else? I didn't learn English till I was in the sixth grade, I think. I could understand it and I didn't talk it until I came out of the eighth grade." Aurora also related, "[My grandmother] knew quite a bit of Yaqui. And that's all they talked, 'cause they didn't know anything else. I didn't learn, though. I just learned how to say 'yes' and 'no,' probably, and that was it. And then I forgot about it. I couldn't. It took me up until I was on the sixth grade, fifth or sixth grade, when I started learning English. I couldn't, you know. I was talking Spanish most of the time."

Art characterized his family as bilingual. "We talked whatever." His mother spoke Spanish and English, "but she never talked the other language [Apache] for some reason." She had nine years of school, having attended boarding school in Benson. She could read and write both English and Spanish, and even learned German from her stepfather. Art's maternal grandmother was Apache. His description of the family of his paternal grandmother, who was from Patagonia, Arizona, reflects the region's ethnic diversity: "I think they all were Spanish people. You know, there's people they're Spanish, and there's other people that are more Indian than Mexicans. But these folks were more Spanish and they're light-complected, like my father and my aunt. Almost like *güeros* [fair-skinned, fair-haired people]."

Martín and Carlos, men of Seri ancestry who had always lived among the Yaqui, spoke Spanish and English; they had not learned Yaqui. Martín's mother spoke Spanish to him, and English was used at school. Carlos hadn't learned Seri from his father, because he died when Carlos was very young.

I asked Aurora about the long walks she had mentioned with her grandmother.

> **L:** You mentioned that when you were going on long walks with her, she would try to teach you [Yaqui]. . . . Where would you walk?
>
> **A:** Up on those mountains in back of Green Valley. Green Valley was all pure . . . monte [land covered with underbrush]. . . . It had only mesquites and those palo verde . . . trees. And a lot of washes. And it's real pretty where we used to go walking, 'cause there was a lot of cactus. And then she would show me the different kinds of plants that were good and that. But I didn't learn, though. I was so dumb, I forgot everything. The only thing that I can remember is the onions from the monte over there. They're sweet little onions.

In another description of the walks, Aurora related,

> We would just go walking, me and my grandma, and sometimes me and my aunt. Or my grandma, my aunt, and me and kids . . . my other cousins. My sisters sometimes. But not usually. Most of the time it was just me and her walking around. . . . We would make wood, too. Wood for the stoves. And then we would go have somebody pick it up after we had made it. . . . I used to love to take those walks with my grandma, because I learned a lot of stuff. Stuff that I wanted to stay with, I would stay with. But like she wanted me to learn Yaqui; I didn't; . . . I just didn't. I don't know why. Now I regret it.

Such forms of socialization contrast dramatically with contexts being imposed to socialize individuals into completely different cultural, political, and economic practices, those of U.S. industrial capitalism. Delia described the physical plant and activities of a Tucson public school she attended in 1929: "La Drachman tenía, pues, cuartos así que tenía uno que ir así al arithmetic, al spelling, aquí venía con la maestra que estaba todo el tiempo. Pues, ella nos entretenía, ¿no?, diciendo qué era esto y el otro y haciendo historias, y asina, ¿no?, pa' que estuviéramos ahí en la escuela pa'prender, yo creo." (Drachman [school] had rooms like this that you had to go this way to arithmetic, to spelling, here; here you went to the teacher that was always there. Well, she would keep us busy saying what this and that was, and telling stories,[9] and so on, so we'd stay there at school to learn, I think.)

For the Indian languages, contexts of use became so rarefied due to the imposition of other varieties or the pragmatic necessity of using them, that in two interviewees' families, the Indian language became the language of secrecy and inaccessibility. Aurora explained, "My grandfather on my dad's side, he used to talk like that when they didn't want the kids on the family to know what they were talking; they would talk *Yaqui*." Art's account also appeared to associate Apache language in his family with secrets or marked privacy.

From participants' comments on language acquisition and use, a picture emerged of cultures and identities rapidly losing ground and viability, with harsh implications for individuals, families, and other kinship and social units. The volatile linguistic environment was experienced by many young people moving into early adolescence, in the process of beginning to form an adult identity. The implications for self-image and development are profound. Utilizing a U.S. national ideology of individualism, Aurora explained that she had not learned Yaqui because she was lazy or dumb. She did not describe herself as a child juggling multiple language varieties in an environment that was often hostile.

History and Dissemination of the Pachuco Language Variety in Tucson

The earliest an interviewee recalled hearing Pachuco/caló in Tucson was 1929, so the variety has been spoken in this city at least since that time. The earliest speakers among consultants had learned from people "passing through," probably as a function of the migrations related to the Mexican Revolution, labor contracting, and then the Great Depression. Delia learned the language at school when she was around eight years old. She said, "Hablaban mucho asina en la escuela. . . . Se juntaban muchos, y muchachas también. Y comenzaban a hablar y todo ahí. Y nosotros los oíamos; queríamos hablar una que otra palabra." (They used to talk like that a lot at school. . . . A lot of them [kids] would get together, and girls too, and they would begin to talk there and all, and we would hear them. We would try to speak a word or two.)

I asked Martín if his generation was the first generation of speakers. He replied, "Pues, ya había. Antes había otros *antes* de nosotros . . . porque, pues, yo los miré a ésos. Ya 'staban mayores ya cuando nosotros oíamos a ellos. Y nosotros, se nos pegó eso, también."

(Well, there already were others *before* us . . . because I saw those fellows. They were already older when we used to hear them. And we started talking like that, too.")

Those older fellows passing through Tucson from different places (Texas and California were mentioned) spoke an unintelligible language. Martín continued, "A veces los oíamos nosotros. Nosotros nos juntámos riendo de él, porque nosotros también [chuckling] no les entendíamos. '¡Amen!' les decíamos. 'No sé qué 'stá hablando ese muchacho, o señor ése.' Ahora no. Ahora nosotros lo usamos también." (Sometimes we would hear them. We would get together and laugh about it, because we could not understand them, either. "Amen!" we would say to them. "I don't know what that boy or man is saying." Not now. Now we use it, too.)

Pachuco/caló has been characterized as an urban variety, and while urban centers may have been the primary sites of its development, this study finds that it was spoken early on, at least in Arizona, in rural areas and mining towns. Delia, a young Tucson dweller, carried Pachuco/caló to a ranching and mining area southeast of the city in 1929. Her family sent her there to live with her grandmother at eight years of age, so she would not be sent to La Corrección, the reform school at Fort Grant. I asked if any people at the ranch spoke Pachuco. She replied, "No; no hablaba así la gente. Yo en veces hablaba con, ahí con los locals y ellos comenzaron a hablar como yo." (No; the people didn't talk like that. At times I would speak with the locals there, and they began to speak the way I did.)

Two people recalled early use of Pachuco in mining towns. Louie's older brother spoke the language in Jerome, Arizona; it had been spoken there even before the dress style arrived. Gilberto Arrieta, a lifelong resident of Morenci, Arizona, recalled that Pachuco/caló was spoken there in the 1930s.

Most of the older men said World War II brought about changes in the language. Martín and Carlos alluded to the effects of the war on languages and language use in general during one discussion. Carlos began,

> **C:** Allí en la guerra, you really learn different.
>
> **M:** Yo conozco uno que vive todavía ahí; dice que cuando él entró al servicio, se le olvidó la lengua Yaqui. "¡Nooo! ¿Cómo, si tu eres Yaqui? ¿Cómo se te va a olvidar?" ¡No quería él hablar Yaqui porque "se le olvidó"! [**C:** chuckles] ¿Cómo?
>
> (**C:** Over there in the war, you really learn different.
>
> **M:** I know one fellow that still lives there [in his neighborhood, Old Pascua]; he says that when he went into the service, he forgot the Yaqui language. "Nooo! How is that possible? You're Yaqui! How can you forget it?" He didn't want to speak Yaqui because "he forgot it"! [**C:** chuckles] How can he forget?)

Martín's account may reflect one man's changed attitudes about language varieties, a shift in language preference, and/or shifted competencies in different language varieties as a result of experiences in the military.

Pachuco survived after the war, though some vocabulary changed. New generations continued its use, although, as for many groups, the pre–World War II generation and those following the war had significantly different life experiences.

Interviewees' Characterizations of Pachuco/Caló

Interviewees described Pachuco as a young people's or teenagers' language, characterizing it as humorous, innovative, at times nasty, and unintelligible to speakers of more standard varieties of Spanish. Many individuals pointed to relexification as one of its salient characteristics, the need to know a whole new vocabulary. As Carlos put it, "you had to throw a lot of words." Rudy explained, "It's a lotta difference in the *words* when you're somebody that speaks ordinary language, like say, '¿Cómo estás?' [How are you?], and all this. *They* would do it very different." Martín said that when one says something to a nonspeaker in Pachuco, "haz de cuenta que les pegaste en las nalgas; ¡amen! No más no." (It's as though you slapped them on the butt. Amen! They just don't get it.)

A picture emerged of Pachuco/caló as manifesting variation according to region, nationality, city/town, barrio, internal barrio social boundaries, and generation. Carlos thought a particular accent on the Barker recordings represented the town the speaker was from. "It's like a different version," he said. "We talk one way; that's another. But we're the same way."

A number of people mentioned regional differences. After listening to a segment of the recordings, Rudy said, "That sounds like El Paso. Texas language. . . . It's a difference from all the way to the coast, to Texas. 'Cause you don't hear words like this in California; they're different; they *sound* different. . . . They talk like they were raised somewhere in Texas, somewhere close to the border. . . . The verbal of the words . . . they sound like they're what they call Tejanos."

Two men said they became more familiar with other regional versions of Pachuco through life in the military shortly after World War II. Bob spoke of distinguishing differences between Arizona and New Mexico speech. He had listened for familiar regional Pachuco forms in order to make friends while away in the service. At that time, for him, Arizona speech was "like a magnet."

Differences based on nationality were described as being apparent in intonation and in norms of appropriateness in interaction.

Some persons described interbarrio differences in Pachuco/caló. Rudy's brand of Pachuco was different from that of one of his brothers who had hung out in another barrio. He explained, "Even now me and my brothers don't understand him when he comes over. . . . Thirtieth and Fortieth [streets] was two different barrios, different guys. Their ways was different. Their language was a lot different from ours. [The barrios] were pretty close [in physical distance], but not the same guys was hanging around with each other. Everybody had their different ways. Words were different." He added that the two barrios were different environments. Armando and Julie also mentioned language differences between barrios when they described differences in Chicano neighborhoods in town.

In addition to the types of variation mentioned above, social boundaries within barrios created by age-grading were reflected in differences in language usage. Rudy and an older brother belonged to different age-graded groups, which he referred to as cliques. He said his older brother would, "[come over to] our side and he'd be talking different; we couldn't understand him. *He* could understand *us* 'cause he was older than us, 'cause he knew already. But we weren't *allowed* to go; there was a point there, we couldn't go over there unless we were a certain age."

Differences in Pachuco/caló usage between generations were perceived primarily in terms of differences in a relatively small set of key vocabulary and also in terms of language shift, described as a progressive tendency toward the use of more English in the Pachuco of younger speakers.[10]

A number of distinguishing factors intersected in Art's description of the speech of older pachucos: "I think that the pachuco, you know, the old pachuco had a style of, ah, from the other side, of Mexico, you know. . . . Because of their, how they talked. And you can tell people when they come from Mexico; they have a *cola* [reference to a different intonational pattern], and that's Pachuco. And the, the pachuco here, you know, would say it different, you know, without a *cola*." Perhaps the speech of the earliest generations possessed prosody that was closer to that of speech in Mexico. The grandparents or great-grandparents of many participants in this study had come from Mexico. (For many, generation, nationality, and region overlap here, due to historical factors.)

Language also was, and continues to be, a marker of boundaries between sectors of youth and different youth culture identities. When asked if there was a big difference between kids that were into the pachuco phenomenon and those that were not, Lydia responded, "Oh, yeah. I think they wouldn't mix with them, you know. Because, see, they'll say a word that the pachuco would say; the other person wouldn't understand what they're saying."

The Morales family teenagers mentioned some contemporary dynamics of youth groups and language use and named different youth cultures extant in Tucson's high schools in 1985. Among those mentioned were cowboys and punk rockers. Their comments foregrounded the role of language in youth culture identity.

Son: At Pueblo [High School] there's a lot of cholos and cholas, but here at Sunnyside [High] there's just the punk rockers, you know.

Daughter 1: That's what's mostly around here, too. That's why I guess we can't relate to them and stuff, 'cause they'll come out with, "Gag me with a spoon" [she laughs].

Speakers

Among speakers of Pachuco/caló in Tucson in the early days, according to interviewees, were children, youth, women, and men (young men passing through and local young men). Ethnically, speakers in Tucson were Mexicano/Chicano people and multilingual, Spanish-speaking Indians. Many were speakers before the dress style came along that became associated with the youth culture. Recall that Delia said the pachucos she saw at school in 1929 "didn't seem like they were pachucos," but she could tell by the way they talked. Many speakers never adopted the pachuco dress style even after it arrived. In 1950, Barker wrote, "Many of the writer's informants have pointed out that the word 'pachuco' is a colloquial way of saying El Paso. . . . Of course, this does not necessarily mean that the pachucos were the first group to speak the jargon. . . . Three of the writer's older informants have pointed out that the jargon goes back at least to the early 1930s, thus antedating by several years the pachucos themselves" (Barker 1950:21).

However, the older interviewees in the present study consistently referred to people who spoke the language before the dress style caught on as "pachucos" and "pachucas." It appears that the term pachuco is multivocal and was present in the region before it became a label for the visible youth culture of a particular historical period, associated with a dress style.

Rudy commented on the language/dress style continuum during one interview when I noted that it seemed that many folks who did not dress pachuco nonetheless spoke the language. He explained by analogy with conditions for present-day cholo youth: "A lotta people didn't dress like that, but yet they know how to speak it. They don't wanna; like if you put a bandanna on, they mark you as a *cholito* [a reference to police harassment]; that's why a lotta people didn't want to wear that kinda clothes, but yet they come from that kind of environment. . . . That's what made a lot of people change their dressing way."

From this study's information, it appears that a dress style caught on with a segment of Pachuco speakers. The dress style per se was not the defining marker of speakers.

Pachuco/Caló: A Male Language?

At a backyard barbecue in Tucson one afternoon in the late 1980s, I commented to two Chicana friends in their forties that the academic literature says few women speak Pachuco. The two friends looked at each other and laughed. One of the women said, "You had to know how to talk that way to survive in our high school!" A ubiquitous and grossly inaccurate claim in the academic literature is that Pachuco, with few exceptions, is spoken by males. The most-cited works on Pachuco/caló (Barker 1950; Webb 1982; Sanchez 1983; and Ortega 1991, among others) make this claim. For example, Barker said, "The usage of Pachuco in Tucson may be defined in terms of a particular sex and age group. . . . The speakers of Pachuco are very largely adolescents and young men of Mexican descent who move in lower class social circles" (1950:16). This claim is not borne out by empirical research. Letticia Galindo's (1981, 1992) research confirms the widespread knowledge and use of Pachuco/caló by contemporary females, while my own research in Tucson, Arizona; Tijuana, Baja California, and Ciudad Juarez and Chihuahua, Chihuahua, Mexico confirms the widespread knowledge and use of the caló by female teens of the 1930s, '40s, and '50s, following strikingly similar patterns of use (Cummings 1994:172).

Letticia Galindo pointed this out in 1981 in her brief article "Perceptions of Pachuquismo and Use of Caló/Pachuco Spanish by Various Chicana Women," which appeared, like a voice crying in the wilderness, in *La Red/The Net*: "Most studies on the use of caló/pachuco Spanish have been conducted from a male perspective with a primary focus on male subjects. There is a noticeable lack of research on the Chicana, and those studies that did indeed mention women as users of caló have categorized them as being either prostitutes, barmaids, or mates of gang members" (1981:2). Galindo published the interesting results of a larger contemporary study in her article "Dispelling the Male-Only Myth: Chicanas and Calo" (1992).

Among academic studies that contributed to the stigmatization of pachucas and cholas on both sides of the U.S.–Mexico border by portraying them as prostitutes were those of Coltharp (1965) and Barrera Bassols (1979). These researchers were cultural outsiders whose research methods and contact with the culture were so marginal that their characterizations of female speakers were unwarranted and in no way based upon familiarity with the phenomenon. The claim that the only female speakers of Pachuco/caló are prostitutes is about as accurate as saying, "The only women who speak English are prostitutes." The claim may say more about where these particular scholars were hanging out, or had sought or found subjects, than it does about women who speak the language. Such academic stigmatization of pachucas may account for the fact that many females, especially from generations of the 1930s and '40s, at times conceal knowledge of the language.

Galindo's voice has gone unheeded, for some recent, ostensibly exhaustive studies of Pachuco/caló continue to claim that it is almost exclusively spoken by males (Sanchez 1983; Ortega 1991; Ornstein-Galicia 1995).

The ways in which the women of Galindo's sample characterized female speakers was "far from what the literature has described the Chicana use of caló to be" (1981:2). My research concurs with her finding. Galindo points to "stereotypes and myths" created "especially in an educational environment." Ten of the eleven Chicana participants in her first study and the majority of the thirty-five women (in their late twenties and early thirties) in the second study viewed caló in a positive manner. A small minority did not view the language variety favorably. The women were also asked to identify settings where it was spoken and the people with whom they used it. Galindo found that "places such as bars, dances, restaurants, and social gatherings where spontaneous, uninhibited, free-flowing speech occur were the most prevalent responses. They also indicated girlfriends, family members, close friends (both male and female), and pachucos as the people most likely to be included in these social and linguistic interactions" (1981:2). These findings coincide strikingly with the observations of participants in the present study on female usage in the 1930s and even as early as 1929 in Tucson. Galindo's and my own observations would suggest a more thorough study of the use of these varieties by females and of the implications of caló use for the expression and maintenance of identity.

Recent work in linguistics and anthropology is closely examining differences in language use by gender, including socialization, power and politeness norms, conversational interaction, and use of intonational patterns and vocabulary (Philips, Steele, and Tanz 1987; Thorne, Kramarae, and Henley 1983; Folb 1980; Eble 1977). To these, I would add the need for research on access of males and females to different contexts, rarefaction of closed-sphere male meanings and topics in mixed-gender contexts, the differential range of sanctions that females and males may face in various contexts of use; functions of caló use by females; and the implications of male meanings expressed, for caló use by females. One consequence of that use is the reproduction of male-structured meanings about the nature and place of females in the prolific use of metaphors that reinforce the semantic content of *female* as "negative," "undesirable," "inferior," "trivial," and "amusing" (Cummings 1991). Pachuco, then, may be a "male language" in much the same sense that English and Spanish are male languages, that is, in that many expressions and metaphors are androcentric, not essentially in the variety's use by males or females.

Use of a dominating form by members of a subjugated group can be interpreted in a number of ways. One might be as an attempt to appropriate a position of strength through the appropriation of the form. Appropriation of the forms of the dominating, however, can be a double-edged sword. The positive intentions of pachucas and cholas crossing boundaries, even seemingly innocent incursions into contexts, activities, and cultural usages defined as male, have often resulted in forms of disenfranchisement as a consequence of the women's divergence from prescribed female qualities and roles. Disenfranchisement can occur as social censure in the form of talk affecting the reputation of the individual, such as attributing the "aggressive" qualities of pachucas and cholas to imputed masculinity or lesbianism. Attempts to enjoy freedoms that most males take for granted may find women branded *putas* (whores), with consequences affecting their interpersonal relations and safety.

Obviously, if the gender boundaries of language and behavior were as "natural" as popular wisdom teaches, such sanctions would be superfluous. (Of course, many of these issues and practices are not unique to Pachuco but are found in other language varieties and cultures around the world.) Perhaps acute awareness of the stigma and sanctions occasioned by certain types of language use accounts for why females that I knew in Tijuana in the 1980s, when in the company of males of even their own cohort, appeared to tone down their vocabulary or not use caló at all. Nevertheless, in all female situations, the same women would speak caló (Cummings 1986, 1990a, 1990b).

Lydia, one of the Tucson interviewees, said that some young women of her time (the 1940s) wouldn't speak Pachuco because "the way they use the words sounded *muy bajo* [very low]." In an anecdote about pachucos stealing chickens from her aunt's yard in about 1929, we see that Delia was virtually *accused* of knowing the language. When she was able to translate the speech of pachucos, her aunt found this highly suspicious. Delia employed a diversionary tactic to cope with the accusation.

However, stigma surrounding the language variety was not limited to its use by females. Many interviewees, both male and female, spoke of their parents' disapproval of their use of Pachuco language, of the language variety itself, and at times of speakers in general. Lydia said, "A lot of parents didn't like the way they talked." Art's mother referred to pachucos as *pachucos raspas.* He explained, "*Pachucos raspas* means people that don't have class, you know, *raspas*; they talk crap out of their mouth. When they talk, they can't talk decent." He described Pachuco as "a nasty language." "Nasty" not only referred to Pachuco's sexual metaphors but also appeared to equate with blatant directness, frankness, or explicitness, qualities inappropriate to mainstream language conventions.

Rudy's mother disapproved of her sons' use of the language and modeled "proper" speech to them. Upon hearing the Barker recordings in which the word *borlo* (dance, party) was used, Rudy related, "My mom used to say, '¡No digas *borlo!*' (Don't say *borlo!*). Sounds real bad. 'You say, "Voy a ir al baile"' [I'm going to go to the dance]. Some word, well, you know, more appropriate. And I says, 'Nah; yo voy a ir al *borlo*' [I'm going to go to the borlo]. Y my mom would say, 'No al borlo; *baile*'" [Not to the borlo, the *baile*]. He added, "She was always against us talking like, '¡Chale, carnal!' [No, bro!]. 'You don't say, "Chale, carnal"'; you say, "No, hermano" [brother].'" She didn't like that. '*All* you have to do is say "*yes*" or "no"; "*sí o no.*" None of this "Simón, carnal" [Yeah, bro].' [laughs] She'd get mad!"

These parents' strong reactions point to the material nature of sound and its differential attachment to affect. In these cases,

Pachuco use evokes negative meanings and emotions, at times producing intergenerational friction. Nevertheless, young women and men used the language variety, especially with peers; however, they were careful with whom they used it. Rudy said many young women wouldn't speak Pachuco but would just listen during caló conversations. Lydia said some people would judge a young woman harshly if she used Pachuco, while others would only interpret it as teenage speech. She herself had used Pachuco at times at the soda fountain where she worked during the 1940s:

> Once in a while [at work] I'd say, "Nel ese; No, no hay" [No, dude; No, we don't have any]. "Cálmate," be quiet. Or, "Cálmate," I'll be there like [in] a while. I had to tell 'em. . . . "Es que yo llegué primero." "Órale. Espérate." O, "Cálmate; tu sigues" ["I got here first." "OK. Wait." Or, "Wait; you're next"], like that, you know? . . . But otherwise, if other people'd come in, of course I'd talk to them *right*. . . . And so you know, *friends*, that you have to talk with, most of 'em understand the way they [speakers in the Barker recordings] talk.

From the women's comments, it appears that females spoke Pachuco/caló to friends who were also speakers (male and female), and in addition, would use Pachuco assertively to make a point. Patty gave such an example of her contemporary use of Pachuco when she described the cruising scene on South Sixth Avenue. At two or three in the morning people cruise and park on the residential side streets off Sixth Avenue, where she lives.

> And sometimes they take a lot of time to pass by . . . to even cross the *street*. . . . I remember one time when I was coming home from a bar and they wouldn't *let* us pass. And I said, "Ese vato! ¡Déjame pasar, ese! ¡No me dejes aquí no más, hombre! ¡Muévete, ese!" le dije ["Hey, dude! Let me by, dude! Don't leave me just sitting here, man! Move, dude!" I told him] [mimicking calling out]. Y que, "¡No seas tan gacho, man!" le dije yo. Y no lo retiró ni nada. Creía que estoy en la onda. [And, "Don't be so rotten, man!" I said to him. And he didn't move it or anything. He thought I was cruising, too.] I *had* to talk to them like that. . . . And he let us pass. No problem, when you talk to them the same, you know?

I asked what would have happened if she hadn't talked to him like that.

> ¡La *madre*! [Hell, no!] He wouldn't even let me pass! [she chuckles] He *wouldn't!* You know, that's somethin; you've gotta get hip with them, because you know what they are and all that; you've gotta really get *to* them, because, you know, si no [if you don't], if you're like a square, dicen, "Esta vata 'stá todo 'scuadra" [They say, "This chick's a complete square"]; you know, she isn't hip to it. But you've gotta talk to them the way they talk, 'cause I know that they wear those [makes gesture indicating bandanna headband] and I say, "Yo conozco el vato" ["I know the guy"], because *I* wear it, you know?

So we see that males and females used Pachuco/caló selectively with male and female peers to express solidarity, and both used Pachuco for added assertiveness. The additional stigmatization of use of Pachuco by females led to many more hedges on the part of women interviewees than with the men. For example, most of the older women interviewed initially denied knowledge of the language.

Life-Cycle Dynamics

Socialization

Interviewees spoke of different types of language socialization contexts. Many persons used contagion metaphors to describe the process, like, "se te pega" (fig. you catch it) and "it goes around." The new language seemed to enjoy tremendous popularity with many young people. Delia heard the language at school among her peers and became an early agent of dissemination and socialization of others when she moved to a rural area. She was also instrumental in teaching her daughter Aurora the language. Much of Aurora's language learning took place within the family, including through siblings. When asked whom she learned from, she answered, "by hearing the young guys like my brothers. Their friends talked a lot like that when they were in their teens and they were already in high school. And that's how I started, more or less. And then if I heard something I usually would ask my mom and she would tell me [she would translate]. . . . A lot of that stuff, my mom, she was the one who would tell me more."

During one interview, Ida spoke a few sentences in Pachuco/ caló. When I asked her where and when she learned the vocabulary, she nodded toward her husband, Louie, and said, "From him." (Ida and Louie laughed.) She didn't know the language before she met him. Louie added, "but there's a lot of girls that maybe they're [in their] late sixties, early seventies [at the time of the interview in 1991], that they were part of the pachuco group."

Dora learned the caló from peers and friends and did not mention any Pachuco use within her family. She said, "Tenía muchas amigas que eran pachucas." (I had a lot of friends that were pachucas.) She later married a Pachuco-speaker. When asked how she learned the caló, she said, "Es muy común *entender*, porque si yo hablara ese lenguaje, y tu no la hablas, ¿no?, pero yo te hablo asina; con el tiempo la ibas a entender. No necesitabas *hablarla*; ibas a entenderlo." (It is very common to *understand*, because if I were to speak that language and you don't speak it, right? But I speak to you that way, over time you would understand it. You wouldn't have to *speak* it; you would understand it.) She added, "It's the same as any other language. You pick up some of it."

Carlos and Martín had heard older fellows talk who were just passing through Tucson, and they picked it up, too: "Se nos pegó también" (lit. it stuck to us; fig. we caught it, too). When asked how one learns, Carlos said, "Tiene uno que juntarse con ellos. Si no te juntas, pues, no te das cuenta qué 'stá pasando. Tiene que *oírlo*. Si no lo oye, pues, sabe, pues, de qué están hablando." (You have to hang around with them. If you don't, well, you aren't aware of what's going on. You have to *hear* it. If you don't hear it, well, who knows what they are talking about.)

Bob described his own language learning situation: "You can pick it up easy, you know? . . . But it's the *big* guys. I used to hang around just *behind* them." These accounts stress the importance of immersion and of absorbing contextual information as part of the learning process.

"Calming Down" and Aging

Some participants in this study seemed to have used less Pachuco as they moved into more mature roles. Ida called this process "calming down" and noted that her husband, Louie, wasn't dressing pachuco-style anymore when she met him. He was already working in the mines.

> Sometimes he still would talk to me like that and say, "¡Esa!"[11] or "Qué bonitos los tramos," or "¡Qué tramos, esa!" [What a sharp pair of pants!] or whatever. Sometimes the old *image* that he used to portray comes back . . . every once in a while. Well, when Adrian [grandson] was born, they bought him a beautiful little hat, and he'd say, "¡Ei, que bonito tando, ese!" [Hey, what a beautiful hat, guy!]. Sometimes he brings those words back. Or, "nel" [no]. "Do you want something?" "¡Nel, esa!" [No, *esa*]. But I didn't really get to see that side of him. When we met, he was calmed down, I guess.

Some people claimed to have forgotten much of the vocabulary over the years. Delia's memory was activated upon hearing the Barker recordings. She indicated she had lost conversational fluency with age but remembered the words upon hearing them. When I asked Dora how a particular word was said in Pachuco, she responded, "Pos, no te puedo decir, porque no me acuerdo. Ya tanto tiempo, ¿tu crees que me voy a acordar?" (Well, I can't tell you, because I don't remember. So many years; how am I going to remember?)

Both of these women spoke Pachuco in their recorded interviews, principally in the form of reported speech, and did so very fluently. Both gave long, running paraphrases in more standard regional Spanish of what was being said in the Barker conversations. As the recording played, Delia even translated for her two-year-old great-granddaughter, who was very curious about the speech on the tape.

A number of older individuals, especially males, said that they and their male peers still speak some Pachuco at times. Lydia, now in her sixties, is still called *esa* by some of her older friends and still uses the language with one of her neighbors. Rudy said he has heard older females use Pachuco, at times, if they become involved in a heated argument with a spouse.

Pachuco Conversational Dynamics

Some early, influential work on conversational interaction in anthropological linguistics is based on a dyadic (two-speaker) characterization of interaction (Goffman 1974; Sacks, Schegloff, and Jefferson 1974). The validity of that approach as a general model has been challenged by authors like Reisman (1974). The organization of Pachuco oral discourse certainly challenges dyadic notions of conversational dynamics. Pachuco conversations are often multiparty, taking place in groups of as many as fifteen or more active participants. The pace in such conversations can be very fast when compared with middle-class, Anglo interaction. Carlos used the word *refuego* (lit. crossfire) to describe the group conversations at his house.[12] During a discussion, he and Martín described conversational dynamics in which individuals participate in a group conversation and also in the conversations of subgroupings via the simultaneous monitoring and sharing of multiple conversations:

> **C:** Refuego. Es como una bola, ¿no?, toda la bola, ¿ves? Una bola es refuego. Allá tu también estás, todos the same way, you know? Verás, cuando vienen aquí, asina es lo que hacemos. Puro refuego entre todos. (**L:** Yeah.) Unos se ponen a platicar aquí [signals with hand to one side], y luego otros por acá, ¿tu sabes?
>
> **L:** Yeah.
>
> **C:** Y la plática sale aquí y sale allá [reference to separate conversations going on on his different sides; he signals opposite sides with his hands and head; points at his ear with his finger] pero están poniendo oreja, so you can hear what they're saying, ya que están poniendo oreja a lo que están diciendo por aquel lado o a los que están enfrente, así, ¿ves? De modo que se ponen de oreja a oreja. Cada quien tiene su orillita por un lado, y de otro color. Están mirando y hablando, ¿no?
>
> **M:** Diferentes teóricas.
>
> **C:** Ehi.
>
> **M:** Tienen junta teórica muy enganchada.
>
> **C:** Pues, la tienes que enganchar, you know . . . get the whole word.
>
> **L:** ¿Entonces, una teórica, qué viene siendo?
>
> **M:** La plática.
>
> **C:** No más.
>
> **M:** Como aquí 'stamos platicando; esa es la teórica.

L: Oh. ¿Pero usted dice que en un grupo grande puede haber diferentes teóricas?

C: Sí.

[In what follows, Martín and Carlos are talking at the same time:]

M: Pues, sí. Y luego unos 'stán allá hecho bola, y otros aquí.

C: Se ponen en la tarde por aquí ellos . . .

M: . . . y ellos aquí, asina. La conversación.

C: . . . es teórica. [overlapped] Pero están oyendo. Ponen atención a los que están hablando. Y por acá 'stá el otro lado. Pero tienen que estar hablando con todos, ¿no? Pero siempre tienes que meterte a hablar, tu sabes. (**L:** giggles)

C: El metichi, cómo dicen, ¿no? (laughs) . . . se tiene que meter también a, "¡Ehi, yo también!" tu sabes.

[**M:** Overlapped.]

C: . . . Porque quieren, "¡Eh! ¡Tu cállate!"

M: "Mete la cuchara," dicen.

L: Oh.

C: "Ya metí mi cuchara," dicen.

The conversation continued:

L: Oh. ¿Pues, entonces pueden estar oyendo diferentes conversaciones a la misma vez?

C: Sí.

L: ¿Y participando en diferentes?

C: Sí. Siempre tiene que, you know, meter tu cuchara allí. "¡Hey, yo también!" tu sabes.

(**C:** *Refuego.* It's like a group [dynamic], you understand? The whole group. A group is refuego. You are there, too, all the same way. Let me explain; when they [his friends and relatives] come here, that is what we do. All refuego amongst everyone. (**L:** Yeah.) Some begin chatting here [signals with hand to one side], and then others over here, you know?

L: Yeah.

C: And conversations are going on here and there [reference to separate conversations going on to his different sides; he signals opposite sides with his hands and head; points at his ear with his finger.], but they are listening/paying attention (**L:** Mhum.), so you can hear what they're saying, since they are listening to what they are saying over on that side or to the people that are across from them, see? So they are ear to ear. Each person has something going on to one side, and it's a different color. They are watching and speaking, see?

M: Different conversations.

C: Yes.

M: Together, they have a very engaging conversation.

C: Well, you have to pay attention . . . get the whole word.

L: Then, what is *teórica*?

M: Conversation.

C: That's all.

M: Like we are talking here; that is la teórica.[13]

L: Oh. But you are saying that in a large group there can be different conversations?

C: Yes.

(Martín and Carlos describe the configuration of the people that gather on Carlos's patio in the afternoons; people sit on different sides of the patio.)

C: It's conversation. But they are listening, paying attention to the ones that are talking. And over here is the other side. But they have to be talking with everyone, see? But you always have to jump in to talk, you know. (**L:** giggles)

C: The *metiche* (someone who butts in), as they say, has to jump in, too, and [say], "Hey, me too!" Because they will try to shut you up.

M: "Take your turn," they say.

C: "I put in my two cents.")

The conversation continued:

(**L:** Oh. Well, then they can be listening to different conversations at the same time?

C: Yes.

L: . . . and participating in different ones?

C: Yes. You always have to put in your two cents over there. "Hey, me too!")

In the account above, listening, observing, paying attention, speaking, and conversing with all present are foregrounded. In pachuco culture, salient value is placed upon individuals' language use, and verbal interactions are focused upon as events in and of themselves worthy of being recounted. The direct-quotation strategy (reported speech) is the primary manner of reporting events and portraying interactors. High value is attached to creativity, transmutations of form, and the creation of humor, irony, and exaggeration through novel juxtapositions, played off immediately evolving contexts. Transvaluation and remodeling of lexical items from Spanish, English, and Indian language varieties are important strategies of symbolic manipulation. In transvaluation, also called "masking," people take on forms from the immediate environment as a mask behind which, or through which, alternate meanings are conveyed. "Remodeling" reshapes forms to maximize the resemblance between historical source and current usage, to mediate multiple sets of cultural identities and meanings (Reisman 1970). Hill and Coombs (1982) have noted that these strategies can ambiguously invoke several norms at once, thus the close participation and attention required of interactors.

In Pachuco-speaking groups, the collective construction of discourse is often observed, even the group construction of single sentences, like the two examples that follow, taken from interviews:

L: Cómo han cambiado las cosas, entonces . . .
[**M:** ¡Iiii . . . ! **C:** Sí.]
L: . . . de los tiempos de ustedes . . .
C: . . . de pachuco, acá . . .
M: . . . a los de ahora.

(**L:** How things have changed, then . . .
[**M:** Ooooh . . . ! **C:** Yes.]
L: . . . from your times . . .
C: . . . as cool pachucos . . .
M: . . . to today's times.)

The second sentence is from the Morales family interview and involves Aurora, her two teenage daughters, and a son:

> **A:** I've noticed that every time there's a place where the young people hang around, you know . . .
>
> **D1:** . . . someone has to come . . .
>
> **Son:** . . . close it down . . .
>
> **A:** . . . and then all of a sudden you hear that the police are constantly there.

Meaning in Conversation

Bakhtin's ([1929] 1984) theory of dialogicality offers some of the complexity necessary for looking at the production of meaning in Pachuco/caló discourse. His multiple-voice theory and elaboration of categories of ways that voices can engage one another provide some means of beginning to examine the "dialogic angles" at which voices and discourses are "juxtaposed" and "counterposed" in Pachuco conversation. However, Bakhtin's analysis addresses largely monolingual, monocultural contexts (however complex), whereas a number of systems are in play here, encompassing different semantic structures, interpretive frameworks, and mechanisms for the creation of meaning. As these are juxtaposed, counterposed, and angled, possibilities for generating and/or implying meaning are exponentially increased.

A Pachuco word for "police": *la capirucha*, for example, plays on the English word *cop* and the archaic Spanish *capirote* (hood of a garment; *hood* in turn being cop-slang for *hoodlum* (Michael Silverstein, personal communication, 1989). The *-ucha* suffix can add a connotation of age, insignificance, or ugliness.

Another example of juxtaposition emerged as I was compiling a list of names of Tucson barrios when I first arrived in Tucson. One young fellow wrote the name "Barrio Snavagon" in my notebook, among others. Another day, in a different part of town, other young people were reading my list. One young man paused when he came to "Snavagon," saying he could recall no such barrio in Tucson. He read the word in English, thought about it for awhile, said it a few times in English, then slowly pronounced it with Spanish phonetics.

It came out "son of a gun," with a Spanish accent. He broke into raucous laughter, as did the others present.

Another example comes from a woman who remembered when she and her brothers and sisters, as children, wanted to know more about their Indian heritage and asked their grandfather, "¿De qué indios somos?" ("What Indians are we descended from?") He answered, "¡Somos de los indios masculeros!" (We're descended from the Masculeros!) (a play on Mescaleros [Mescalero Apache] and the Pachuco/caló phrase *más culero*: "the worst, the meanest, the 'baddest'"). The woman's family was in fact of Mescalero Apache ancestry. The layers of meaning are conveyed with a graphic anatomical and sexual image.

Silverstein (1985) has provided a framework for examining embedded layers of meaning in language use and has identified two functional levels of language. The first, $function_1$, refers to purposeful use of language or "what speakers think or believe they are doing with language," such as questioning, declaring, giving an order, and naming someone/something, etc. The second, $function_2$, refers to the fact that a speaker or hearer must know something about the contexts in which a linguistic signal is used in order to understand that signal (i.e., to be able to interpret a particular word, phrase, gesture, intonation, etc.). Also, once one hears a linguistic signal and recognizes it, one *automatically* knows something about (and can presuppose the existence of) certain entailed aspects of the speech situation. For example, if we hear or say the word *soldiers*, we know, without explicitly saying so, that they wear uniforms, work with firearms and weapons, have officers and enlisted men, may be sent here and there, fight in wars, etc. That previous, subconscious knowledge helps us understand things that are being communicated when we hear someone use the word *soldier* in a conversation. We take that kind of background information into account when we infer meaning from what a speaker is saying, and also when we convey information to others. Silverstein and also Briggs (1988) have argued that $function_2$ generally lies beyond the limits of awareness of native speakers. That is, that it operates at a subconscious or "automatic" level. However, it can be said that Pachuco/caló and similar language varieties pay more explicit attention to these things. Due to a juxtaposition of systems, there are a greatly increased number of possible contexts and interpretive frameworks that may be being referenced, and a corresponding array of possible co-occurring elements. There are, therefore, a greatly increased number of possible interpretations. Because of this, a heightened level of attention and mental alertness is required. This is why I say that standard monolingual interaction may seem comparatively slow or even boring to speakers of these language varieties.

Systems may intersect in a word, in a phrase, in prosody (intonation), in nonverbal signals, or in the manner in which discourse is organized. This may be precisely where the "symbolic ambiguity" lies. Knowing about copresence of referents (unspoken contextual information) for Pachuco speakers in Tucson means knowing this for multiple systems, varieties, and registers; multiple regions; nationalities; ethnic identities; tribal entities; and interbarrio and cohort differences, including semantic differences related to these *and* new dimensions created by their interplay in speech interaction.

Characterizations of Pachuco/Caló in the Academic Literature

Trejo (1968), González (1967), Ortega (1991, 1977) and others have noted that the language variety is spoken widely throughout a socioeconomic class, of which "criminals" or gang members are but a small subgroup. Ortega states that "it may be that a more significant distributive feature of Caló is not so much its real usage by Chicano youths and/or by Chicano gangs, and/or by Chicano criminals—granted these uses are empirically resolved—as much as the usage by a lower class group, distinctly a working class" (Ortega 1991:xiii). The political nature of labeling this variety a "criminal" language is evident in the following quote about caló in Mexico, written by Guerrero de la Rosa shortly after the Mexican revolution of 1910:

> Spanish slang . . . has its origins in the lowest, most uneducated and dangerous classes: criminals, thieves, ruffians and all the 'ne'er-do-wells' who dedicate themselves to carrying out illegal and dishonest activities and have found the necessity to invent a certain terminology that only they know. They use strange expressions as a way of covering up their ill intentions. This slang is generally composed of insolent, rude and even obscene expressions . . . In reality, its use is one of the characteristics

> that distinguish our 'indigents' from decent people. (1939, cited in Ortega 1977:8; author's translation).

Here, the language variety and socioeconomic class signal danger and indecency. Since the Mexican Revolution can be characterized as class warfare, one might ask why certain classes were "uneducated" and which classes had guaranteed that for centuries.

Barker, on the other hand, found that the use of caló wasn't restricted to gangs or criminals but reflected a need to meet the challenges of biculturalism. (The present Tucson study suggests that many youth in the region were dealing with the challenges of being in at least *three* cultures at the same time: Indian, Mexican, and Anglo.) Ortega (1977) feels this caló resulted from a rejection of the rigid and conventional social standards of Mexican and Anglo communities. For Rafael Gonzáles (1967), the caló reflects a reaction to cultural intolerance and serves as a form of identification. My analysis concurs with Gonzáles's characterization and finds that a good deal of the stigma ascribed to Pachuco language appears to be due to its routine and blatant violation of the politeness conventions of dominant sectors of Mexican, Mexican American, and Anglo-American societies. This is evident both in interactional strategies and in the graphic sexual and anatomical metaphors habitually employed. Those strategies have led me to view the continuing use of Pachuco/caló as a metacommentary on what that culture may well consider to be the hypocrisy or the inapplicability of the politeness conventions of "proper" Mexican and Anglo-American societies. Such usages convey political commentary and cultural critique.

By way of example, two jokes told by interviewees portrayed vatos speaking Pachuco with respected religious authority figures. Much of the humor generated comes from foregrounding the gross inappropriateness of use of the language variety in such contexts and with religious figures or deities. One joke portrayed a pachuco praying to a saint in church, requesting a favor in Pachuco. He flattered the saint, saying, "¡Ora, vato! ¡Tu eres a toda madre!" (Hey, dude! You're really cool!) The other joke portrayed a pachuco speaking to a priest at a convent in caló.

The graphic expressions ubiquitous in Pachuco include such words and expressions as *a toda madre* (lit. to every mother; fig. really great/cool/fantastic); *no hay pedo* (lit. there's no fart; fig. there's no: problem, trouble, fight); *culón/culona* (lit. person with a big anus or derriere; fig. coward, person that can't be depended upon, not a team player); and *cagar el palo* (lit: defecate on the stick; fig. to screw up, mess up). Of course, Pachuco's conversational practices often violate elite and middle-class Mexican, Mexican American, and Anglo-American discourse protocols and may in part be intended as a commentary on those protocols. It should be noted, however, that explicit anatomical or sexual references are not necessarily considered inappropriate in mixed-gender contexts in many of the region's Indian societies, while in Euro-American societies of the 1930s and '40s, such references in polite, mixed-gender contexts would have been out of place.

In addition to being saddled with the labels "criminal" and "indecent," Pachuco/caló incurred further stigma by virtue of being both an oral and a mixed language variety. Until recently, academic work in linguistics has traditionally been concerned with "standard" languages, a concern probably derived from attitudes that stigmatized oral and mixed varieties (Hill and Hill 1987; Hill and Coombs 1982).

Pachuco Language Use by Contemporary Youth and Children

Although, in the course of research, I heard many young Tucson Chicanos and Chicanas conversing fluently in Pachuco/caló, I was surprised to find that a good number of older individuals had the impression that young people don't understand or speak the language today. This study found evidence to the contrary. Indeed, some young people used multiple registers of Spanish and English and were also fluent in Pachuco. Older individuals who felt the caló had died seemed no longer to use caló or used it very little and only with persons of their own age. However, others were familiar with younger people's caló use and were able to describe those usages. This is probably a function of intergenerational dynamics, in which some folks do not speak Pachuco across generations, while others do, whether in family contexts or with younger friends. Older individuals familiar with Pachuco as spoken by the young described different practices. One was an increased use of a code-switching variety of Pachuco, one with a lot of English mixed in. Carlos gave the example, "¡*Órale*! You know what?"

Young adults and teens, however, were quite familiar with Pachuco language and saw little change in the variety as spoken now compared with that spoken in the 1947 Barker recordings. Veronica said, "That's the same thing they used to talk over here, the method of talking and *'órale vato, simón.'* They're still talking like that. Nothing's changed; the words are the same. They haven't invented anything new." Her husband said, "I know a bunch of guys that still talk like that. It hasn't changed. . . . It's never gonna fade." The Morales' son and Lydia's daughter, both in their early twenties, used Pachuco in some contexts with friends and found no unintelligible vocabulary or usages in a segment of the Barker recordings they listened to.

Veronica observed, "Rap music now is using it, and it sounds hip, so contemporary music is keeping it popular."

Patty and her sister shared their observations of their own small sons, both around six years of age. Patty's nephew would ask his mother,

> **S:** "What's that word?"
>
> **P:** [giggles] The *both* of 'em do it.
>
> **S:** Ahuh. Her little boy and my little boy, sometimes we hear 'em talking like that. "¡Ese vato!" and all that, and I go, "Well . . ." So I guess they're picking it up from Patty and my husband.

Most of the persons interviewed seemed pleased or at least amused to see the language variety continue to be used by successive generations. Perhaps Carlos put it most eloquently during one interview, when speaking of how one speaks Pachuco/caló: "Tiene que componer un, como un corrido. Para que siga el corrido todo el tiempo. Es lo que quiere decir, 'El corrido, que siga; que no se *acabe*,' see? Como dice el corrido, 'el corrido viejo.' Que no se acabe. Que quede fuerte." ("You have to compose, like a *corrido*.[14] So that the ballad/story will always continue. That is what it means to say, 'May the corrido continue; may it not *end*,' see? Like the song says, 'The old song.' May it not end. May it continue to be strong.")

6

EDUCATION

The public school system profoundly affected the lives of most interviewees. In Tucson, public schools were segregated until the 1970s. In his report of 1920–21,[1] Tucson superintendent C. E. Rose characterized the public schools as follows:

> The school situation in Tucson is an unusual one in the fact that over 50 percent of the school children as a whole are Spanish speaking. The 24th St. School (Ochoa) just established this year, is entirely made up of children of foreign blood, Mexican and Indian, who could not speak nor understand a word of English at the opening of the school year. The Drachman school is 99 percent foreign, the Davis school about 85 percent, the Mansfeld about 60 percent, and the Holladay about 30 percent. (cited in Sheridan 1986: 223)

Tucson and other communities had "Americanization" programs that conformed to national education policy aimed at the large population of immigrants in the United States in the years following World War I. However, ethnic groups native to the Southwest were included in this agenda. The goal, as voiced in 1909 in the philosophy of Ellwood P. Cubberley, dean of the School of Education at

Stanford University, was to "assimilate and amalgamate these people as a part of our American race, and to implant in their children, *so far as can be done*, the Anglo-Saxon conception of righteousness, law and order . . . and to awaken in them a reverence for our democratic institutions" (cited in Sheridan 1986:226; emphasis added). Adhering to this policy, Superintendent Rose stated in his 1920–21 report that "the Supervisor and teachers of these children have been persistent in their efforts to get English into the homes and to awaken in the parents an interest to learn English and to learn and to assimilate the high ideals and customs of this country" (cited in Sheridan 1986: 225–26).

Ironically, it was within the context of the segregated reality that educators of the time advanced a policy of obligatory assimilation as the only way "Mexican" and other "foreign" children were going to succeed in U.S. society. Sheridan writes, "To that end, the Tucson public school system devised a number of programs to teach Mexican students 'American' values, as well as the English language" (1986: 219). The 1C program, for more than four and a half decades, was the foundation of the school system's attempts to incorporate "foreign" students into the mainstream of U.S. society (1986:224).[2]

This national and local educational philosophy was based on scientific studies and opinions of the time. Sheridan describes four master's theses approved by the University of Arizona's College of Education during the first half of the twentieth century that addressed the nature of the educational situation in Tucson. Erik W. Allstrom's 1929 thesis had identified a "Mexican problem" and proposed that the people's "weird superstitions" be broken down. He felt that the educational system could produce individuals "able to 'rearrange' their 'customs' to 'conform as far as possible to those which are here current'" (my emphasis). A 1931 thesis by Esther Calloway focused on the Latin character, recommending "moral instruction" for "desired character traits." She listed traits needed by Latins as "cleanliness," "honesty," and "industry" (implying that members of that group were dirty, dishonest, and lazy). In 1931, George Peak tested students and concluded that "the English race is superior in general achievement to the Spanish race." Finally, Rachel Riggin's 1946 thesis found that a subsistence diet, lack of medical care, and economic limitations led these ethnic groups to associate more closely with their own kind, perpetuating racial viewpoints (1986:227–32). This last analysis, though appearing to be more benign than the others, neglects the active social dimension of segregation (Brakette Williams, personal communication, 1992), a phenomenon not exclusively economic. Qualifying phrases such as Cubberley's "so far as can be done" and Allstrom's "as far as possible," used with reference to assimilation and the rearrangement of customs, suggest the authors may have had reservations about whether such assimilation was possible or desirable.

Nuances of discourse in many of the participants' interviews in the present study revealed quite a bit of resistance to, and disapproval of, the manner in which the policy of assimilation to the "high ideals" had been put into practice in Tucson's schools. A number of individuals, for one reason or another, made reference to school policy on language use. During one conversation, Martín said to his lifelong friend,

> ¿Te acuerdas que antes dicían que no puedían que hablaran en español en la escuela porque acá y que? ¡nooo!
>
> (Do you remember that before, they used to say that you couldn't speak Spanish at school because of this and that? Nooo!)

He continued,

> El tribu. ¿*Cómo* van a . . . quitarle a uno el tribu de uno? *pues.*
>
> (Your tribe. How can they take your tribe away from you?!)

Martín had once expressed his indignation about the lack of linguistic reciprocity in general to an Anglo at a bar:

> Un día le dije a uno allí en una cantina, le dije a un amigo . . . "Mire," le dije, "yo hice un sacrificio de mi parte, ¿no?, de aprender tu lengua, que tu eres americano, ¿right? ¿Y por qué aprendí el tuyo, y tu no puedes aprender la mía?" "Ohh . . . ," que de acá y que pa'llá. Le dije, "No, no. Asina como ustedes dicen, yo también," le dije. "Yo aprendí la tuya. No bien, bien," dije, "pero no me engaña cualesquier persona. ¿Por qué tu no puedes aprender la mía?"
>
> (One day I told a guy there in a bar, I told a guy . . . "Look," I told him, "I made the effort on my part, didn't I? To learn your language, and you're an *americano,* right? How come I

> learned yours, and you can't learn mine?" "Ohh . . . ," this and that. I said, "No, no. Just like you folks say, I say it too," I told him. "I learned yours. Not real, real well," I said, "but I can't be fooled by just anybody. . . . Why can't you learn mine?")

Teachers' and principals' use of physical violence against students, along with other forms of humiliation, as routine means of ensuring compliance with school language policies were frequently noted in participants' interviews. Sheridan and others mention students having their mouths washed out with soap; Carlos Velez-Ibañez (personal communication, 1992) recalled methods such as spanking, paddling, detention, and social coercion, including surveillance. One elementary school teacher in Nogales, Arizona, made students eat one extremely hot chile pepper (*chiltepín*) for every word of Spanish they spoke. Different methods were used in different schools and time periods. Language prohibitions were in effect through the 1960s, with change coming only during the 1970s.

For some individuals such tactics produced a lifelong aversion to particular dynamics related to "white" language and culture. Aurora said of her seventy-one-year-old mother, Delia, "My mom didn't like school. She knows English; she talks it but she doesn't like to talk it, and she'll understand you, but [laughs] she tries not to listen!"

Dora had described her own school situation:

> Aquí tuve toda mi escuela hasta el nueve. Gradué del nueve. Tengo diploma del nueve. . . . Ya no fui a la escuela porque, porque fue durante, fue durante el Depression. Yo hice graduated en '34 ya pa'l '35, ¿no? y mi papá no tuvo dinero para, para mandarme a la escuela, allí para que fuera al high school. . . . En ese tiempo todo tenía uno que comprar, hasta pagar por la toalla de physical ed., y no, pues. No se pudo. Me puse a trabajar con una americana ayudándole en su casa a hacer housework y a cuidar a una niña.

> (I went all through school here up to ninth grade. I graduated from ninth grade. I have a ninth-grade diploma. . . I didn't go on to school because it was during, it was during the Depression. I graduated in '34, it was almost '35, and my father didn't have money to send me to school, so that I could go to high school. . . . At that time you had to buy everything.

You even had to pay for the towel for P.E.,[3] and we couldn't. We couldn't. I went to work for an *americana* helping her with housework and taking care of a little girl.)

Martín had said,

> Yo fui a tercer grado y ni lo acabalé. No más me cambiaron. Y luego de allá no volví a ir. Pues, tenía que ir a trabajar.
>
> (I went to the third grade, and I didn't even finish that. They just transferred me. And after that I didn't go back. I had to work.)

He said he was fifteen or sixteen years old at that time. I asked him whether he had entered school as an older child, and he answered:

> Pues, no me daban chanza de ir a la escuela, porque nos sacaban pa' fuera a trabajar. No había tiempo de ir a la . . . y luego cuando veníamos de las piscas, agarrábamos un mes, dos meses de escuela; ya teníamos que ir otra vez pa'cá. No hubo escuela.
>
> (Well, they didn't give me a chance to go to school, because they would take us out of town to work. There wasn't time to go to . . . and then when we would come back from picking [cotton], we would get a month, two months of school, then we would have to go out here again. There was no school.)

Louie had left school in the tenth grade, in 1942, to go to work in a mine.

Post–World War II Interviewees

Subsequent generations in school before the 1970s continued to be subject to the same language policy. Patty modeled her elementary-school teacher's interaction with students on the subject of language use: "You speak Spanish, say 'Hey!' you know, she used to tell me, 'You wanna keep on wanting to speak Spanish? you go to the principal.' I remember Mrs. [name], my *third*-grade teacher. Boy, I used to have bumps on my head, 'cause she used to hit me with that stick. [laughs] A big old long stick, well, you know, thin stick:

'pum!' 'Patty! Don't be doing that!' 'Pum!' She used to hit me on my head." She had learned English, but with a detrimental result in her adult life today: "See, I had trouble when I went to school, in my English. So I had to talk in English in my school, but the teachers told me that I had to speak English more often, you know, because I had too much Spanish, and now, I have more English and I can't even speak Spanish very well."

While telling about where she had gone to school, Veronica related her account of language use at school. Her mother had divorced when she was very small and moved to a border city in Mexico, where she attended first grade at age six. Her mother then moved back to Tucson, and in Veronica's words, she was sent "right back to kindergarten, and that was hard, because you're a big old kid, you know, and all these little kids; and that was bad." She had been seven years old when they returned to Tucson.

> **V:** I know that I was always a grade or two behind the rest of the kids that I shoulda been with. But since you didn't know English, you didn't, they're gonna put you back where you started at, you know, learn English. Now they don't. I think like they have that bilingual thing now. And I remember too that if you spoke Spanish, you got spanked for it.
>
> **L:** That even happened during your time?
>
> **V:** Yeah! Sure, 'cause I got paddled a lot of times, 'cause you didn't know anything else but Spanish, man. And if you needed to ask where the bathroom was at or something, and you got caught, you got paddled for it.

Describing his own school experience, Art said he began school at Davis elementary and then (evidently because of the desegregation decision in the 1950s) had gone to "John Spring, the black school that used to be Dunbar, when they passed the new law that all public schools could be, everybody could use them. John Spring used to be called Dunbar. And I was one of the first *in* there. The blacks used to *go* there, and the Mexicans and the Indians used to go to all these other schools." When talking about having dropped out of high school in the ninth grade, Art said,

> **A:** I just couldn't grasp *English.*
>
> **L:** It was still a language thing?

A: Barrier, yeah, right. For some reason, I had this, this chip on my shoulder.

L: About speaking it?

A: About everything.

He explained further, saying, "Well, that was all my, my problem in my life, you know. Ahh, I had a lot of hate, you know; it's caused by . . . the city, the church, the priests, the nuns, or by teachers, or this society,[4] you know." He added, "I've been a fighter all my life, you know. . . . If I didn't like something, I would tell the Anglos, you know." When asked why he ultimately dropped out of school, Art stated, "Well, I didn't like school, to start. I think it was imposed on me as a young kid. I think the first day I, I still remember when my father took me to 1C [the class for Spanish speakers], and my father took me to school down to Davis [Elementary School], and he greased down my hair, and I only spoke Spanish or Mexican. Teacher looked down at me and sent me home." When asked why, he said, "'Cause of my hair, I guess. I just know I went home. There's things you don't forget, you know."

The segregated schools had existed within broader contexts of social and economic segregation. In one conversation, Dora described the town this way:

L: El otro día Usted dijo que cuando Usted era niña, que las razas vivían bastante separadas. Que Ustedes no tenían mucho contacto con Anglos.

D: Oh, no, no, pues. Eran barrios americanos, barrios mexicanos, barrios negros. No estaba revuelto. No estaba revuelto.

L: ¿Cuándo empezó la revoltura?

D: Pues, no sé cuándo, pero comenzó comenzó. . . . Los negritos tenían que ir hasta atrás en las tranvías. Ellos no se podían sentar enfrente de la tranvía.

(**L:** The other day you said that when you were a child, the races lived virtually apart. That you didn't have much contact with Anglos.

D: Oh, no, no. There were *americano* barrios, Mexican barrios, and black barrios. It wasn't mixed. It wasn't mixed.

> **L:** When did the mixing begin?
>
> **D:** I don't know when, but it began, it began. . . . The black people used to have to ride in the very back of the streetcars. They weren't allowed to sit in the front of the car.)

Art also described a segregated town: "You know that Mexicans used to, and Indians used to go to one school. And then the Anglos would live in, ahh, in the other part of the city. Just lately, and probably in the late '50s, they started moving to the west." He recalled what an older Apache man had told him:

> **A:** John's father used to tell me that in Globe they used to have signs, you know, "Service to Dogs but No Indians Allowed and No Blacks."
>
> **L:** They used to have those signs, right in Globe?
>
> **A:** Yeah, in Texas, too. It says, "No Mexicans and Indians."

Art made reference to the legal status of Indians in the United States when telling about the signs excluding Mexicans and Indians from places of business: "In 1924 they changed the laws; they passed the law that the Indian was a citizen. In its *own native land.* You know, this is ridiculous."

Resistance

Given the irony of obligatory acculturation within a context of residential, social, and occupational segregation, perhaps the most insidious dynamics of the educational system played themselves out in daily interactions in the definition and enforcement of "the proper ways" that things should be done, that is, in the definition of acceptable forms of interaction.

Individuals of different generations expressed similar perspectives on appropriate and inappropriate forms of interaction. Episodes recounted in many interviews contain allusions that index unspoken social norms. Interactions with authority figures at school were being compared to those tacit norms and evaluated. For example, when telling of getting into fights at school and of subsequent punishment, two women of different generations made similar allusions, exemplifying this type of indexing. Delia said she had fought at school because "no me quería dejar de nadie" (I didn't want to let anyone mistreat me.) The phrase *no dejarse* describes an interaction strategy of not allowing oneself to be treated unfairly or badly. Patty had characterized herself by saying, "I used to think I was bad, you know, 'Nobody messes with me.'" She used "bad" the way it is used in inner-city black street English. She used an instance of her own or a fictional person's reported speech to define that attitude as "nobody messes with me." ("Messing with someone," like the phrase "no dejarse," implies mistreatment in the sense of instigation of uncalled-for, inappropriate interaction.) Both women, therefore, appear to imply they felt they were being treated unfairly or inappropriately.

Patty, when describing an incident that occurred at a Tucson reform school when she was a girl, said that she became very angry at a matron there. She felt the matron had assumed a profound knowledge of her character, when in fact she had made erroneous assumptions. She described the matron as acting "like she knows everything." Patty's characterization of the matron, and her intonation while delivering the phrase "like she knows everything," suggested that where she came from (or to her way of thinking), acting like you "know everything" is not an acceptable behavior, even for adults in their interactions with children. Thus, these women had tacitly alluded to socially unacceptable or inappropriate forms of interaction.

During another interview, Louie described how one *should* get along with others, referring specifically to pachuco contexts but generalizing to others: "It's like any place you go. If you know how to treat the people you're with, you know what I mean?, they'll treat you the same and you're accepted. But if you go in there and you say, 'Hey! I'm the king here,' no; they'll put you down right away. . . . You don't go in and, and say that you're better, or you're the king or whatever. No. You go in there and treat people like they're supposed to be treated, and they'll treat you right. Any place you go." In his statement, he described some "right" and "wrong" ways to treat people.

Rudy had alluded to behavior considered inappropriate while discussing vocabulary used in conversations in the 1947 Barker recordings. Such behaviors included being *sura*,[5] a know-it-all; being someone that shows off: *se maderéa* (which Rudy also described as to "walk around like King Kong or somebody"); and being *sangrón* or *pesetón*: a person that "thinks he's high and mighty or that he's high-class."

Two men described pachucos as upholding standards of appropriate conduct, that is, neither being out to treat others unfairly nor allowing others to do so. When commenting on contemporary lowriders, Louie said, "When you have something that you cherish, if somebody else goes and does something wrong with it, it makes you mad. Like the pachuco, he liked his dress style, and he wasn't out messing with nobody else."

In his characterization of pachucos, Bob said, "There were mean pachucos and there were, I won't say *mean*, they just didn't let nobody fool around with nobody."

Bob's teenage children said that contemporary cholos would "act bad and stuff" so that people would "think [they're] bad." The eighteen-year-old daughter added, "Then they can't push you around."

In all of the above-mentioned descriptions, some phrases characterize what are perceived as inappropriate or antisocial interaction styles, while others characterize strategies (being *bad, mean, no dejarse*) intended to avoid being "pushed around" or "messed with" by people who don't "treat people right," that is, those that "walk around like King Kong," who "know it all," who "think they're better," or who act like they're "the king."

Upon finding themselves subject to such interactions at school as children, a number of individuals of different generations spontaneously fought back. In elementary school, Delia fought with a boy who harassed her. A teacher hit Lydia with a ruler. Lydia responded by throwing a desk at her. Patty, who was "bossed around" by the reform school matron who acted "like she knows everything," was so angry that she was going to throw a chair at the woman. Art was always fighting and would tell the Anglos what he thought (a strategy he said he later abandoned).

Armando told of an incident at his Douglas elementary school: "Este americanito, you know, was calling us 'f—in' Mexicans,' was calling us 'beaners,' 'dirty Mexicans' or something. So what we did, me and this other Chicanito, see? We got these little popsicle sticks and got some gravel and started shooting this gravel at this kid. 'You don't call us stupid Mexicans!' you know. I still remember that very vividly. And then the teacher coming over, grabbing us, and spanked us, and we tried to explain and, 'No. No "buts" about that,' and I'm going 'Bullshit' and, you know, and stuff. I remember all these kinds of bullshit stuff."

Because of their actions, Delia was assigned to a reform school; Lydia dropped out of high school to avoid being expelled or otherwise disciplined; Patty was sent to a reform school. Art was also sent to reform school and subsequently dropped out of high school in the ninth grade.

Art and at least one other woman interviewed stated or suggested that the versions above of the strategy of being "bad" were not ultimately successful, over time, in producing the desired result (i.e., not being pushed around, messed with, etc.). After telling about his persistent attempts over time to fight back, Art said,

> **A:** Probably in the last ten years I gave in.
>
> **L:** Really?
>
> **A:** There's too many; you can't beat them. [said with a smile]
>
> **L:** [laughs.]

Art continued with a marked note of sarcasm in his voice. "So I, I decided I'll be one of the flock and get grants, and work for the system rather than, ahh, gettin', get beat, put in jail, and beat up, kicked out of, ahh, this and that."

One woman, when telling about the group of chuca-style girlfriends she hung out with in high school in the 1970s, said: "We used to put eyeliner like this, lines going down, like that. 'We're cool. We're bad,' you know? We were . . . at *that* time, but . . ." Her emphasis of the past tense seemed to suggest that different times and circumstances had come later.

In an even more contemporary case, Bob and Aurora's seventeen-year-old son had dropped out of high school as a sophomore, explaining that there was "too much trouble." His sister added, "He didn't like school." The son said, "I didn't get along with the teachers. They'd always get me in trouble." Later, I asked him, "Do you ever think about going back to school?" He shook his head no.

So a number of individuals interviewed had negative feelings about particular interactions with authority figures at school and had responded by resisting or being oppositional: telling them what they thought, fighting back, or dropping out. Thus, they had attempted to define and defend a sphere of authority over their persons, using strategic responses.

Comments made by Delia during a linguistic interview suggest that in 1929, Pachuco-speaking children and adolescents used a sign language repertoire at school to enhance their personal and group autonomy within an institutional setting that stressed close monitoring and control of interaction. Possible intervention of adult authorities was circumvented through silent communication of which teachers and authorities were unaware. Telling of her Pachuco-speaking schoolmates in elementary school, Delia said, "Le hacen asina [signals with thumb], porque no se daban cuenta, la gente grande, ¿no? Cuando no querían hablar, que no los oyeran hablar, entonces ellos hacían señas, tu sabes, así, y se hacían señas." (They would do like this [she gestures with her thumb], because the adults wouldn't realize [they were communicating], you understand? . . . When they didn't want to speak, so they wouldn't hear them talking, then they would gesture, you know, like that, and make signs to one another.)

Notwithstanding the negative experiences mentioned by some persons interviewed, a number of individuals had not wanted to leave school when they had been obliged to for economic or other reasons, as in Ida's case. She described her older brother as "a real scholar," who held down an after-school job because he wanted to help his dad. His school life was cut short at the age of sixteen when he contracted polio, which the family attributes to his work-related conditions. He passed away at age eighteen. When she was in ninth grade, Ida and her sister dropped out of school for two years to care for him while her parents worked to pay medical bills. Ida said, "And when finally about a year or two years later I got a chance to go, some teachers found out, and, and they came and asked my dad to let me go. I was too embarrassed, because I said, 'All the girls that were with me in school, they're ahead. They're two years ahead of me.' And pride kept me from going, and now I could kick myself." At another point in the conversation she said, "I will never, ever stop regretting that I didn't complete high school and get a job, because right now I know what I am up against."

Louie, Dora, and Martín had dropped out of school for economic reasons and gone to work.

Reform Schools

A number of persons interviewed mentioned reform schools while speaking of their own experiences or of the experiences of friends or acquaintances. The two schools most mentioned were the State

Industrial School for "wayward boys and girls," referred to as La Corrección or Fort Grant, and Mother Higgins, operated by Pima County. A Catholic girls' home located in Phoenix, referred to as "Good Shepherd," was also mentioned. Fort Grant is at the foot of the Pinaleño Mountains near Willcox, Arizona; Mother Higgins was located near the present I-10 freeway and Congress Street in downtown Tucson.

Two persons interviewed had been sent to Fort Grant. Delia was to have been sent there at age eight. Art had been sent there as a teenager in the early 1960s. The brother of a close friend of Veronica had also been sent there. When Aurora told about the places her mother, Delia, had resided as a child, the reform school came up as she spoke about the barrio in Tucson.

> **A:** She lived in that area most of her life (**L:** Is that right?) until my mom was so bad that they were gonna send her to the juvenile, you know, to the, at that time they used to call it the reform, for girls, La Corrección. . . . They were gonna send my mom there.
>
> **L:** When she was a teenager?
>
> **A:** When she was a little girl.
>
> **L:** And your tía was raising her.
>
> **A:** Ahá. And when they were gonna send her away, my tía called the, ah, told my grandfather that she would have to, he would have to do something about my mom because they were gonna send her away, and she couldn't control her, you know? So my grandfather came.

The grandfather (her mother's stepfather) had taken a new wife around this time (the mother had died in childbirth), and they were living in the mountains southeast of Tucson, working on a ranch.

> **A:** So my grandfather told my [step]grandmother that they were gonna put my mom away because they couldn't handle her. And so my grandmother said, "Bring her to me. I'm going to straighten her out," you know?
>
> **L:** Do you have any idea what kinds of things she was doing, that they were considering sending her to the Corrección?
>
> **A:** Oh! My mom was real mean.

L: What was she doing?

A: She got to be mean, well, to defend herself, you know? Little kids were mean to her, you know? She was so mean that she would pull their hair, cut their hair.

The mother had been transferred to a number of different elementary schools, Ochoa, Carrillo, and Drachman.

A: They kept changing her because they couldn't handle her, you know. The teachers couldn't handle her. (**L:** Hum.) Ah, she would, she tells me that one, that the last straw was when she got, um, you know those *picos* [pointed things] that you make a circle with? You know, with a pencil?

L: Yes, ahuh. Compass.

A: Oh. She got a guy in the back with one a those . . . because this guy pulled her . . . *trenzas* [braids]. (**L:** Oooh.) And she turned around and got him in the back. Cut him, you know, with it. And that's the last straw. They couldn't handle that, you know, the teachers. That's what they told my tía, you know, that they were gonna put her away. So that's when they sent her back to the ranch with my grandmother. And my grandmother kept her. And then she went back to another tía, and then, and then, she went back to my grandmother and then she went with my dad.

Delia herself had spoken about these events when I interviewed her later with her daughter, Aurora, present. She said she had thought, at first, that she was just being transferred again to a different school, but that Mr. Meyer of Drachman school had come to her house to talk to her aunt and uncle. (Aurora described Mr. Meyer as being "like the policeman of the school.") Delia was in kindergarten at the time. She had only recently entered school at age eight, because until that time she was taking care of her sick aunt, doing the cooking, housework, and yard work. When the aunt recovered, she entered kindergarten. I asked her,

L: ¿Entonces, qué cosas pasaron cuando todo eso de que la querían mandar a la Correccional?

D: Pues, es que porque, mmmm, pues, vivían muchas criaturas ahí. Tenía ella casas de renta, ¿no? mi tía. (**L:** Yeah.) Y se peleaban conmigo, yo también me peleaba, y en la escuela también. (**L:** ¿De veras?) Pues, yo no me quería dejar de nadie. (**L:** Oh, yeah.) You know, I fight for myself. [laughs]

(**L:** What things happened then, when all of that happened that they wanted to send you to the reform school?

D: Well, it's because, mmmm, well, a lot of kids lived there. My aunt had houses that she rented out, you see? (**L:** Yeah.) And they would fight with me, and I would fight back, and at school, too. (**L:** Really?) Well, I didn't want to let anyone treat me badly. (**L:** Oh, yeah.) You know, I fight for myself. [laughs])

Her intonation while speaking the phrases "también me peleaba, y en la escuela también" (I would fight back, and at school, too) conveyed the message, *understandably* or *logically*. While telling the story about her mom and the reform school, Aurora stated that her mother had "learned street ways" in the neighborhood where she lived as a child. She said, "When she started being real mean, you know, because she said that she didn't know. Nobody told her, you know, nothing. My tía was the kind of person that, she hardly even talked to her own daughter, you know? (**L:** Yeah.) And she [Delia] was an orphan. Or maybe she didn't *care*, you know, what happened to my mom, you know. You know how orphans are, at the time they were (**L:** Sometimes they get passed around) even worser. Yeah." After explaining in her own interview that she got into fights at school, Delia added,

D: Pero, a mí me querían quitar de mi tía, ves mi'jita?

L: They did?

D: Ajá, me querían quitar otras gentes, ¿no? porque veían que me mandaban dinero, ¿no? (**L:** ¡Oh, por algo!) Por eso me querían encerrar mejor en la esta, en La Corrección. Porque todos me querían a mí criarme asina como mi tía, ¿no? Entonces mi pa', ahem, habló con los señores; le preguntaron a él que si yo qué era de él, y no me parezco a él, no era mi pa' él. (**L:** Oh, yeah, yeah.) Y entonces es, es una bola, ¿no? Entonces, mi tío se enojó con mi pa', porque me quería llevar con mi nina. Y mi tía, pues, se enfermó porque quería que me estuviera yo con ella. Entonces dijo, "Pues, aquí usted no habla por ella," le dijo mi pa'. "No habla por ella, que se la quieren llevar. No sé por qué, qué hizo ella." Y luego ya vino el Meyer por mí, ¿no? (**L:** Ajá.) Y ahí estaba el, el patrón de mi pa' [Anglo man]; estaba ahí y entonces se pusieron a hablar el (Anglo man) y él, él que venía por mí, el Meyer, y entonces le dijo, "Sí; aquí vive ella; no más que es envidia de la gente," le dijo. "Y todas la quieren a ella," dice. "Quiere que se vaya con ella a vivir, con ella por la gente que la quieren mandar pa' La Corrección." Porque veían que me traiban, pos me traiban mucha comida, ropa, y todo, el (Anglo man) y todo, porque es él que compró el rancho, ¿ves? Y, y envidia, tu sabes.

(**D:** But they wanted to take me away from my aunt, you see, mi'jita?

L: They did?

D: Yes, other people wanted to take me away, you see? Because they saw that money was being sent for me, you understand? (**L:** Oh, that's why!) That is why they wanted to lock me up instead in this, in La Corrección. Because all of them wanted to raise me like my aunt was doing, you understand? Then my [step]father spoke with the men; they asked him what relation I was to him, and I don't look like him; he wasn't my father. (**L:** Oh, yeah, yeah.) And then it's, it's confusing, you understand? Then my uncle got angry at my [step]father, because he wanted to take me to my godmother. And, and, well, my aunt got sick because she wanted me to stay with her. Then he said, "You don't speak for her," my father told him. "You don't speak for her; they're trying to take her away. I don't know why, what she did." And then he, then Meyer came to get me, you see? (**L:** Ahuh.) And my [step]father's boss [an Anglo man] was there; he was there and then they began to talk [the stepfather's boss] and the one that had come to get me, Meyer, and then he told him, "Yes, she lives here; but it is just people's envy," he said. "She wants her to go live with her, because of the people that want to send her to La Corrección." Because they would see that they would bring me, well, they would bring me a lot of food, clothes, and everything, the [stepfather's boss], because he is the one that bought the ranch, you see? And it was envy, you know.)

Delia said that she lasted only for a month at school "porque luego hicieron un escándalo" (because then they made a big scene). Her aunt was sick at that time.

> **D:** Yeah, y se enfermó mucho y todos creían que era de los riñones. You know, everybody was talking about her, that she was sick. So luego vino el Meyer, y vino las nursis, y las maestras a verla y todo. Y entonces,porque me estaba haciendo muy huilita yo, ¿no? Que porque yo no comía y creían que ella era floja, ¿no?; que no me daba comida y todo eso. Pero, no; pues yo no más comía cualquier cosa y ya. Y por eso querían ponerla a ella en el hospital y mandarla pa' allá pa' su tierra. . . . Y me querían mandar al, a La Correción. Me decían a mí; I don't know.
>
> **L:** Yeah. ¿Entonces cuál fue la solución de toda esa situación?
>
> **F:** Pues, ya entonces mi papá, stepfather, you know (**L:** Yeah.), me llevó allá con mi madrina que me confirmó. Me llevó pa'l rancho [place-name] y ahí había una escuela. . . . Y ahí fui y lo que aprendí poquito, ¿no? to write my name.
>
> (**F:** Yeah, and she got very sick, and everyone thought it was her kidneys. You know, everybody was talking about her, that she was sick. So Meyer came and the nurse and the teachers, to see her and all. And then, because I was getting very thin and weak, you see? That was because I didn't eat, and they thought that she was lazy, you see? That she didn't feed me and all that. But that wasn't it; I just used to eat any old thing, and that was all. And that is why they wanted to put her in the hospital and send her back to where she was from [Mexico]. . . . And they wanted to send me to, to La Corrección. That is what they told me; I don't know.
>
> **L:** Yeah. So then what was the solution to that whole situation?
>
> **F:** Well, then my father, stepfather, you know (**L:** Yeah.), took me over there to my godmother that had confirmed me. He took me to the ranch [place-name], and there was a school there. . . . And that is where I learned a little bit, see? To write my name.)

Figure 11. Juveniles in the cafeteria of the State Industrial School for wayward children at Fort Grant, Arizona, "La Corrección," late 1950s or the 1960s. (Arizona Department of Corrections)

These events had occurred in the context of a hectic, orphaned childhood. As a girl she had been moved around and always worked. Her uncle in Tucson (in whose household she was living when the events took place) worked as a custodian at a Tucson bank. The aunt did not work, due to the illness. Aurora said her mother had moved around a lot as a child.

This had been her life as a small girl, before going to school and then ending up at the ranch with her stepmother.

Art had told of his experiences at Ft. Grant (La Corrección): "I was sent there for a long time, for about six months." When asked why, he said, "fighting and drinking."

> **L:** Was it a history or a specific thing that happened?
>
> **A:** No, I guess I had a history of, ahh, fighting and drinking . . . against whatever, whoever got in my way, in those days.

I asked Art to describe life at Fort Grant.

> **L:** Would you describe that reform school and what it was like staying there; what you had to do and all that, at that Fort Grant?
>
> **A:** March to breakfast, lunch, dinner. March like soldiers. Make our beds, clean, ahh, our salón, ah, what do you call it, dormitory? Work in different departments, plumbers. Some went to high school, depending how, when you came in, where were you in life; that's where they stuck you in. If you got in trouble when you were going to school, they went back to school, to finish your high school.
>
> **L:** How many guys were up there?
>
> **A:** Over 300.

He described the process of being sent there: "Mother Higgins used to be downtown, the center that holds you before you go to reform school. And after that, when they, ah, when the judge found you guilty, he'd turn you over to the state, and you'd do time over there [at Ft. Grant]." Of the reform-school experience, Art remarked,

> **A:** I mean [sighs], I guess I was sort of an abnormal person, but from those years to this present time I've really changed.

In his attempts to understand why he behaved the way he did, Art mentioned as possible causes both "this society" (the phrase he often used to refer to U.S. Anglo society and, at times, to Chicano society) and the fact that his father used to beat him.

Since a number of persons interviewed mentioned Fort Grant, a friend and I took a drive there one Saturday to see the place. It is 131 miles from Tucson, over two hours by car. When we arrived, we were greeted by an armed guard. I was not aware that Fort Grant is now a minimum security state prison for men. I told the guard about my research, that some people I interviewed had been in Fort Grant when it was a reform school. He finally let us enter the administration building of the prison, where there was an exhibit of historical photographs.

Inside, black-and-white photos lined the walls of a reception area and a long, rather dark corridor. Some glass cases held objects (sabers and canteens, etc.) from the era before the reform school

(1872–1905), when Fort Grant had been a U.S. Cavalry post charged with subduing the area's Apache Indians. Cavalry soldiers and Apache scouts looked down from the photographs on the walls. Many of the soldiers were African American. We learned from the pictures that although it was located in an incredibly isolated area, Fort Grant had possessed such amenities as lovely officers' homes arranged along a wide avenue ("Officers' Row"), looking out on "Lake Constance," an artificial lake constructed at the fort. In 1888 the officers even had a hunt club and rode to the hounds in style.

When the task of physically subduing the Apaches had been accomplished, the fort was virtually abandoned in 1905. In 1912, the year of Arizona statehood, the federal government deeded the fort to the state for use as the State Industrial School for wayward boys and girls. Before my visit to Fort Grant, when Delia had told me she was to be sent there in 1929 at age eight, I had wondered if her memory might be deceiving her. Nevertheless, an informational sign with the exhibit read, "Until 1941 children as young as eight were often committed to the Industrial School, often simply because they were neglected or abandoned. This practice was finally outlawed by the State Juvenile Code that required juvenile court approval prior to sending a youth to the School." In 1944, vocational training and a placement service became part of the school program. (Art remembered being sent to work nights as a dishwasher in a Willcox, Arizona, restaurant.) The school was placed under the Department of Corrections in 1968, and in 1973 a new juvenile facility opened and Fort Grant was converted to an adult prison.

Four other women had been put in reform schools when they ran away to escape difficult situations at home. Veronica was sent to Mother Higgins, as was Patty when she ran away to avoid being paddled at school. Patty's orphaned mother had been placed in a convent for the same offense, and Julie's high school friend spent time in the Good Shepherd home. (Three of the eleven female consultants had been sent to reform schools.)

Resistance in Context

The United States government annexed southern Arizona in 1854 through the Gadsden Purchase, shortly after achieving victory in the war with Mexico, 1846–48. Although Tucson's Mexican and Indian inhabitants outnumbered Anglos for the next few decades, and the groups are said to have lived in relative harmony, those populations began to experience a sustained loss of control over important aspects of their lives after the arrival of the Southern Pacific Railroad in 1880 and an influx of Anglo outsiders. It was during the subsequent period that institutionalized patterns of discrimination began to appear (Sheridan 1986:89). Raquel Goldsmith (1994) describes this period as characterized by a loss of control of public space by the Mexican community and a retreat of their cultural ways into the intimate contexts of family and friends.

From comments on experiences in the educational system, it seems apparent that by the early twentieth century, the state, now in the form of the U.S. federal and state governments, was increasingly usurping authority from individuals on matters that might previously have been settled between persons, or by previously extant institutionalized processes (features of local or regional Mexican and Indian cultures). The public school system functioned as a space into which the state funneled children for large blocks of time not only for teaching literacy and other skills, but for indoctrination and habituation to particular practices and modes of thought.

In these "educational" reserves, during appropriated blocks of time, community interaction and communication practices were forcibly prohibited and supplanted with modes stipulated and formalized by the colonizing society's ruling elite. Conventions of appropriateness having to do with communication and interaction were taught, all carrying underlying definitions of, and assumptions about, the nature of personhood. The logic and social norms that these conventions supplanted were those relating to reciprocity and other notions of appropriateness in interaction as understood and practiced in Indian societies, and still practiced in poorer, rural sectors of Mexican society.

The dynamics of this imposition cannot be explained in terms of simple cultural misunderstanding or miscommunication, nor do they correspond exclusively to the realm of economic domination. The active social and political dimensions of Anglo-Saxon expansion and supremacism as played out in the racial politics of Manifest Destiny underlie social and occupational segregation and preclude such benign explanations. The public schools' Americanization programs, inculcating through violence "official" modes of thought and interaction, were palpable twentieth-century extensions of the supremacist racial agenda of the nineteenth century. But whereas culturally different, impoverished European immigrant groups, if compliant, at some point could hope to blend into the mythic white "American" national identity, culturally different nonwhite groups could not, no matter how well they learned or displayed school-taught lessons of "civility." The suppressed conventions of their societies continued to speak to them of notions of appropriateness and fairness within the controlled environment of the public school system. Given the policy enforcement practices employed historically by schools for much of the twentieth century, it should not be a surprise that in contemporary Chicano English street-gang slang in Los Angeles, *to school* someone means to give them a beating to enforce proper behavior, to ensure adherence to gang rules.

As it systematically attempted to supplant community norms of interaction and thought, the state increasingly appropriated the function of conferring important aspects of personhood, especially (judging from many individuals' remarks) "intelligence" and "dumbness." Not graduating from high school came to mean lack of intelligence, circumstances notwithstanding, even though at least one woman said she knew she shouldn't feel that way. Perhaps her contradictory thoughts and feelings are indicative of the weight the state brings to bear on people's psyches, emotions, and lives.

A number of interviewees reacted to school authority figures in certain instances by resisting or being oppositional at school out of an apparent sense of indignation. In almost every case this brought unintended consequences for the individual and for family members. Such behaviors can be seen as refusal to respect restrictive or offensive boundaries, be they physical or social. In all cases individuals attempted to escape from or to impose their will in unacceptable or intolerable situations, thus aiming to achieve a degree of personal emancipation. Some tried to do this by using violence (as did school personnel), though resisting students quickly learned that they were not in a reciprocal situation.

The consequences of resistance or oppositional behavior for some persons was reform school. The state branded these individuals "wayward," "incorrigible," and "delinquent" at different periods of time. They were "sent away," "put away," *llevados* (taken away), *encerrados* (locked up), "sent to the juvenile," "put in jail," "kicked out of this and that," "caught," "held," "detained," "found guilty," "turned over to the state," "treated like shit," and "bossed around," and they "did time." Art had said that in the case of Fort Grant, "they stuck you in" depending on where you were in life when you got in trouble, as though "stuck" into some obligatory life trajectory.

The reform schools and the role of the state in these and similar cases can be understood in terms of what Corrigan and Sayer (1985) call *moral regulation,* which describes how state activity makes and symbolizes the permissible, the sole imaginable, parameters of individual identity. In the United States this is based on elite Anglo ideals, so moral regulation also sets the sole imaginable parameters of cultural identity. Feminist literature on the state and morality takes its analyses further, recognizing that state-defined normality is informed by patriarchy.[6]

In their comments about why they had behaved the way they did, or about why they had been sent to reform school, most individuals focused on family dynamics or their own personal qualities. This is in tune with elite national discourse on causality, a discourse of individualism that points to the individual or family to explain difficulties or failures. It was said that Delia had not received adequate guidance from family members or guardians; she was said to have been bad and mean but that she was trying to defend herself. Art thought perhaps he had been an abnormal person. Patty's sister attributed Patty's situation to problems at home and to not being treated right at home. The sister said Patty had "made herself bad" out of frustration. Veronica mentioned that her mother had been very strict.

However, individuals and families do not exist in a vacuum, they are embedded in larger systems. More systemic, structural causes rooted in broader sociopolitical contexts are hinted at in a number of explanations, for example, in Art's speculation about "this society" (Anglo society) and in the comments of persons who referred to aspects of "problems at home." In the case of Delia, who was raised by guardians, there was speculation that perhaps she wasn't truly cared about and that the motivation of would-be guardians was to appropriate child-support payments sent by her biological father. The state's solution to such custody battles at the time was to send the children to the State Industrial School at Fort Grant (La Corrección). Veronica, who had described her mother as being strict, mentioned prominently that her mother had been in an unhappy marriage, had divorced and chosen to remain a single working mother. Given the mother's socioeconomic class and racial/ethnic group, Veronica had been obliged to carry heavy child-care responsibilities for her brother and sister from a very early age. This had made her want to "get away." Her statement about things having been harder on women then than now pointed to gender-related dynamics.

In their interview, Patty and her sister attributed Patty's habit of running away to violence in the home and at school. Their mother had also had problems having to do with being orphaned as a child and taken in by relatives who were not happy with her presence. All of these situations speak of structural problems, poverty and accompanying stress, lack of occupational and educational opportunities; illness and lack of adequate health care; oppressive institutionalized gender relations; lack of child-care options for working mothers, and lack of protection for orphaned children and those embroiled in custody battles.

The children that became the first generations to introduce pachuco style were modern, twentieth-century kids, most of whom were first-generation urban dwellers and the first generation of these ethnic groups in that century to be subjected to sustained institutional Anglo-American cultural influences. Their attitudes were nontraditional in the sense that some at times took things into their own hands, thus breaking with previous patterns of respect for authority figures, including teachers and parents. Their motivations may have come from notions of both appropriateness and justice in their traditional systems and also (ironically) from the school-taught nationalist ideology of liberty and justice for all.

Giroux has called oppositional behaviors at school *resistance*, and he states that "resistance in this case redefines the causes and meaning of oppositional behavior by arguing that it has little to do with the logic of deviance, individual pathology, learned helplessness (and, of course, genetic explanations), and a great deal to do, though not exhaustively, with the logic of moral and political indignation" (1983:107). He locates the basis for such behavior in "the meaning of common sense," which in the case of subordinate groups, he says, is based on "a different logic" (1983:108). This different logic grows out of historical conditions, the collective values of a peer group, or practices embedded in other social sites" (1983:110). While Giroux focuses almost entirely on socioeconomic class, the Tucson peer groups examined here involve differences not only of class, but also of cultural practices.

A *different logic* was hinted in the accounts of some persons that were involved in reform school situations. Patty, who was sent to

Mother Higgins, said that "they treated you like you committed a *murder* or something." When describing the events surrounding the effort to send her to La Corrección, Delia said that the authority figures involved "hicieron un escándalo" (made a big scene). Both comments suggest the women felt the punishment was exaggerated or had not fit the "crime." Art had characterized the director of the reform school as "nothing but a educated mafia," an interesting reversal of labels, being that reform school youth were characterized by the state as "delinquent."

In this case, collective peer-group values, those mentioned with reference to groups of pachuco youth, seem to be those that are being tacitly referenced in individuals' comments in interviews (although a principal source may well be found in Indian interactional practices in general). These peer-group values are those that were espoused by a cohort of Mexican and Indian youth under particular historical circumstances: the early twentieth-century institutional onslaught against their cultures, their persons. From a number of individuals' comments, those values can be summed up as to defend oneself in unfair situations, *no dejarse*: to not let people "push you around," "mess with you," "fool around with you;" to fight for oneself against those that behave inappropriately: the "know-it-alls," people that are *sura*; show-offs (*se maderéan*), the "King Kongs;" the *sangrones* and "*pesetones*" that think they're "better," "high and mighty," "high-class," or that they're "the king."

In the case of schools, Giroux sees emancipation as the guiding interest of resistance, whether personal or social (1983:108–9). Yet he does not suggest that teachers are monolithic enforcers, but rather that they are mediators within a system. In the case of Delia, who was to be sent to La Corrección, a teacher and the school nurse had objected to the effort to send her away.

Changes in the Educational System

In 1974 black and Mexican plaintiffs brought suit against Tucson School District Number 1. The suit would lead the schools to desegregate, and it marked the beginning of profound changes in the lives of Tucson residents. The plaintiffs charged:

> Traditionally, the District has operated a tri-ethnic school system. While Black children were segregated by State law, Chicano children were originally segregated by the District's

> school board policy, with the acquiescence of the State Board of Education. Deliberate efforts to segregate Mexican children under color of State law have their genesis in the Nineteenth century and became more elaborate in the Twentieth century. (*Mexican Americans for Equal Education v. Tucson School District Number 1,* Plaintiff's Amended Complaint, March 23, 1975, p.6. TUSD Archives, cited in Sheridan 1986:219–20.)

In the changing political climate after World War II and the Korean War, and especially in that of the late sixties and seventies, federal programs began to address social and economic circumstances not institutionally addressed before. This was a time when cultural enforcement was relaxed and the legitimacy of other cultures was "officially" recognized, or at least tolerated. These changes came about during a political climate fostered by the dynamics of war, the presence of ethnic power movements, assassinations of public figures, urban riots, etc. World War II veterans returned home in the late 1940s with a less provincial view of the world and enhanced attitudes about their own self-worth and rights as citizens. The Sputnik scare in 1957 had occasioned a national atmosphere in which educational philosophy and practice came under serious review, especially in the crucial areas of science and language, where previous policies were now seen as having produced weakness. The successes of the civil rights movement and the political climate surrounding ethnic politics after the Kennedy assassination in 1963 led to the creation of the Office of Economic Opportunity (popularly known as the War on Poverty), through which more federal funding was made available in these areas, with new priorities. It was in the climate produced by these events that language and cultural policies began to change (Adalberto Guerrero, personal communication, 1992) and that government programs began to address the specific needs of sectors of the national population that had been politically, economically, socially, and educationally marginalized.

By the mid-1960s, programs that addressed education, employment, and housing became available in Tucson. The Youth Opportunity Center served as an employment referral center for teenagers. It operated out of trailers set up in parks in the communities. Neighborhood Youth Corps served as an employment agency but also offered federally subsidized jobs. Job Corps, a residential job training program for youth, grew out of the experience of Neighborhood Youth Corps when it became apparent that there were some youths whose home situations were so dysfunctional that they would benefit most from a residential program. The Model Cities Program, although primarily addressing housing needs, provided day care and preschools. It also set up a scholarship fund at Pima Community College (the Educational Enrichment Program) through which individuals could obtain the GED (high school equivalency) or study to become paraprofessionals. Many of these students went on to complete further studies and become professionals. The program at times also paid for material improvements at neighborhood schools and, in the case of the school in the Pascua neighborhood, offered Yaqui language classes. The Migrant Education Program addressed the particular circumstances of schoolchildren of families that traveled working different crops. It helped children catch up on missed schoolwork when they returned from periods of agricultural labor and also kept track of families even if they moved to different districts. Thus, children were tracked, monitored, and tutored so that they would still receive a basic education despite frequent relocation and missed school. Night and adult school programs had existed previously in Arizona on a small scale but expanded tremendously in Tucson when Neighborhood Centers began to be established. The El Río Neighborhood Center was the first to open, in 1971. It was established only after sustained community efforts began in 1967. The most intense period of community activism was from 1969 to 1971, during which time there were demonstrations, petitions, confrontations, and arrests. The center opened in 1971, with other Neighborhood Centers following: El Pueblo Neighborhood Center, Pascua Neighborhood Center, "A" Mountain Neighborhood Center (now Fred Archer Neighborhood Center), and Northwest Neighborhood Center. Through the centers, Arizona Basic Education (ABE) offered GED classes, English as a Second Language (ESL), and citizenship classes. There was such demand for these classes at the El Río center that ABE outgrew the available facilities within two years, and a portable classroom had to be installed in the parking lot (Salomon Baldenegro, personal communication, 1992).

The importance in people's lives of the opportunities made available through these programs is evident in the narratives of people I interviewed. Ida, whose brother had polio, had returned to school as an older adult. She explained,

> I went back to school ten years ago, at the neighborhood center here. I told my daughter, my youngest daughter, "Go with me. I'm so nervous." I just needed her as a crutch. So I went in, and the teacher gave me a little test, and this test started from 7; 7 to 9. So, at 8 o'clock we used to get a little break, and we were on break; I said, "Go home. Go home. I don't need you." And I felt secure and, boy, I really got into math . . . oh, geometry! I loved it and I excelled in that subject. I really did. But at that age I went. I did it because, I don't know, I've always felt like everybody else,—I don't care who you mention, who you talk about—everybody else is above me; that's the way I feel, just because I didn't complete high school. Because I didn't graduate with my class. I always feel that I'm not as superior, call it if you want to, and I know I shouldn't.

Art had returned to school in Tucson as an adult after living on one of the Apache reservations for "ten glorious years." He had gotten sick from drinking and was brought to Tucson and hospitalized with bleeding.

> **A:** And I found myself in this society, and I said, "When, who, what. . .? What am I gonna do?" So, I didn't drink for almost eight years, nine years. I got reeducated; I have a GED and I got about three years of college.
>
> **L:** Really? Where did you go to do that?
>
> **A:** I went to Pima College. But, ah, I wish I could learn more, but, ah, I think I did what I had to do just to get a job. More or less influence people in that I could do a good job. . . . I took auto mechanics and I took a number of courses—drafting, writing, proposal writing, thesis—but like I said, my English is not so great . . . writing.
>
> **L:** Oh, the writing part, huh?
>
> **A:** Yeah, I love to write; sometimes I think and write it out.

The consequences of his previous status as a high school dropout had been harsh. In the context of telling about how he had been drafted, Art commented,

> See, I had a eighth-grade education. And I, you know, I thought it was, life was so important to me, to be macho and,

> you know, beat up people, get drunk, this and that, that I never paid attention to my life of learning to read and write in this society. So I could never pass a test of the army. So they had me classified as I-Y, in case of emergency. So when this Vietnam War started, I accidentally went and reported that I got married. And they says, "No problem. We would never take a guy like you, in your standards." I said, "Fine." Thirty days later they drafted me; sent me, president sent me a notice. Sixty days later I was in the army in Fort Bliss, Texas.

The existence of programs through community colleges had later permitted him to "reeducate" himself, a process about which he showed great enthusiasm.

Patty, who had run away rather than be paddled at school, was finally able to complete school with the assistance of one of the government programs that offered jobs for young people:

> When I graduated from high school, I worked for it, because I joined the Neighborhood Youth Corps. And my mother didn't believe me that I was going to graduate, 'cause I used to work for [a city agency]. I was a clerk-typist. Neighborhood Youth Corps helped me a heck of a lot, because after I'd get out of school, I'd go straight over there and then learn, you know, filing and all that stuff, from [the city agency]. And I saved my money, and I bought my graduation clothes; I paid for my gown, cap and gown, stuff like that, you know. My mother didn't even believe I was going. She thought I was gonna be dumb, you know, but actually, I thought so too, but I found out that [laugh] I passed the grades, you know. And it shocked me when they told me I was gonna graduate. But, ah, at the time when I went to school, there were more, more, they helped you more. In other words, they'd get involved with you to teach you.

Veronica gave the following account:

> **V:** I didn't graduate. I dropped out as a junior.
>
> **L:** What did you do? What was your plan, or what was going on?
>
> **V:** Well, you know, at that time, you know, the thing for girls was that you got married and had a lot of babies and stayed

> home and took care of your husband. That was *it.* But it doesn't work out that way [laughs], you know?
>
> **L:** Yeah. So that's why you left school.
>
> **V:** Left school and then I went back and got my GED.

In the Morales family, in the 1980s, the eighteen-year-old daughter first dropped out of school, then worked hard going to night school at Tucson High in order to graduate. To graduate on time she went to regular classes during the day and attended three classes every evening at adult school. The seventeen-year-old son who said he didn't like school had been placed in the "extended day" program, where he attended classes from 2:30 to 6 p.m., before finally dropping out.

The continuing significance of availability of programs to persons who may have left school for various reasons or who desire to improve their education was evident in Rudy's interview. He was discussing the internal dynamics of groups of contemporary young adult male friends that hang out together. Rudy said that some young men put pressure on the others to pursue a party-style existence that includes a large investment of time and a lot of beer drinking. Nevertheless, some of the men take a different course.

> You look at the guy, and then you say, "Well, he's trying to change his life," you know; that's what he's trying to do. Like he might go back to school or something, you know, or take some kind of a typing class or . . . it's happened. I've seen a guy do that; say, "I ain't got time; I'm goin' to this mechanics school." So it's kind of a situation that, for some guy they say, "Hey, man," you know, "Cállate el ocico. Shut up. He's doin', he's doin' right." There's always one guy that says, "He's turnin' chickenshit on us." Like when we used to have, you know, we'd have fifteen, ten guys together, one guy'd say, "Hey, man. I gotta go, man." "Where you going?" "I gotta go see about this business that I got. Gotta get into this program," and stuff.

All of these people characterized the federally sponsored programs as a positive influence in their lives. They had to make a personal effort, but the opportunity was there to be taken advantage of if they were willing, unlike before, when as Martín had put it, "*No hubo escuela*" (There was no school). In his words, "En ese tiempo no había lo que hay ahora. Pues, que no había ayudas como ahora en el tiempo que yo crecí." (At that time, the things they have now didn't exist. Well, when I was growing up, there were no programs of assistance like there are now.) It is obvious from people's accounts that the institutional changes addressing educational and economic issues were largely positive and enhanced individuals' and families' life trajectories.

In the years since 1980, conservative Republican administrations have engineered the dismantling of many such programs, portending a throwback to conditions similar to those described by individuals whose lives were negatively affected by the lack of opportunity. The present alarming dropout rates for Indian and Mexican youth in Tucson and in the United States in general suggest that serious structural barriers must still be addressed.

7

THE POLICE

Police and the Meaning of Pachucos' Clothes

Since before the Second World War, law enforcement agencies have had an emotionally charged, institutionalized view of pachucos and their clothes. The present-day targeting of reputed "gang" clothing and colors is only the latest version of an old law enforcement practice. The zoot suit and pachuco-style clothing were targeted since shortly after their appearance on the scene in the 1930s. Young Mexican American males with a preference for an ethnic/race-related, youth-culture clothing style were targeted for harassment by dominant-society police officers who marked and enforced interethnic boundaries through their law enforcement practices and a justifying ideology that defined pachuco youth as "deviant" or delinquent. The historical and ongoing harassment of pachuco-style-wearing Mexican American youth by police is an experience central to pachuco identity.

A number of interviewees referred to that harassment in their comments. Rudy said of the early pachucos, "Well, at that time, you know, the way they dressed was an attraction to the policemen, and then if somethin' would happen, the finger'd be pointing at *them.* It could be somebody else, but that harassment was there all the time. They finger this guy; 'He's down there and we saw him down there, so let's catch him.' So they go into the barrios and they harassed everybody. . . . They *still* do it."

Louie alluded to the practice of targeting youth wearing the clothing style when he said, "There's a lot of people that wear a jacket because that's the style. . . . There was nothing *wrong* with the style."

Rudy said this kind of harassment caused many people to stop wearing the styles that they liked. He gave the following example of continuing police harassment of young Mexican males in Los Angeles: "Now, what they're doing is they're putting everybody in jail in L.A. if they have a bandanna on; they catch 'em and they put 'em away . . . " He added, "It's everywhere."

Many community-oriented, concerned parents I spoke with feel that the targeting of clothing styles and colors per se is an unfair restriction and additional burden placed on Hispanic young people and their families. However, those who say this publicly (especially in the context of the politics of the "war on drugs" and accompanying ideology) risk being labeled "apologists" for gangs or gang sympathizers, something far from the truth.

Notwithstanding the concerns of these citizens, this law enforcement ideology places a priori blame on youth of ethnic minority groups who wear clothing styles defined by police agencies as signaling delinquency. At the center of these practices is a thinly veiled racism that carries the authority of the state and is ubiquitous in all forms of media, including news and entertainment. The ideology and police practices place community members and persons associated with the youth culture at a pragmatic and ideological disadvantage. Our legal system stipulates that a person is innocent until proven guilty; the assumption of a priori guilt based on race and a clothing style marks a clear boundary of inequity. One parent I spoke with said he wants to bring his son up to be law-abiding and to respect law enforcement officers. However, given the realities of police interaction with young Mexican males, he finds that he must also teach him to be wary of officers.

The Institutional Culture of Law Enforcement: Ideology and Practice

In their comments, a number of interviewees referred to what police think about pachucos and contemporary cholos. Historically, law enforcement ideology portrays Hispanic and African American persons wearing certain clothing styles as a criminal element or as gang members. Such definitions of "gang-related individuals" amount to a less-than-sophisticated assessment of actual dynamics and both play into and create stereotypes. However, many everyday law enforcement practices depart from these assumptions. For example, a manual used in the mid-1980s by the Arizona Department of Corrections, *Chicano Street Gangs*, lists as signs of gang membership a cross tattoo on the hand at the base of the thumb and index finger, and tattoos of peacocks, the Virgin Mary, butterflies, spiders, a cholo, or a girl's face and head with long hair (Mendez 1983:16). Driving 1950s or '60s Chevrolets or Buicks that are lowered, have a chrome steering wheel (a chain), and perhaps a fur dashboard and mag or spoke rims, also places one in that category (1983:22–23). Bandanna headbands, watch caps, hairnets, baseball caps, khaki pants, white T-shirts, plaid Pendleton-type shirts, baseball shirts, grey or dark-colored sweatshirts, topcoats, and zoot suits are listed as "the basic clothing (uniform) worn by the street gang member" (1983:7 13). According to the Department of Corrections guide, gang members also listen to "Oldies but Goodies" (1950s) music (1983:19) and write in various styles of "cholo lettering."

Such guides to gang-member identification are absurd and tremendously discriminatory, since these styles are widely popular in working-class Chicano youth culture and have been for some time—some styles for decades. They do not intrinsically indicate gang membership or gang activities. Many young people wear popular youth-culture clothing styles and symbols; only a minority commit criminal acts, while the great majority do not. To use popular dress styles as a gauge of a priori guilt or suspicion is unconstitutional. The effect of this policing practice is that what has been taught about the legal system in civics, government, and history classrooms is often undone in one encounter with police on the street.

Gang identification manuals such as the one mentioned here are used widely in the socialization of police in academies and in police work later on. Such teaching and identification manuals can be seen in terms of Jacqueline Urla's *social technics*, which, like statistics, operate simultaneously as technologies of scientific knowledge, of government administration, and of symbolic representation (1993:819). She points to the examination of this conjunction of functions as an important site for inquiry into the social construction of identity.

Marjorie Zatz finds manufactured social imagery at the root of the labeling of Chicano youth groups in Phoenix, Arizona, as deviant (1987:130). Joan Moore discusses Hagedorn and Macon's documentation, on the ground, of such stereotypical images driving public policy and law enforcement practices in Milwaukee, Wisconsin, practices that, rather than stemming the formation of hardcore gangs, contributed to their creation and growth.

The following comments from interviewees addressed law enforcement ideology, or "what police think" about pachuco and cholo youth. A pachuco in the Barker recordings mentioned a police officer's thinking when he told of an incident in the park when he went there with a girl: "'Stábamos teoriquiando, ese, y luego llega la jura, ese. Pues estábamos al oscuro, ese, y creía que estábamos haciendo algo mal, ¿ve?; creyó la jura. (**S2:** Simón.) Llegó y luego, pues, nos dice, '¿Esos, qué 'stán haciendo?' dice. 'Pues nada. ¿Pues qué se trae?' le digo yo." (We were talking, guy, and then a cop came up. Well, we were in the dark, and he thought that we were doing something wrong, see? . . . He came up and then he says to us, "You there! What are you doing?" I say to him, "Nothing. What's your problem?")

A Morales family teenager mentioned police thinking when I asked the siblings about contemporary cruising on Tucson's Sixth Avenue, saying that cruisers are often portrayed in the media as troublemakers. "Well, out here they're not causing trouble, but that's what the cops always think. That's why they break it up."

Police–Vato Interaction

In reported conversations between pachuco males and police officers in the Barker recordings and in interviewees' comments,[1] a finite number of modes of interaction emerged: an officer approaching a person without cause, taunting or insulting the individual; an officer trying to "put something on" the young man; the young person "retaliating" against or "confronting" the officer; or the young person trying not to play into the police officer's attempted setup (including opting for the strategy of fleeing or avoidance of interaction altogether). In police-initiated interaction with pachucos and cholos, contempt is often conveyed by officers through the breach or absence of common courtesy. In addition to violation of constitutional rights, reported police practices include ridicule, insult, and humiliation, at times including the destruction of meaningful symbols of identity, especially culturally significant symbols of male identity.

The repercussions of this type of policing can be seen in the comments of a number of individuals. One is a general fear and distrust of police officers and a desire to avoid interaction with them. One middle-aged man said, "Like, you see the car, 'Uh-oh, a *cop*.' You get *scared*. It's *there*. You *live* with it. Who can change it?" Indeed, when discussing vocabulary referring to the police, a number of individuals gave examples like "Run! Here come the police!"

One woman spontaneously gave an example of usage for *capirucha* (cop) when the word came up in a discussion of vocabulary after listening to the Barker segment: "Dice, '¡Oiga, ahí viene la capirucha, oye!' y arrancaban luego (**L:** Oh.) todos. '¡Ándale, la pata!' o '¡El huarache! ¡El talón!' Ansina decían . . . que tenían corrida, ¿no? Al talón le daban." (He says, "Hey, here come the cops, hey!" and they would all take off right away. "Hurry, hot-foot it!" or "El huarache! [lit.: The sandal!]. El talón! [lit.: The heel!]" That's what they would say. That they were going to run).

Many young men were angered by the harassment and kinds of interaction to which they were subjected by police officers, and they responded in a nonservile manner. Take, for example, the reported response of the vato in the park with the girl, in the Barker recordings:

> "¿Esos, qué 'stán haciendo?" dice [el policía]. "Pues nada. ¿Pues qué se trae?" le digo yo. "Pues, yo no cargo nada," me dice. "Pues, yo sí, ese. Yo traigo par de aces, ¿y usted?" "Pues, yo no traigo nada." "Pues, yo lo jodí; ¿por qué no se descuenta?" le digo.
>
> ("You there! What are you doing?" he [the policeman] says. I say to him, "Nothing. What's your problem?" "Well, I'm not saying I have anything on you," he says. "Well, I have

> something on you, guy. I have a pair of aces; what have you got?" "I don't have anything." "Well, I beat you [lit. screwed you]; why don't you split?" I said.)

One man gave the following explanation of the vato's reported response in this interaction: "He was just sittin' there; he's not bothering nobody and he's not really into getting into a hassle with the policeman at all, you know; he's just kicking back. In other words, he doesn't have . . . [any] intention of doing wrong with the policeman, against him. He's just sittin' there talking with a girl." I added that the vato said he had a pair of aces. The man responded, "That means that he's not doing nothin', you know; he can't charge him; he can't put nothing on him. . . . The cop can't come over and say, "Well, you're violating something." So that's why he says, 'I've got the pair of aces." In other words, "If you can't charge me with nothin', leave me alone." This interviewee anticipates that the officer may "put something" on the young man (try to charge him falsely with some violation). The man continued, "So if he harasses him . . . with no reason, then he [the pachuco] could come back on him." I pointed out that he said the cop left. The man responded, "Well, he confronted him pretty good . . . "

In his continuing comments, this interviewee elaborated upon what he meant by "he confronted him." "He mighta confronted him in some ways, but he let him know before anything got outta hand that he wasn't doin' nothin'. . . . 'You try to charge me for something, you better have something on me.'" "He confronted him" here is defined as a nonservile response to a police officer possibly "trying to charge (a person) for something" when no violation has occurred. The interviewee pointed to the Barker vato's analogy of poker, a game with rules and standards of fairness.

According to one interviewee, one strategy used by police officers to "put something" on someone is "to get you mad so they can arrest you." Stopping persons who are not violating any law is one way. Taunting or insulting interaction is another. A vato in the Barker recordings tells of being stopped by an officer under such circumstances. He tells another pachuco how he dealt with the policeman, saying, "le tiré a loco." One interviewee explained,

> That means he tried to ignore him [the cop]. Like, a lot of times cops will make you mad and see if you ignore them or give him a bad time, see? . . . In other words, he's not

> gonna argue the point. . . . He's not really gonna ignore it, but he's gonna . . . like, a lot of these kids they retaliate back to the cop, see? And then the cop gets mad, and that's when everything starts. They arrest them for whatever, resisting, or information. That's what he was referring to. . . . So the cop couldn't get him mad, so he told him, "Bórrate," like saying "Get outta here!" you know. "I couldn't get him mad."

Note that the phrase "retaliate back" implies that the police officer already did something to the young man that was inappropriate.

Another example of a young man "retaliating back" or "confronting" an officer in one of these situations appears in the conversations of the Barker recordings, in this case in the form of an insult. One vato tells another of being stopped by a policeman for no apparent reason. He quotes himself as saying to the officer, "¿Oiga, por qué me anda siguiendo a mí? oiga. *Yo*, sí, soy vato." (Hey, why are you following me? *I* am a man.)

I asked one man about police–community relations back in the 1930s and '40s in the barrios. Similar dynamics are evident in his comments on police–vato interaction in his neighborhood. He foregrounded two possibilities: "I don't know if that police force had it against the guys, or maybe the guys made them mad and whatever, and they'd pick one up for anything, maybe some misdemeanor. They'd shave his head." Here, an institutionalized practice of bodily humiliation is visited upon the person in the destruction of cherished symbols of identity. The practice continues in many places today in locally specific forms. In Nogales, Sonora, Mexico, for example, municipal policemen in the mid 1980s cut cholo males' long hair and/or would take their earring from them when they were detained because of their appearance and harassed under the a priori labels *sospechoso* (suspect), *antisocial*, or *delincuente* (delinquent). (The earring was given to a young male by his steady girlfriend as a symbol of their relationship. The actions of the police amount to a symbolic appropriation of the young man's girlfriend.) Interaction in such cases is calculated provocation: insult, ridicule, and humiliation. In Mexico the policing practice marks socioeconomic-class and youth-culture boundaries, rather than the racial/ethnic and class boundaries marked by similar practices in the United States.

Blatantly insulting interaction (Brown and Levinson's [1978] "bald on record") violates standards of social appropriateness and politeness for Mexican, Indian, and Anglo cultures, the hybrid youth culture included, and as Louie had said of lowriders, "when you have something that you cherish, if somebody else goes and does something wrong with it; it makes you mad." Interaction of the type exhibited by police officers in these cases—harassment, insult, and humiliation—is uncalled-for and fits the definition of "messing with someone," and a *no dejarse* [don't passively accept it] response is considered appropriate or even mandated. Such deeply rooted, widespread law enforcement practices, coupled with the differential dispensing of justice by the criminal justice system, can be said to be one of the central causes of events such as the L.A. uprising following the beating of Rodney King.[2]

Brackette Williams (1989) points out that the state continually marks and maintains boundaries between racial/ethnic and class groups under changing circumstances in various ways. Applying different policing practices to various groups is one of the ways in which this is accomplished. Such policing of ethnic minority groups puts individuals in a double bind, for communities are subject both to overpolicing (harassment) and underpolicing (failure on the part of police to respond when assistance is requested).

Overpolicing/Underpolicing

Most comments made and episodes recounted by persons mentioning the police testified to less-than-cordial relations between officers and working-class members of these ethnic communities in general. Accounts testified to police utilization of different procedures based on race and/or clothing style of the individual, such as harassment (being approached/stopped, interrogated, asked for identification when no violation has been committed), tickets differentially issued on the basis of race, or being falsely charged with violations.

One man told of parking tickets in his neighborhood issued on the basis of race during the 1970s. He had parked his car on his lot (as he and others in his area were in the habit of doing). One morning he looked out his living-room window and saw the neighborhood policeman ticketing his car. The interviewee had gone out earlier and had seen two other cars in the neighborhood parked in the same way. He followed the policeman down the street to speak to him and observed that one such car (belonging to an Anglo teacher at the local school) had not been ticketed, although the policeman had already passed that way on his beat. He demanded that the policeman ticket that car or destroy his ticket. The policeman declined. When the interviewee challenged the ticket with the officer's superior, the officer was obliged to write a ticket for the teacher's car. Although angered by the incident, the interviewee was pleased that at least some possibility existed of contesting such an injustice.

Another policing practice is the prohibition or overpolicing of culture-specific social events. Members of every generation commented on the increasing encroachment of police into social life. Carlos told of changes in permitted social activities when Tucson municipal jurisdiction came into his neighborhood:

> Nosotros todos cantámos, más antes. Aquí en la iglesia esta. Llegáron los sheriffs. Y, we had a big fire, con guitarra y cerveza, y nunca nos decían na'a. "¡Cántame una canción, muchachos!" "¡Bueno; buenas noches!" He took off. Now that the city's around, you can't even sit around the churches like that. We're kicked out for some'n. Or make a bonfire. No hay. Se acabó.
>
> (We all used to sing, before. Here at this church. The sheriffs came. And we had a big fire, with guitars and beer, and they would never say anything to us. "Sing me a song, boys!" "Well, good-night!" He took off. Now that the city's around, you can't even sit around the churches like that. We're kicked out for some'n. Or make a bonfire. Not any more. That's a thing of the past.)

Martín added, "No quieren nada." (They don't want you to do anything.)

Indeed, in the process of the Anglo appropriation project, even the place from which the law emanated changed. Carlos pointed out that the state capitol had been located in Tucson before it was moved to Phoenix. When speaking of the law today and the place from which it emanates, he said, "Esta ley viene de Phoenix, no de aquí. [This law comes from Phoenix, not from here.] That's the capital. And the capital was over here [Tucson]; it's supposed to be down here."

Julie told of the response to the dance parties at the abandoned house across from where her friend's parents lived:

> One time we got raided by the police. We were jumping out of these windows, 'cause it was like an adobe house, too! So it's just cuts in the wall. And we were jumping through these holes, and the policemen were over there with their flashlights and cops all over the place and everybody goes running to cars and running down the streets and everything. . . . Usually the guy that lived there got caught. . . . They'd take him to his parents' house, and they'd scold him and stuff y todo. And then the following weekend, he'd be doing it again, and we'd keep going to these parties.

Many interviewees spoke of police harassment of cruisers. When I asked one interviewee whether she thought cruising and parking with friends was dangerous, she answered, "Cruising, caravaning, that's not dangerous. 'Cause you're going so slow! [laughs] Unless somebody comes and hits you! [laughs]"

One teenager said there had been a lot of car clubs in Tucson. He and his sisters named "Old Memories," "Street Pride," "Royal Expression," and "Sophisticated Few." He spoke of a decline in the number of clubs, saying most people cruise Sixth Avenue now on their own. His mother added, "Isn't that that the police are breaking them up, that's why?" When asked if lowriders are gang-related like some people say, the son replied, "Bull."

Louie had spoken of contemporary lowriders, alluding to the problems with the police. "Nowadays you got the lowriders. . . . They got the dress code almost like the pachucos, same thing. And what they do, they drive their cars down [lowered]; that's *all.*"

A mother thought the police were trying to stop cruising because "they just don't like to see people having fun." Her children commented on a popular dance craze at the time of the interview in 1985:

> **D2:** Now it's breaking.
>
> **S:** But now it's going away, too.
>
> **L:** It's going away?
>
> **S:** I think it is, 'cause there used to be kids that used to get out on Sixth [Ave.] and put cardboard up there, and they used to have all kinds of people around [watching them dance], but you don't see that no more.
>
> **D2:** Thanks to the cops.

In 1993, Tucson had a number of court cases challenging unequally applied police practices. Four officers were using adhesive tape to attempt to find cocaine on the noses of people they stopped on weekend nights on South Sixth Avenue, the predominantly Hispanic cruising strip in town. The court dismissed all the cases brought in which evidence had been gathered in this manner, not objecting to the method itself, but ruling that the practice had been unequally applied by Tucson police. The method was not being utilized elsewhere in the city. On a weekend soon after this ruling, cruisers were targeted by police on Speedway Boulevard, the predominantly Anglo cruising strip. Interestingly, a number of parents immediately complained of police harassment. Sixth Avenue, unlike Speedway, was routinely targeted.

Other individuals spoke of another phenomenon experienced in their neighborhoods, underpolicing. One man made the following comments on police–community relations, past and present, also emphasizing the factor of socioeconomic class:

> The law, at that time, between the forties and the fifties, it was chickenshit. You could get away with anything. Especially if you was in a predominantly minority area, like a community, buncha low-income people, you know, can barely survive. And you get people that stick to their own, and there's a lot a crime. The law says, "Well, as long as there's no killing, we won't go over there. But let 'em do what they want. We'll protect *this* guy; he's got a $50,000 home. We'll protect *him,*" you know? [Mimics police talking to rich man:] "Pick up the phone. Just *call* us. We'll *be* there." Even now, that I know of. You pick up the phone, and somebody's getting' killed across the street; cop says, "Hey, I ain't got time," you know, "I ain't got enough men." By the time he comes over, he's probably down the block, and then he says, "Well, by this time I think somebody's already got their head cut off, so I'll go in there like I'm the law."

The differential policing of subordinated groups puts them at a pragmatic disadvantage by placing additional logistic and economic burdens on group members in the form of limitations on movement and activities, subjection to harassment, beatings, court appearances, fines, jail and prison sentences, additional health-care costs, and accompanying stress on family and social dynamics. As residential and occupational segregation began to break down, it appears that the state increasingly policed racial/ethnic minority populations and, through law enforcement ideologies and practices, have had a negative effect in defining their identities.

Law enforcement agencies have policed, and continue to police public space along racial/ethnic lines utilizing differing policing practices, especially with males of subjugated groups. Their historically rooted, institutionalized police ideologies justify those practices. Along with schools and reform schools, in informal practice, police define individuals who do not conform to dominant society models of identity and interaction as deviant. These notions proceed from racially conceived notions of "American" in which nonwhite groups are seen as not American or less American than whites, citizenship notwithstanding. One example can be seen in the continuing practice of targeting popular youth clothing styles worn by members of minority racial/ethnic groups, a form of racial profiling, that continues to be a problem, rather than waning.

8

POWER RELATIONS
CULTURAL REPRESSIONS

The word *barrio* in Tucson captures attachment to place, kinship, history, and culture. The feeling was summed up in comments Rudy made when I asked why pachucos always seemed to greet or challenge young strangers with the phrase, "¿Qué barrio?" (What neighborhood?). He said, "I guess it's pride in their barrios. 'My ancestors lived there, so I'm living there, too.' It carries a tradition. It's like a place where their roots are at. Mainly. Predominantly in the Mexican culture, that's what you find. The roots are there. 'Oh, *la familia* [Spanish surname], there's a lot of them. That's their barrio right there.' And they all grow up with the image of being proud of their barrio. I come from Barrio El Hoyo. A guy could be sixty years old and he would *still* say that." Barrios were described as being composed of, or bounded by, certain streets. Interviewees characterized the groups as a "*bola*" (bunch), "*ganga,*" "group," or "group of friends." A number of people used the phrase "like a club." Rubel (1965) discusses basic organizational features of these voluntary friendship associations in his article "The Mexican-American Palomilla." The small, gender-segregated cohorts might have been referred to as cliques, or not labeled at all, had they been composed of Anglo youth.

However, the press, law enforcement, and social-science literature characterized the groups early on as "gangs," a practice which continues today. A relatively recent example of this is seen in an article appearing in the *Los Angeles Times* and the *Tucson Citizen* on June 13, 1992. A group of four affluent students, "at prestigious Polytechnic High School" in Long Beach, California, three of them white, were arrested for the execution-style murder of a fifth group member. The boys were carrying out burglaries, and the fifth boy had cooperated with a police investigation. The other boys killed him because he violated the group's "loyalty oath." Despite their organization for the purpose of committing burglaries and other illegal acts, this group is characterized in the article and by a detective representing the Los Angeles Police Department's South Bureau Homicide Section as a "group" and a "club." Yet, consistently in the media and in law enforcement practices, incidents involving Hispanic and black youth are often presumed to be "gang-related."

Although many interviewees used the word *gang* with reference to their cohort, it became clear that they did not use the term the way it is used in deviance literature. Martín called the cohorts *puros grupos* (just groups). Carlos added, "Le decían 'gangas'" (They called them *gangas*.) Their comments appear to parallel Lydia's definition of *ganga*: "If we had a gang, I mean it like, 'la ganga,' but we weren't a *gang*. 'La ganga' that hang around with each other, that's what they meant." Her distinction between *gang* and *ganga* suggests she uses *ganga* the way the word *gang* is used in the song "Hail! Hail! The Gang's All Here." This meaning exists in English but is not the one that was applied to Mexican American and Indian adolescent cohorts, especially in the Southwest.

The groups varied in number of members and ethnic composition. However, the average hangout group was composed of about six to twelve individuals. Some groups were all Mexican Americans, some all Indians, and at least one group had both.

The early pachucos living by the river that Delia spoke of were an exception in Tucson, since it appears they were not originally from the city and were transient, living on the margins of local neighborhoods. Their presence seems to have been a function of the Great Depression and related migrations.

No interviewee mentioned any kind of initiation practices such as contemporary Los Angeles cholo groups' *jumping in*; the *bautizos* (baptisms) or dunkings practiced in contemporary Chihuahua,

Chihuahua, Mexico; or the kind of *bautizo* mentioned in at least one early El Paso, Texas, pachuco group.[1]

In the stable neighborhoods dating from before the population movements of the 1950s, male peer groups were characterized by lifelong friendship and intimacy. Martín and Carlos of the pre–World War II era, both retired and receiving Social Security, had known each other since childhood ("*desde chavalos*") and still socialized on a daily basis. Martín told Carlos, "¡Yo te miré en zapeta, hombre!" (I saw you in diapers, man!) Carlos demonstrated his tendency to talk with his hands and sign certain expressions without speaking, adding that Martín nonetheless answers him back. "But I already know what he's saying," interjected Martín. Carlos added, "He knows everything about me, you know."

Rudy spoke of such friendships in his generation, saying, "You've known this guy since you were from grammar school or from junior high. . . . All those years you've known the guy. . . . There's guys that you know, like from sixth grade on. Talking about till your fifties; you still know each other. You get to know a guy like the palm of your hand." (It must be stressed that this is true of Tucson, where Mexican and Indian communities have deep roots, unlike the dynamics of places or neighborhoods composed of more recently arrived families and immigrants.)

The intimacy of the male groups is expressed in the term *carnal* (brother/bro), which appears to have undergone changes in semantic content in Tucson, reflecting political and philosophical changes, along with changes in the neighborhoods. The earliest meaning of *carnal* that Rudy recalled reflects the literal kinship relation it described in the Southwest: "Some people react on that if you call 'em 'carnal.' 'Specially a family that's got about fifteen, sixteen in it; they'll say, 'You're not my brother,' you know. 'Tu no eres mi carnal, so don't call me *carnal.* I *got* brothers.'"

Another early meaning given for the word *carnal* was: "A lot of guys that hang together, they would call 'carnales' like, you know, they go to their house and they eat at their table; those are the guys that would call each other 'carnales,' say, 'mi carnalito.'" One man described this as a "term of endearment," similar to the way young men use the word *cuñado* (brother-in-law). However, with the advent of the Chicano movement, use of the term foregrounded a political dimension that had been present in Tucson at least since the 1950s, but which during the movement came to be called *carnalismo,* reflecting cultural nationalism: "If he's raised Mexican, he's a 'carnal,' like the blacks call each other 'brothers.' Then the *Chicano* would call themself a 'carnal.'"

Leaders and the Male Group

Participants overwhelmingly stated that each male group had a leader. Of the earliest pachucos camped near the Santa Cruz River, Delia said, "Había gente grande, más mayor que ellos y los mandaban. . . . Mandaban a los chiquillos. Eran como hermanos mayores." (There were big people, older than [the younger boys], and they were the leaders. They had authority over the younger boys. They were like older brothers.) She alluded to hierarchical organization and used a family metaphor to describe that relation. (Recall that this group was almost certainly not a local, Tucson-barrio-based group, but was composed of transient young men and boys.)

Speaking about the Tucson barrios, Martín and Carlos said a leader "named/imposed himself" (*él se ponía*) and invited others to join him.

> **C:** 'Y él que quiere andar conmigo, vámonos.'
>
> **M:** Es como hay un ejercito y un capitán, algo asina. Tiene el mando. Tu le tienes que obedecer. Y si no, a *ti* te pegó.
>
> **L:** ¿De veras?
>
> **M:** Mmhum. [chuckles] Se arrancaba de la bola donde están peleando y a *ti* te agarraba.
>
> **C:** Ea. Y éste con más power, and somebody could, más fregón, se aventaba pa'rriba.
>
> **M:** Es cierto, ¿no? . . . Aquél lo bajan pa bajo, y aquél subía. ¿See?
>
> **L:** ¿Él que podía fregar?
>
> **C:** Pues, si es más abusado, él que, you know, better than him.

> (**C:** 'And the guys that want to follow me, let's go.'
>
> **M:** It's like there's an army and a captain, something like that. He's in charge/gives the orders. You have to obey him. And if you don't, he would hit *you*.

L: Really?

M: Mmhum. [chuckles] He would come out of the group where they're fighting, and he would start hitting *you.*

C: Yeah. And this guy with more power, and somebody can, who is stronger, would propel himself to the top [the leadership position].

M: That's true, right? . . . They would knock that guy out of power, and the other one would move up [to be leader]. See?

L: The guy that could hit [was physically a better fighter]?

C: Well, if he is smarter: the one that, you know, better than him.)

Two kinds of leadership emerged from the comments of men in the study: (1) one dependent upon the use of physical force (by a person labeled "the bully," "the dominator," or "the physical type") and (2) a style relying on intelligence, strategic planning, and artful use of language. The goal of both types is control of the group. One man explained that "the strong tries to control the weak, always." The male variously labeled as the "bully of the flock" or "dominator" was quoted as saying, "'I'm tougher than *all* of you! Anybody give me any BS, I'll kick *all* your butts.' And they look up to that, 'cause there's some guy that say, 'I don't know; I don't think he can, but I'm not going to try it.'" The bully intimidates to gain a "respect" that grows out of fear. "He wants you to be scared of him. Right then he wants to dominate you with that."

The second type of leader gains respect via *la teoriqueada* (the way they talk),[2] "lingo," or the ability to *maderear* (use persuasive rhetoric, bullshit, persuade through deceit). He must be *abusado* (smart) and *trucha* (quick thinking and acting/alert). "He's there; the right words. And the other guy, no. The other guy will do it with fists." At least two individuals suggested that the second type is the superior leader, since such a person may be able to control even the bully with planning and psychology. One man explained, "The guy that's gonna be the leader of every group, he talks his way, really. . . . It's a bunch of BS, but it's there." He said a group might choose to recognize the "intelligent one" as the de facto leader, even though someone else was more dominant physically. He explained the intelligent guy's approach, saying, "That's what you use. You use him [the bully] as a fool to kick somebody's butt, and you use yourself to control the group with your language, your strategies." He illustrated how the second kind of leader can manipulate the physical type. "You motivate him to think that you're there to help him, 'cause he doesn't *know,* but yet he knows how to fight and all this and be violent. But the other guy sits there . . . all cool and he waits for him. . . . It's like a plan."

This second type of leader was portrayed as calm, calculating, and adept at using various "tools of control." He is patient, likable, and capable of self-control. The bully, on the other hand, is volatile and has only one way of dealing with situations: an immediate, violent response. The ability to plan ahead, use psychology, and wait patiently are qualities he does not possess.

Rudy suggested the violent male may have a vulnerability factor that can be manipulated. He may have to depend on others, whose motives could be less than altruistic, for some things. He illustrated the vulnerability of dependent individuals to deceit and betrayal, saying, "Some of these people [bullies] never really got very intelligent. They would depend on the *other* guy. They say, 'Well, he can do it; don't worry about it; he'll show me how to do it.' And there's some guy that would say, 'Well, I'll do it all wrong for him and do it right for *me,*' you know. [laughs] It *happens.* . . . Then, 'What happened?' 'I don't know.' You get some kind of excuse."

It appears that the first type of leaders were deferred to out of expedience, since many men seemed less than happy with dynamics they created. The second type of leader, however, seemed to be more universally admired.

Historical Discourse on Pachucos

The negative discourse about pachucos must be seen in historical context. The production of negative images of Mexican people in American, English-language media, politics, and popular culture is not new. Such discourses serve to debase and discredit sectors of the nation's population. Pachuco demeanor is better understood when viewed in the context of entrenched practices of discrimination in employment, education, and policing, together with characterizations of such youth by the media as negative, ridiculous, or criminal figures. Academic versions of these discourses appeared in force immediately after the so-called zoot-suit riots. Sociologists, social workers, and psychologists contributed to the process, working with state agencies of social control: police, courts, reformatories, and jails. The school of thought known as the "sociology of deviance" is particularly related to the process and is where the bulk of literature on pachuco youth culture can be found.

Marjorie Zatz has summarized critiques of "deviance" approaches to pachuco and contemporary "cholo" youth cultures, describing the phenomenon through the concept of the "creation of a moral panic." In this view, a manufactured social imagery, rather than actual behavior, is the root of the labeling of Chicano youth groups as deviant (1987:130). A number of authors have noted an anti-"minority" and anti-working-class bias in the selective labeling of individuals and groups as criminal or deviant (Black 1976, 1984; Michalowski 1985; Pfohl 1985). Pfohl sees the categorization of groups and actions as deviant as a complex political act located within a particular framework of social, economic, and political power relations (1985:334). Spitzer (1975) names as factors in the process the size of the state control apparatus, the size and level of threat the population presents, and the social utility of "problem populations" as "tension drains" or scapegoats. These shape the likelihood that potentially problematic populations will be officially defined as deviant and subject to police control.

In light of interviewees' comments about, and hedges surrounding, definitions of pachuco identity itself, it is useful to understand the stereotype in terms of Brackette Williams's construct of ideological disadvantage, the power of the dominant group to decide what significance is to be accorded appropriations (Williams 1989:433). With law enforcement, media, and academic stereotyping of pachucos, the dominant society has appropriated the definition of the identity itself, which, proceeding from outside the community, has carried more weight than definitions originating with community members themselves. The reality of that weight is seen in interviewees' constant hedges, the fact that persons can rarely refer to the identity at all without the stereotype intruding upon what they are saying.

The portrayal of pachucas in the Los Angeles press soon after the "zoot-suit riots" was part of a newspaper campaign against Mexican juvenile delinquency in which it was reported that a dreadful situation existed. This included exposing the fact that "young girls were tattooed with various 'secret cabalistic symbols' of gang membership" (McWilliams [1948] 1968:231). Portrayal of pachucas in the press during the "riots" and in some academic writing since then as prostitutes (Coltharp 1965; Barrera Bassols 1979) adds a dimension of stigma for these women above and beyond that faced by Mexican and Mexican American women in general, who are routinely and predominantly represented in English-language popular music, media, and dominant-society male folklore by the image of the prostitute. Take, for example, the songs: "Down in Mexico" (The Coasters), "Come a Little Bit Closer" (Jay and the Americans), "Just like Tom Thumb's Blues" (Bob Dylan), and country-western songs such as "Laredo Rose" (The Texas Tornados), "Lost and Found in a Border Town" (Brooks and Dunn), "A Clean Shirt" (Willie Nelson/ Waylon Jennings), "El Paso" (Marty Robbins), and other songs ad nauseam, along with box-office hit movies such as *The Old Gringo, Born on the Fourth of July,* and *La Bamba,*[3] to name only a few. The stereotype of the pachuca carries a double dose of this image, along with the female version of the bloodthirsty, savage Mexican, which surely proceeds from the image of the bloodthirsty, savage Indian.

Pachuca Identity and Gender Boundaries

A gendered dimension not present in male groups was the fact that pachuca behavior included a number of activities and practices considered inappropriate for females in middle- and upper-class sectors of Anglo-American, Mexican American, and Mexican societies. Veronica recalled girls of her age group rolling up their pant cuffs and dropping cigarette ashes into them when they smoked. Many women spoke of the culturally prescribed necessity of not backing away from fights with other girls. Some of the pachucas' other behavior and practices also shocked middle- and upper-class notions of gender appropriateness on both sides of the border, such as the practice of tattooing crosses on their hands or foreheads. It must be recalled, however, that females of a number of Indian groups in the region tattooed their faces and bodies with various designs and that gender roles were quite differently defined in those societies.

The Morales' teenage daughters described and contested the insinuations of masculinity or lesbianism to which contemporary cholas are at times subjected. "Some [guys] back off and say that it's [being chola is] not nice 'cause it's not feminine. It's not a girl. . . . Not how a girl should be. It's like trying to act like a guy; trying to imitate a guy." When asked if that was true, they answered, "No! We're girls! [they laugh] We like guys. [she laughs] And that's cholo."

For the early pachucas who didn't dress much differently than other girls their age (regardless of ethnic group), the cross tattoo between the thumb and forefinger on the hand (or, for the more daring, between the eyes on the forehead or below the lower lip) was one of the most patent symbols of pachuca identity. More than the other practices, tattooing seemed a lightning rod for feelings about such gender-boundary crossings by females. If family members may not have looked upon tattoos on young males in an entirely positive light, at least they were part of a young manhood ritual related to militarism, recognizable to mainstream sectors of Anglo- and Mexican American society. Dora so strongly associated tattoos with males and masculinity that when she tried to remember the words for "tattoo" in Spanish and English, she thought of the Marines! No males in this study mentioned negative family reactions. However, tattoos on females seemed to provoke especially strong negative reactions on the part of several women's family members, or fear of such reactions. Parents were unhappy with daughters' tattoos, whether due to their own feelings or out of fear of repercussions for the young person.

There is ongoing contemporary evidence that much tattooing in this youth culture involves an institutionalized practice of purposefully etching a memory-triggering image onto the skin, just as expressed in Julie's account of her group's tattoo. Lydia and Julie's stories of group tattoos suggest a female cohort ritual reminiscent of a blood-sister pact. (The group tattoos seem to have occurred only in female cohorts. Males apparently preferred to have different, distinctive tattoos.)

Both males and females did their own tattoos with India ink during early to mid-adolescence. To the young people, the popular tattoos were a marker of peer-group identity. To female cohorts with identical tattoos, they were a symbol of unity, equality, friendship, and collective daring. (Recall that these girls were doing this long before it became fashionable in middle-class Anglo society. Here, we see a change in meaning when members of the dominant group take up a practice, another example of subordinated group members' ideological disadvantage.)

Gendered differences in the meaning of having a tattoo proved difficult to overcome, although the young people defied both those and the cultural meanings attributed to tattoos by dominant elements of society. Accounts suggested that individuals ultimately may not have been able to completely overcome the "weight" of the dominant social meanings and were thus at an ideological disadvantage. Dora spoke of older women wanting to remove the tattoos. One woman referred to tattoos as "shit." A man spoke of having to "drag it around for the rest of your life," implying a weight.

The accounts of female cohort friendships suggest a striving for more freedom (even if at times vicarious), daring together as a group to cross boundaries of prescribed appropriateness. The girls seemed to desire sophistication and knowledge about "the world beyond" to which they did not have access or which perhaps was declared off-limits to them. The girls collectively encouraged each other to dare against restrictions. A few even dared to run away to extricate themselves from difficult situations at home or school. Such efforts were often carried out as a pact with a female friend.

All in all, through their cohort activities and relation to pachuco identity itself, it appears that while males sought to enhance or consolidate their male identity in line with rather mainstream standards, pachuca females sought to go beyond the imposed bounds of appropriateness for their gender.

Social Life and Courtship

In their interviews, members of different generations gave assessments of other generations' courting behavior. Dora said, "Now it is very different. . . . Now the girls don't even like for the mother to go along . . . or to be where their mother is. They want to be by themself, by themself. They are embarrassed to be seen with their mother." Other persons of that early generation said young people now go off alone (*se van solos*), do whatever they want (*se dan vuelo*), and that they don't ask their mothers' permission any more. Carlos described contemporary young people's courting behavior as coyote-like, implying that it is sly, sneaky, or tricky: "Ahora es puro acoyotada. El coyote viene y se mete. '¡Ay! ¡Tu! ¡Va!' Entró con ella y allí se quedó." (Now they're just like coyotes. The coyote comes and goes in. "Oh! You! How did you get here?!" He came in with her and stayed there.)

Younger people had their own assessments of the older generation's ways. Two middle-aged women spoke about their mothers' attitudes toward sex, saying women of that generation tended to feel that "sex is dirty." Veronica also remarked (perhaps by way of explanation), "Before, guys didn't want to marry a girl if she'd had *sex* with some guy. That was kind of ridiculous." One of the younger women felt that when she was in high school in the 1980s, attitudes about sex still hadn't changed all that much. She spoke of what would happen to a woman who was thought to be sexually active: "It's nothing nowadays, but in those days, if they did put you down, then you were the biggest whore in the area. . . . You have a baby or somebody just had a baby, it's nothing anymore. You're pregnant, she's pregnant [two or three women present say all at once: 'Oh, my God!' mimicking people's response before], 'And she's not married to him?!'"

What seems evident over the generations is that the good girl/bad girl dichotomy has prevailed, albeit with shifting markers of female decency. For gender, as in the case of ethnicity, the pragmatic and ideological disadvantages for the subjugated group take the form of differential application of rules and meanings. The same act may define a male as "only human" and may render a female "the biggest whore in the area."

Public and Private Patriarchy

During the post–World War II years, as women moved into spaces and activities previously reserved for men, the state (at various levels) stepped up its policing of gender relations, and violence against women increased. Silvia Walby described this change as, "part of a shift from private to public patriarchy, with male control of individual women in families and households giving way to public patriarchal control through the state" (Walby 1990:89). During the post-war period, resistance to private (family) patriarchy is increasingly evident in young people's attempts to elude control. Older women spoke of the post-war years as a time when they moved beyond previous limitations, yet they also expressed the need to be increasingly concerned for their safety.

Corrigan and Sayer (1985) call the role of the state in this process, "moral regulation," which imposes a definition of "normality" on constructions of gender and sexuality. Feminist literature on the state and morality adds that state-defined normality is informed by patriarchy (see Ortner 1976).

That male interests don't always coincide with either those of private (family) or public (state) patriarchy is illustrated in a number of examples from men's interviews. Some men had had difficult and they felt unjustified encounters with young women's fathers, uncles, brothers, and also with their mothers (as in the A-Mountain incident). Two of the older men had not liked the imposed role of "sisters' keeper." (Some interviews even showed evidence of male-female sibling collusion in eluding those roles.)

The limitations on female mobility at the time of the Barker recordings, and ideological and pragmatic consequences of violating those limits, were described by Rudy: "Back in those days the girls' parents would be real strict. You'd see a lot of the guys out in the street but its very, very rare you'd see one of these girls out in the street, 'cause that's when they would call her a *putita* [whore] or whatever." He noted that such girls would be the targets of rape and gang rape; "[Daughters were] just s'pozed to come back home and iron and wash the dishes and stuff." This may account for why so many of the female groups met in homes or at school.

Historical Change in Conflict Dynamics

Pre–World War II Generation

The eldest interviewees perceived stark contrasts in the conflict practices of the early pachucos vis-à-vis those seen in contemporary times with hardcore cholos.[4] Martín, Carlos, and a friend (M3) commented:

> **C:** Ya se acabó el pleito. Ahora los chavalos son, you know, *diferentes.*
>
> **M3:** Estos tiran balazos.
>
> **C:** Ellos sacan (**M:** pum, pum) cuete. . . . Nosotros usámos las ondas, slingshot? Esa nosotros la usámos pa agarrar codorníz cuando estábamos chavalos también. (**M:** Sí.) ¡Paasss! Íbamos al traque a agarrar piedras.
>
> **M:** ¡La piedra! ¡*Duele* ésa! ¡Es fierro! [chuckling] Puro fierro.

L: ¿De éso a los cuetes de ahora?

M: Ahora sacan pistola de oro.

L: ¿Cómo wachan el asunto de los jóvenes ahora? . . . Que tanta pistola . . .

C: No los calmas. . . . Han cambiado *mucho* los chavalos.

(**C:** There are no fistfights anymore. Now the young fellows are *different.*

M3: These guys fire bullets.

C: They pull out (**M:** bam, bam) a firearm. . . . We used slingshots. We used that to hunt quail too, when we were boys. (**M:** Yes.) Wham! We would go to the railroad tracks to get stones.

M: A stone! It *hurts*! It's [like] metal! [chuckling] Pure metal.

L: From that to today's firearms?

M: Now they pull out a gold pistol.

L: What do you think about the subject of young people today? . . . that there are so many pistols?

C: You can't control them. The young guys have changed *a lot.*)

Martín and Carlos mentioned specific weapons used in the past, such as ".38 special" pistols and shotguns, noting that the firearms today are more powerful. They told of drive-by shootings now in the neighborhood; then Carlos added,

C: They think they're pachucos, you know.

M: . . . *más smart* . . .

C: . . . *pero* drugs's *stupid.*

M: Si cuando están en la carcel andan llorando que la mamá que "Llévame éste," que "Llévame este otro." ¿Quién se lo buscó? Él mismo. ¿Por qué no comprenden que hacen algo malo? ¿Por qué andan llorando?

(**C:** They think they're pachucos, you know.

M: . . . *smarter* . . .

C: But drugs's *stupid.*

> **M:** And when they are in jail they are crying to their mother to "Bring me this" and "Bring me that." Who got himself into the situation? He himself. Why don't they understand that they are doing something bad? Why are they crying?)

Martín and Carlos continued:

> **M:** Y aquí, [**C:** overlap] venga en un Año Nuevo y verás qué plegaria de cuetes oyes. Parecen cañones. [chuckles] [makes pinging bullet sound]
>
> **M3:** Y ahí va la chota en friega.
>
> **M:** ¡Y no; no salen! ¡No andan aquí! En las puras doce del New Year . . . no miras a un vato d'esos. (**L:** ¿No vienen?) Pues, tienen miedo que les den.
>
> (**M:** And [**C:** overlap] come by here on New Year's, and you'll see what a *plegaria* of firearms you will hear.[5] They sound like cannons. [chuckles] [makes pinging bullet sound]
>
> **M3:** And there go the cops in a hurry.
>
> **M:** And no. They [the police] don't come out! They don't come around here! At exactly twelve midnight on New Year's Eve, you don't see one of those guys. (**L:** They don't come?) Well, they are afraid that they will be shot.)

All the older interviewees said that in the early days, fights were infrequent and violence was not random. Confrontations occurred for rather predictable reasons within or between social groupings, usually taking place in private or semiprivate settings between two individuals, without the use of weapons. If others were present, they did not join the fray. On the contrary, they kept others from entering and checked conflict escalation. Most fights appear to have been gender-segregated, although the Barker conversations relate one instance of a woman fighting a man. As for the use of weapons, Delia's mother had told her that watch chains were mostly twirled to intimidate. There were no accounts of pachucas actually using the knives they reputedly carried inside their pompadours. The only recollection of a stabbing in the early days was of a man who cheated in a card game. It was not clear if that incident involved pachucos. The sole fight Ed witnessed where a knife was pulled occurred in Los Angeles. All interviewees said that homicides were almost unknown.

Louie said he doesn't get along with modern-day cholos, because, he said, "too many [of them are] in trouble." His comments suggest that even weapons that were available in the early days were not used in the ways they are used today: "Nowadays, if you say anything, they'll pull out a gun." "What about back then?" I asked. "No! They wouldn't kill you. I think that there were guns and knives and everything, but like I tell you, if they're going to fight, they'll just let you and him fight."

One woman gave an example of how conflicts are carried out today. One night she heard a boom outside her house. Someone had thrown a bottle of gasoline into a nearby vehicle. She said, "Apparently they knew it was his [her neighbor's vehicle]; they spotted it and did that *para hacerle daño* [to do him harm]. But heaven knows what he did to them, too. They don't know who did it. They know who did it, but you know they aren't going to say. So, I mean, I'm not going to say, 'They did this; they did that.' *Pasado mañana* [day after tomorrow] they blast all your family. Forget it, you know. I just keep to myself around here."

Violence against family members was virtually unheard-of during the early period and was certainly socially unacceptable. In general, persons that were not direct parties to disputes were not legitimate targets. Random violence was not legitimized, either, but Dora pointed to its existence now when she said that one should not even look at a group of young men driving along in a car because they might shoot you. Lydia said, "In that time [the old times] *no había nada* [there wasn't anything]. Now there is. And I think they're worse." I asked what might have made it change. "I guess that this generation . . . the way they pick up things on TV and all that. The way they dress, total different style. And now they *do* have gangs in every neighborhood. . . . And all that marking on the walls, they didn't used to have all that in my days. Now you can't go to a nice neighborhood because, brand-new walls, they build the walls and right now they say 'Blood' or whatever they put on [them]." Now, when they have fights, Rudy said, "[It's] five, six on one; five on two, a gun or a knife."

Immediate Post–World War II Generation

Interviewees of this group shared perceptions of changes in the objective of confrontations, in the underlying ideology or code, in the presence and use of weapons, and in the social organization of conflict.

Rudy said things have changed radically from the old code of honor. In his day it was still in place and largely respected in practice. As he said earlier, "Ese es *hombre.* [That guy is a *man.*] He's a man. He'll fight you and get over it. You beat him, he respects you; that's *it.*" He goes on to say, "But *now,* you know, he'll say, 'He won't touch me; I'm gonna *shoot* him,' you know, or 'I'm gonna cut his head off.' . . . Or somebody's always there to strike that blow behind your back. . . . *Now,* kids gotta watch out what their reactions are to trouble. 'Specially the physical fistfights or whatever." He feels drugs are a central cause of the change, that substance use impairs a person's judgment and reactions to situations, along with the ability to defend oneself. A young person may go into a conflict mode on the spur of the moment without being in a condition to think or reason. (Recall that in the early days, appointments might be made for a fight and a place and time chosen. Many times others were present monitoring the progress of the confrontation. They might even stop a fight if too much damage was being inflicted.) Rudy added that many substances used today were not available or socially acceptable in the past. However, he said, at the point when the demand for drugs in American society in general burgeoned and created a lucrative market, an economic incentive began to drive events as young people realized they could make money by going into sales. At that point a very different dynamic began to evolve. Joan Moore, and others, in *Homeboys: Gangs, Drugs and Prison in the Barrios of Los Angeles,* documents in detail precisely this type of change and the accompanying breakdown in the conventions of fighting in old barrios of Los Angeles in the 1940s, '50s, and '60s (1978:71).

Rudy cited easy availability of firearms as another factor in the change. "That's how come all those people are getting blown away. Anybody can buy a gun." Bob spoke of an escalation in types of weapons and in the objective of conflict. When asked to compare fights back then and now, he answered, "The difference is . . . nah; they can't imitate a pachuco anyway. They want to be one but they cannot be real, original pachuco." A number of the older men made similar comments, appearing to equate pachuco identity with the mode of fighting practiced under the code of honorable manhood, which Bob described as face-to-face, one-on-one.

Bob said, "Nowadays instead of help each other, you want to kill each other." Like Louie and others, he alluded to a breakdown of the conventions of fighting and to changes in the ways weapons were used. "Nowadays you get a brawl; the first thing you got is pull out a knife. . . . They got 'em to *kill.* You know, they don't carry it around to clean their fingernails." He also suggests that the previously small, privately mitigated disputes have now moved into public and even family space: "When they used to have fights [it] was outta sight, where nobody would *see* them."

The 1960s

Reasons for entering into physical confrontations given by those who were teens in the 1960s differ from those given by previous generations. These included perceptions of looks or stares, a social imperative/peer pressure to fight, the need to maintain a certain reputation, and intergroup frictions. Art said, "Just people would look at me. And that was the excuse for me."

Veronica's comments alluded to the social imperative of maintaining a tough reputation and fighting: "I guess it's a way of showing bravado. If somebody looks at you bad, '¡¿Qué me 'stas mirando?!' [What are you looking at?!], you know? '¡¿Qué me miras?!' [What are you looking at?!], you know? Or something like that. And then if you back down, then everybody's just *waiting.*" From these comments, it appears that defense of honor and controlled venting of anger and conflict was being replaced by a commodified bravado, in the form of a personal attribute or trait that is somewhat decontextualized socially, at least when compared to the social forms of previous generations.

Veronica also spoke of peer pressure in high school to belong to cliques, and the physical harassment that was part of that pressure:

> I think it was, it was a lot harder then on women than it is now, you know. 'Cause, you know, at that time, you know, the women had to fight, and also the guys, you know, 'cause you had to have your little clique to walk down the school . . . and I was never involved with a little clique, so I was just, I always hung out with that one girl, and it was pretty hard, because then everybody thought that, well, then you were stuck up, well, you thought you were. "All right," you know, "you don't hang around with the rest of us," you know? And if you didn't

> hang around with the rest of us, then you always have to, you know, get into a fight or do something, 'cause every time you were in the hallway, if you didn't belong to one group, you had to belong to this group, and if you didn't belong to any group at all, then you thought you were *it*. They picked on . . . you'd be going up the stairs, and somebody would try to knock you down, or they'd pull at you or . . .

In this generation's accounts, school was the place most mentioned as the site of fights. Earlier generations mentioned places like a vacant lot, down by the railroad tracks, a bit out of town, or in the center of a ring of pachucos—semiprivate, noninstitutional contexts.

Veronica commented on the changes in conflict dynamics and in the objective of fights. "Now everybody tells me they're shooting at each other, stabbing at each other; you can't go to a party now because you get worried, all this stuff that kids do. At that time [the 1960s] you went to have a good time; nobody wanted to shoot anybody or kill anybody."

She also noted changes in conventions of appropriateness in everyday language use. "*Chinga tu madre*" (F— your mother) is now acceptable, she said, whereas before, this made people really angry. She added that if you say that to someone now, they laugh at you and answer, "So what? F— you, too." She continued, "So now in order to get him pissed off, you have to go over and hit him or stab him or injure to have the same effect as *no más echándole* [just saying something about his mother/swearing at him]."

Veronica felt that a lot of what we see on TV is "not so acceptable" and may be responsible for some of the changes, singling out violent, bloody movies. "I think it has to do with people getting so desensitized, and drugs." She also said that "a lot has to do with the lack of respect that people have nowadays for each other. Not even for a human life. They shoot now. They don't *care*. Their values are a lot different." Lydia, too, felt that kids "pick up" things from what they see on TV. Veronica's husband offered the opinion that young people involved in the new brand of violence were trying to be tough. Veronica interjected, "That's not being tough. That's being *insane*. Before they just wanted to beat you up; now they want to put you six feet under."

So, in addition to changes in standards of appropriateness, Veronica suggests that a kind of habituation to drugs and violence has occurred; they are now considered acceptable. She implied that people become conditioned to things they see constantly, especially when presented as "cool" or desirable.

1970s and 1980s

Reasons given as occasioning fights by interviewees who were teens in the 1970s and early 1980s were frictions between cholos and non-cholos, racial or ethnic insults, individuals that want to control things, and persons such as those mentioned by 1960s individuals that "think they're bad" or that seem to have something to prove. Again, school was the most-mentioned site of confrontations.

The Morales sisters explained that they had undergone a change in their thinking about fights at a certain point in high school. Their comments suggest the presence of a debate or reevaluation of conflict dynamics among some sectors of youth in the 1980s:

> **D2:** Us cholas, we started thinking it's not right to fight a Mexican.
>
> **D1:** A Mexican.
>
> **D2:** You know, you can't. You know, it's like hitting yourself.

In the earlier contexts of an intimate community, conflict was seen as undesirable in pachuco groups, a last resort. It was therapeutic in function ("get it out of your system"), and there were practices of containment, closure, and reconciliation. Such practices sustain and may even strengthen a community or social group. Contemporary hardcore gang ideology, however (like much in the commercial media), glorifies violence as a desirable activity in and of itself, something to be pursued to gain a personal attribute. In this domain, too, self-serving profiteers promote acquisition of the attribute. The costs to families and the community are enormous, and the pathology of these dynamics was recognized by all of the interviewees.

Social Change, Controlled Substances, and Racial Tolerance

As in all of American society, the social use of controlled substances had changed radically by the time teens of the 1960s and 1970s were in their thirties and forties. Though relatively young, they seemed amazed by the escalation they had witnessed during their lifetimes in the availability and use of such substances, especially cocaine, and by changes in attitudes about drug use. All recalled a time when drinking beer in Sabino Canyon "was the worst thing you could do."

A woman who was in high school in the late 1960s said,

> We experimented . . . well, *I* did . . . with pot. . . . I always remember a film they showed us in high school. We were just smoking pot earlier, and we were just talking . . . and then they decided to show us this film. I'll never forget this film where this guy, he smokes some pot . . . and then all of a sudden he went *crazy*, you know? . . . And he started, like, looking in the mirror. And he had *rabbit ears*, you know, and he broke a Coke bottle, you know the old-fashioned Coke bottles? He broke a Coke bottle, and he started drinking from it, and he cut his mouth. And you know, we're sitting there stoned looking at this film. I thought, "That's a bunch of bullshit," you know. So the *good* that would've *done*. I'm telling my child, "Don't use drugs because that, you know, the bad thing is that when you find one kind of drug, you find something stronger, and then you tend to experiment." But if you're watching a film where this guy gets *rabbit ears*, and you know, he's all freaked out, you know, you're stoned already looking at this, and you think, "God!" You know, you're not gonna believe anything they tell you.

The woman implied that the ill-conceived antidrug film at school had the opposite effect of what was intended. She contrasted the film's approach with the more straightforward one she uses with her own child.

In the 1970s some people also experimented with marijuana. Others recalled that in the latter part of that decade, cocaine discreetly made its appearance in Tucson. By the late '80s and '90s, discretion had all but disappeared. However, many individuals of different generations mentioned the negative impact of cocaine on people's lives and on social dynamics.

With changing patterns of alcohol use and the arrival of other drugs on the social scene, the desire to push back the boundaries of appropriateness seems to increase. As minors, a few persons who were teens in the 1960s and '70s developed substance abuse problems and went through difficult struggles to overcome dependency. It appears that for adolescents and young adults of those generations, there were more age-segregated, unchaperoned social contexts and, as in much of American society, a growing tolerance for substance use.

Also in the '60s and '70s, as subordinated groups moved out of previously defined spaces, social life changed and interethnic tensions in Tucson grew. Post-desegregation social life is racially/ethnically mixed but often with tense undercurrents. For example, Veronica assessed the possibility that Anglo individuals might want to socialize with an informal-sector Mexican national at a contemporary Tucson club if he were not selling cocaine. Her husband observed, "The people were wearing a trail down to the bar." Veronica added, "Yeah. And I told [the husband], 'And if you *really think* that all these white people here are gonna be talkin' to that stupid Mexican,' I said. *Everybody* was his buddy. Everybody [was], like, 'You're what?' I mean, give me a break. But everybody was his buddy that night; that's for sure." Her remarks provide a candid commentary on contemporary interethnic relations. Many of this youngest age group characterized racism in Tucson as subtle and not out in the open. One middle-aged woman contrasted the Tucson brand with that of the border town of Douglas, Arizona, which she described as blatant. She had taken a trip there with her husband, who described that town as "very racist," a town that had been segregated. His wife added, "It still is." She said, "You know, I never really faced a lot of prejudice [in Tucson]. It's always been kind of like a hidden thing, and I tell him, 'Ahhh no, people [in Douglas] aren't gonna be prejudiced like that with me.' He takes me into a bar, and I can't believe how prejudiced the peo— . . . even the barmaid was talking about the Mexicans and saying it like, 'Eeuuw, a *Mexican*,' like they're *horrible*. . . . I couldn't believe it, that I had actually seen that." Her husband recalled, "You asked [the bandleader] for a Mexican dance [song]; he says, 'Oh, you mean Spanish.'" She added, "I said, 'No, Mexican.' What's so embarrassing?"

Contemporary Social Events

The Morales family teenagers said that young people now party and "kick back somewhere" with friends, at someone's house, a backyard, or in the desert. Electronic DJs are a popular feature at these events.

Cruising was mentioned as a popular activity, but one plagued by constant police harassment.

Veronica's husband implied that there has been a rarefaction of public social contexts for young people. He felt the only places to go now are nightclubs, where younger people can't get in. Even desert parties are discouraged now by the police and can be held "way out on the outskirts " only. In his day young people partied in the desert at Sweetwater and Ironwood, but those are residential areas today.

In 1991 Veronica observed that "for a long time *quinceañeras* were out of style,[6] [but] now they're back in, all the rage." Her young son goes to them now. Although she thinks this new popularity has more to do with "keeping up with the Joneses" than with the "actual tradition," she feels that the quinceañera's return is a sign of young people turning to their roots. "There's, I think, a thing of getting back your *culture* that's going on with the kids."

As for social contexts for adults, their family, and friends, Veronica and her husband said that playing the guitar and singing in Spanish are "still pretty popular." People also get together with family and friends for barbecues in backyards or parks. Occasions such as weddings, baptisms, birthday parties, quinceañeras, graduation, and anniversary parties are mixed-gender gatherings where large extended families socialize. For the many Tucson families that maintain this tradition, such celebrations include young and old alike, so socializing is not age-segregated but cross-generational.

Calming Down and Aging

Both females and males mentioned marriage and family responsibilities as a factor in the cessation or modification of the cohort relationship. They also mentioned the post-high-school demands of a job, training to prepare for one, or educational pursuits. Rudy stated, "Well, lot of guys, when you get married or something, that's the first thing they say. 'Ya te amarraron' or, you know, '*Ya*, they hooked you,' . . . and 'You ain't going to be able to go out with us no more.' . . . In other words, you fade away from your friends. After that, it's not *there*." He added, "After a while you don't mind. That's the past. . . . And you *realize* that."

As individuals looked back on their teens and pachuco days, they seemed to have fond memories and positive feelings about the identity. Martín and Carlos recalled those times as good times. Carlos recalled them as "*beautiful.*" Martín said, "por la diversión que teníamos; [because of the fun we used to have], andar vacilando [out having a good time]." Carlos added, "Es lo único que tenías, you know. [That's all that you had, you know.]"

Armando explained, "Even I, *ahorita* [right now] at forty-nine years of age, a lot of times find myself acting así como poco chuco [sort of a bit chuco]. It's just something that transforms me; . . . all of a sudden you find yourself doing it. . . . And I feel *good* about it." His wife, Julie, felt the same way.

As Louie thought back to the early pachuco days, he said, "We were an ethnic group, and we had to express ourselves, and we did. We were looking for something, and I think we found it; we did find it," he smiled.

Bob mentioned a fellow in Old Pascua he called "an original pachuco." "He's old, calmed down. Like I say, you can't tell they're pachucos anymore." The man still had the pachuco walk. "They used to walk like a duck." Bob's teenage children, however, noted that some older men around town still dress pachuco-style in "baggies" [pants], hats, shirts, and black shoes. One older man they see downtown wears "a little black hat with feathers sticking out, and he dresses like that, too."

Louie had saved his zoot suits until about two years before the interview, when he finally let his wife give them to the Salvation Army. He still liked the style and pointed out his similar haircut (at age sixty-three), albeit shorter, when he was describing pachuco hair. Martín (age sixty-five) was wearing khakis, a *lisa* (dress shirt), a *tando* (hat) with a cross in the center front of a narrow hatband, and black shoes when I met him. Art (age forty-four) was wearing khakis, a white T-shirt, and a tando. He drove a '64 Impala. Some of the women still bore their tattoos, and others said a few sentences in Pachuco as they recalled the good times at the dances and with their friends. The smiles that came to interviewees' faces and the sudden brightness in their eyes occasioned by the memories seemed to convey the overriding message about how they felt about those times.

9

CONCLUSION

This study has attempted to ethnographically and historically contextualize the appearance and development of pachuco culture in Tucson and give some background in the form of historical clues to that development from an earlier epoch in the region, primarily the nineteenth century and turn of the twentieth century. Contrary to the 1940s phenomenon it is often claimed to be, it is clear that older Arizona persons view the 1930s as the early pachuco era. Indeed some individuals have memories of the late 1920s or knowledge that suggests that pachucos were present in Arizona by at least the late 1920s. This points to the need for further research into the regional dynamics of the culture, its development, and its dissemination.

While the culture has been overwhelmingly characterized as a bicultural, Mexican/Anglo-American phenomenon (linguistically Spanish–English), more systematic attention needs to be given to Indian contributions to the cultural mix. Many of the participants in this study knew which tribal groups they were descended from, and a number of persons self-identified as both Chicano and Indian. Significant early roots of the hybrid culture in the greater Southwest appear to be Indian in origin and philosophical orientation (proceeding from both Mexican and Southwest regional groups). Two of the most salient key symbols of the culture, *pachuco,* the word for the identity itself (with a possible Kiowa angle), and *tacuche* (zoot suit), point to Indian presence and influence, in that the terms were preserved as culturally significant symbols. That influence is also seen in their semantic content: Kiowa *Pä'sûñko*: Paso people, musty-smelling ones; Kiliwa *pachugó*: ladino, Spanish-speaking Indian, a person having an outer wrapping or wearing clothes, town dweller; and Tarascan/Pure'pecha *tacuche*: bundle/wrapping of rags, trouble. Indian influence in the culture is also evident in the early cross tattoos.

The culture's persistent critiques, over generations, of "proper" Mexican, Anglo, and Mexican American societies' ways suggest a continuing preference for and persistence of Indian notions of social appropriateness. There is a need to look into, record, and analyze the neglected, specific regional Indian histories and cultural and linguistic influences related to the hybrid culture: histories of groups and regions, of migrations and employment, of communities, neighborhoods, and schools.

Participants in this study held a very different view of the culture and its symbols than that portrayed in the stereotype held by many whose concept of pachucos almost certainly proceeds from sensationalized press around the time of the so-called zoot suit riots (1943). From participants' comments, we see that both male and female cohorts participated in mainstream popular-culture activities easily recognizable to all Americans. However, the groups of Indian and Mexican American youth were defined early on as "gangs" by dominant-society press, law enforcement agencies, and scholars in the social sciences, especially in the fields of the sociology of deviance and criminology. Anglo youth carrying out these same activities were not characterized as gangs.

That pachucos were portrayed as uniquely violent, even vicious, illustrates the power of dominant groups to impose an identity on subordinate groups. Older men equated pachuco identity with practices adhering to a code of honorable manhood extant within the youth culture in Tucson until about the 1970s: one-on-one fights with fists, face-to-face, often monitored by others to prevent escalation and undue injury. The system was not unique to pachuco groups and other Mexican and Mexican American men but was also widely respected and practiced by Anglo men. However recognizable and familiar the system, pachucos have been portrayed as especially vicious and violent. The persistence of negative characterizations and labeling of Mexican and Mexican Americans (especially working-class people), on the part of the dominant society, is a continuing, historically rooted practice. (See Hill 1993.)

Regional people of the greater Southwest have maintained culture and language not only in spite of negative images, but in the face of concerted and sustained institutional assaults on their cultural forms. Schools actively suppressed and supplanted cultural and linguistic forms through stigmatization, coercion, corporal punishment, and incarceration. Pachuco/ caló, being unwritten, unauthorized, and "mixed," and operating with very different standards of appropriateness, was more stigmatized even than standard Spanish. Yet its complex dynamics of use and production of meaning are more sophisticated (as one man aptly put it) than those of monolingual, monocultural phenomena. Its survival, elaboration, and continued use reflect what Hill and Coombs (1982) call "the struggle for control of the symbolic universe."

Obviously, there have been some glaring cultural misunderstandings, a good dose of intolerance, and, unfortunately, ill will has not been lacking. However, if one is able to get beyond the predominating twentieth-century deviance bias, one sees a previously existing regional culture with hybrid elements centered around El Paso, forming since the sixteenth century, growing out of contact among groups. Indeed, geographical transition zones near the Rio Grande were areas of some hybrid cultural phenomena even in preconquest times.

In historical times, the Salinas pueblos' peoples are believed to have moved to Socorro (now in New Mexico) and then down to El Paso with the Spanish who fled the Pueblo revolt of 1680, as did the Tiguas and others who accompanied them. A large group of Mescalero Apache were settled on a tract along the Rio Grande in 1793, near today's Belen, New Mexico (Sturtevant 1988:421). And while the Apache wars raged in what is now southern Arizona during the nineteenth century, first waged by Spain, then Mexico, then the United States, there was a colony of people referred to as Apaches Mansos, or "docile Apaches," who lived peacefully in Tucson while other Apaches were being hunted and slaughtered (Officer 1987).

So the convergence of populations and interethnic, multilingual environment in the region point to a juxtaposition of cultures, discourses, and semantic systems, providing a context in which the possibility existed for diverse forms and meanings to be played off one another.

Situated studies of pachuco culture of a more historical and ethnographic nature are needed, in addition to the extant essays and linguistic works. The need also continues for ethnographic studies of gendered phenomena related to the youth culture, which are only recently beginning to be systematically addressed. Contrary to claims in much of the academic literature, females have been conversant with the culture and language since its emergence.

Historically and at present, persons associated with pachuco youth culture participate strongly in mainstream United States culture and hold many of its values, not the least being an appreciation for liberty, justice, and freedom of expression. Education is esteemed. Monocultural Anglos will recognize and identify with many of the activities, experiences, and values of the older and younger individuals in this study. The participants, however, also have other rich cultural dimensions in their lives.

Today in Tucson and the region there are contexts and milieus where multiple, simultaneous ethnic identities are unambiguously understood, accepted, and respected. The same goes for "mixed" or hybrid identities; they are unproblematic. A somewhat similar situation exists in Mexico's state of Sonora (but to a lesser extent), where, as in Tucson, the origins of large sectors of the population are regional, with substantial time depth of occupation, and where some Indian groups are still quite visible. However, this contrasts sharply with the contemporary population of the border city of Tijuana, for example, in Baja California, which is composed of people of quite recent migrations and of more disparate origins.

The culture continues today in Tucson, in cities and towns of the Southwest and other areas of the United States and Mexico. Many people are conversant with its forms, appreciate its roots, and do not participate in or subscribe to dynamics introduced by contemporary hardcore gangs. Such gangs are not representative of the great majority of individuals conversant with the culture and language. However, the stigmatization and criminalization of the youth culture continues today in forms that are not all that different from the dynamics surrounding the so-called zoot-suit riots of 1943. Notwithstanding, pachuco culture has persisted in Tucson for over seventy-five years.

Early in the twentieth century, informal groups of young Mexican American males were labeled "gangs" by police and in academic studies, although, as Rubel pointed out in 1965, "voluntary friendship associations" called *palomillas* are an important feature of traditional Mexican social organization (1965:92). Similar groups were also a feature of many regional Indian societies and were similarly labeled in the boarding schools they were forced to attend (Lomawaima 1994).

Labels notwithstanding, I find a more plausible explanation than deviance, of the origins or "causes" of pachuco culture, in the particular historical and cultural trajectories of the region's Mexican and Indian populations. Pachuco's protocols and key symbols continue to speak of its regional and Indian influences. However, in the context of ongoing negative dominant-society discourses about people of Mexican ancestry in the United States, and particularly about pachucos in both Mexico and the United States, many individuals conversant with the hybrid culture and language continue to present themselves in such a way as to be exposed to the least possible hostility, danger, and trouble.

Appendix
Interviewees' Dates and Places of Birth

(Pseudonyms)

Dora, born 1920, Tucson, Arizona

The Morales family:

Delia (Aurora's mother), born 1921, Tucson, Arizona
Aurora, born 1942, Tucson, Arizona
Bob (Aurora's husband), born 1937, Tucson, Arizona
Son, seventeen years old in 1985, year of interview, born Tucson, Arizona
D1: daughter, nineteen years old in 1985, born Tucson, Arizona
D2: daughter, eighteen years old in 1985, born Tucson, Arizona

Martin, born 1925, Tucson, Arizona

Carlos, born 1931, Tucson, Arizona

Louie, born 1927, Jerome, Arizona

Ida (Louie's wife), born 1936, Redington, Arizona

Lydia, born 1930, Tucson, Arizona

Rudy, born 1933, Tucson, Arizona

Art, born 1944, Tucson, Arizona

Julie, born 1947, Tucson, Arizona

Armando (Julie's husband), born 1941, Douglas, Arizona

Patty, born 1946, Tucson, Arizona

Patty's sister, born 1942, Tucson, Arizona

Veronica, born 1951, Douglas, Arizona

Notes

Introduction

1. This recording is in the archives of the University of Arizona's Southwest Folklore Center.

Chapter 1

1. The nuns were the Sisters of St. Joseph of Corondelet. These nuns run the present-day Saint Mary's Hospital near the original location.

2. *El Día de San Juan* (the Nativity of John the Baptist on the Christian liturgical calendar) is celebrated on June 24. In Mexico and the Southwest, this celebration often includes a unique blend of cultures and traditions, some Christian, some not. In the Tucson area, for instance, the celebration coincides with the saguaro cactus harvest and the festivities of the indigenous Tohono O'odham people, which include wine-making from the juice of the saguaro fruit and ceremonies to call down the rain. Tucson's annual rainy season, called the monsoon, typically follows these ceremonies right on cue, beginning the first or second week in July. Another feature of Día de San Juan is the custom of jumping into rivers or irrigation ditches—a delightful way not only to cope with summer's heat, but also to commemorate the ministry of John the Baptist. The event also has overtones of other midsummer celebrations and, of course, is only a few days after the summer solstice, an event celebrated by many cultures in remarkably similar ways.

3. *Cumbias* have a rather fast, tropical rhythm.

4. The verb *respetar* in this context carries the connotation that they would not make sexual advances.

5. "No tener nada que ver con" here alludes to the fact that there was no sexual relationship.

6. For information on the deportations, see Mercedes Carreras de Velasco, *Los mexicanos que devolvió la crisis, 1929–1932*; and Abraham Hoffman, *Unwanted Mexican Americans in the Great Depression: Repatriation Pressures, 1929–1939*.

7. The Civilian Conservation Corps was one of President Franklin D. Roosevelt's New Deal agencies, created during the Great Depression. It employed young men in conservation and reforestation projects.

8. In her book *With Good Heart: Yaqui Beliefs and Ceremonies in Pascua Village*, Muriel Painter described the masks as follows: "The mask is

generally an adult male face, carved in relief. It is made of cottonwood, formed barely to cover the face, and is held in place by a string running from each side to the back. It is painted dull black, with white and sometimes red decorations. A few masks have bits of mother-of-pearl set in. A cross is always painted or incised on the forehead or chin. This is a formée cross. No explanation has been found for this type of cross, but it is said that, unless this form is used, the pascolas do not feel protected" (1986:244).

9. Historian Charles W. Polzer, S.J. (personal communication, 1994) told me that he has not seen anything in Spanish colonial documents about cross tattoos on the hand; however, he felt that such a practice, early in the twentieth century, may have been related to the practices of brotherhoods such as the Penitentes.

10. Woodward, *Penitentes*, p. 272. Mrs. Thomas Harwood claims that some of the new Hispano Methodist preachers "have the cross tattooed on their foreheads which can never be erased" (Mrs. Harriet S. Kellogg, *Life of Mrs. Emily J. Harwood*, p. 338). Early in the twentieth century, Lorenzo de Córdova recalls seeing a herder at Valdez who had "the figure of a cross, light gray in color, imprinted in the middle of his forehead." Although he saw only one other man so marked, he notes that "palms or boughs blessed on Palm Sunday were burned and their ashes used as a filler, rubbed into the design of a cross pricked into the skin" (*Echoes of the Flute*, p. 13). Bonney R. Gaastra, describing Chimayo, Cordova, Truchas and Trampas, claims to have talked to a man with "the faint purple cross tattooed under the skin of his forehead" ('The Doorways of Penitente Land,' *Architectural Record* 57 [1925]:187)" (all from Weigle 1975: 257, n. 61).

Weigle felt the facial tattoos, with their high visibility, would have been discontinued by the Hermanos Penitentes, especially after United States acquisition of New Mexico in 1848, because of public opposition to the brotherhoods on the part of newly arrived Protestant sects and the Catholic church. Opposition from the latter was not consistently strong and was probably motivated by political concerns (Weigle 1975:910).

11. Of the environment the young people went out into in Los Angeles, McWilliams says, "Wherever the Mexicans go, outside their own districts, there are signs [excluding Mexicans], prohibitions, taboos, restrictions. Learning of this 'iron curtain' is part of the education of every Mexican-American boy in Los Angeles" ([1948] 1968:216).

12. *Luciéndola* implies just letting it sit there; it was just sitting there.

13. This woman was born in 1910.

14. The information in this section focuses primarily on male conflicts and is based largely on accounts and comments of males.

15. I use *norteño* to refer to the Spanish spoken by people in rural northern Mexico.

Chapter 2

1. In 1953, Bill Haley and His Comets had the smash-hit record, "Rock around the Clock."

2. According to one man of this generation, this gang was like a car club, and members had club jackets. The group may have been more inter-barrio than some others. The man thought that the membership figure given (350) may have been somewhat inflated.

3. The Gaylords were described by one man as a close-knit cross section of people forming a fairly large group. He described the club as well recognized and its members as "good street fighters" who liked physical contact.

Chapter 3

1. The pueblo of Batuc is the seat of Sonora's *Municipio de Ures.* It was founded by Jesuits as a mission in 1628.

2. The Works Progress Administration was one of the agencies of President Franklin D. Roosevelt's New Deal, a host of programs instituted to bring about economic relief from the ravages of the Great Depression.

3. I believe Aurora referred to this camp as Santa Rita.

Chapter 5

1. Zeferino Diego Ferreira, a Villista who was in Ciudad Juarez in 1916, quoted himself as referring to shoes as *calcos* in a conversation with another Villista colonel in that year. In that same year, he crossed into the United States at El Paso and worked as an agricultural laborer in southern California. Diego had been a cavalry colonel in the Second Brigade of the Northern Division (Cummings 1972).

2. The Mexico City vocabulary Gómez Maillefert chose to focus on in his 1920 article has to do with marijuana. A number of those words and phrases are still used in present-day Pachuco/caló but now have meanings that do not ostensibly refer to marijuana. These include words and phrases such as *la cura* and *curársela,* which Gómez Maillefert reported as referring to the process of removing seeds and stems from the marijuana in preparation for smoking. In the United States and northern Mexico today these phrases denote "amusement/laughter" and "to be amused by/laugh about something," respectively. In his article, Gómez Maillefert gives an ethnographic description of the social context surrounding the process of *la cura* in which friends seated on the floor in a circle smoked

cigarettes of the weed, chatted, and laughed as they removed seeds and stems from a pile in the center on the floor.

Due to the publication date (1920), this vocabulary must have been gathered during or before the Mexican Revolution of 1910. The context reported is without doubt an urban one. However, marijuana use and vocabulary may have had origins in rural areas and contexts. Zeferino Diego Ferreira gave the following account of its use by peons on the hacienda of San Nicolás de los Agustinos in Guanajuato where he worked as a peon as a young boy before the Revolution, in about 1904:

> Every morning in a big plaza there, more than five hundred men would line up and go out in groups to work. Almost all the men and women there were *marihuanos.* The women kept their *hierbita* [herb] under the *metate* where the corn was ground. Everyone smoked it! There were some beautiful fields of it there! Tall plants with big bushy-tailed branches! I even had a cousin there that they called Skunk because he reeked of the smoke. . . . One time when we were planting peanuts, he cut his hand on a very sharp tool that we were using. He went on working that way all day, and when we came out of the fields I asked him if it hurt. "No," he said, "because of the *juana.* I work very comfortably and don't feel tired." . . . I was still a little kid when I was going out to work in his group. Each person had their own row, and I had one, too, even though I was really just working along the side. And if they saw that I was falling behind, they would come and help me until I got caught up. And every single one of them was a *marihuano.* But they were the *best* people! Friendly, nice, and very kind in every way! And they all worked.

I present this information because it raises the question of how much caló vocabulary may have rural Mexican origins.

3. In *masking,* also called transvaluation, people take on forms from the immediate environment as a mask behind which, or through which, alternate meanings are conveyed.

4. This place is thought to be Hueco Tanks, just east of El Paso, Texas (Mooney [1979] 1898:305).

5. In the early 1700s, one branch of the Kiowa moved from the Rocky Mountain area of western Montana. By the mid-1700s, they were living in the Black Hills of South Dakota. Driven from the Black Hills by the Dakotas and Cheyennes, in the early 1800s they migrated to the Wichita Mountains in present-day western Oklahoma. From this stronghold they conducted audacious and frequent forays into west Texas and northern Mexico. One raid in the 1860s is thought to have penetrated as far south as Yucatán or British Honduras. Others went as far southwest as Durango

and through Sonora and Sinaloa to the Gulf of California (Winfrey 1971:105, 113).

6. Professor Laurel Watkins of the Department of Anthropology of the Colorado College was working on a Kiowa dictionary when I was writing my dissertation. At my request, she asked consultant Parker McKenzie about the word *Pä'sûñko.* Mr. McKenzie was familiar with the events Mooney recounted, and identified the word as /pʰá:sę̀gɔ̀/, "musty smelling ones." The reference is to body odor, generally an unpleasant one. He confirmed that the word was used to designate Mexican people from El Paso. The second term given by Mooney, *Pasun-T'a'ka'-i,* was defined by Watkins as /pʰá:sę̀-t'ɔkʰɔ̀y/, "musty smelling Caucasians." Watkins also provided the information about the Kiowa suffix -go (-ko) (Watkins, personal communication (1993)).

7. Meigs described the Kiliwa memorial ceremony in which the *pachugós* were worn in the following manner:

> The *niwey* was a men's ceremony held for the purpose of talking to the dead. The fundamental object of the talking seems to have been to satisfy the dead so that they would stay away. All who had died since the previous niwey, maybe six or seven, were included within its scope. It might be sponsored by anyone whose relative had died since the last niwey, although only a shaman could conduct the heart of the ceremony. Judged by the descriptions, the niwey was a community affair, given by all the families of Arroyo Leon together. . . . The ceremony itself lasts for three nights. The first afternoon, toward evening, four or five men put on robes of human hair, called *pachugós,* which are brought from a distant cave. The pachugós cover the wearers completely, from head to foot. Each man also wears a tuft of eagle feathers on the top of his head (1939:53-54).

According to the account, the shamans entered a special ceremonial structure (*tiwa'*). Then the *pachugós* were taken off and spread on low horizontal frames at the back of the structure and covered with junco mats.

> The dead, who are later assembled by the shaman, sit on the *pachugós* under the *t'itesa'* [feathered wands, "head tufts of the dead"] plumes; they seek the shade. Food for the dead is placed on the front part of each *pachugó.* Biznaga seeds and pine nuts are the best (1939:53).

At one point in the ceremony,

> [The shaman's] spirit leaves his body and goes among the mountains, water holes, earth, and sky looking for the *paiajase* [dead] who have died since the last niwey. . . . Finally, just at dawn, the

paiajase are brought. . . . The shaman screams with fear to see the dead. When the paiajase reach him he dies (temporarily), and one of them enters his body. Then somebody puts a pipe in his mouth, and the paiajase in his body talks, in a strange tongue which only certain people can understand. The rest of the people are overcome with grief at hearing the voice of the dead, and cannot talk: the tears just come (1939:55-56).

8. Art appeared to use this phrase to refer to code-switching.

9. This is probably a reference to the teaching of English vocabulary.

10. Many authors writing on the subject of slang and argot, Pachuco/caló included, voice the opinion that their vocabularies change rapidly. However, Folb (1980), in her work on black street English, found that out of 2,000 expressions she collected over a nine-year period, 75 percent were known to black teens, and 50 percent were actively used in their vocabularies. To Folb, this suggested "the degree to which there is continuity of experience" from generation to generation. It also suggested that vernacular vocabulary is more conservative than innovative in its development.

My impression about Pachuco/caló is much the same. On the basis of the vocabulary used in the 1947 Barker recordings, a large amount appears to have survived, remains stable, and continues to be used in the varieties spoken in Tucson, Arizona; Nogales, Sonora; Tijuana, Baja California; and Chihuahua, Chihuahua.

11. *Esa* is the female version of *ese*, which has a meaning similar to "dude" or "man."

12. Trejo (1968) gives the caló definition of *refuego* as "the liveliness and persistence of an action or dispute."

13. *Teórica* can refer to conversation, the topic of conversation, and also to its philosophical content.

14. Historic ballad in the form of a lyric poem accompanied by guitar. In this many-layered statement, Carlos is, by analogy with the corrido, defining Pachuco/caló as a vehicle for preserving and conveying oral history.

Chapter 6

1. Clinton Rose, *1920-21 Report of the Superintendent, Tucson Public Schools.*

2. Sheridan describes the Arizona state-mandated 1C program as amounting to little more than English vocabulary lessons, in practice (Sheridan 1986:223).

3. Children in Arizona were required to pay for most of their school materials up until the 1980s.

4. Art used "this society" to refer to Anglo society.

5. *Sura* has a number of different, strong negative meanings, among them *simple* (simpleton), a disagreeable person, *asqueroso* (someone that causes one to have a sensation of nausea), or *fastidioso* (someone who "rubs you wrong").

6. See Ortner 1976.

Chapter 7

1. This section refers to interaction between dominant society male police officers and pachuco males.

2. For more extensive accounts of police practices see Acuña 1984; United States Commission on Civil Rights 1970; Morales 1972.

Chapter 8

1. In Los Angeles groups, *jumping in* practices vary. A new member may run a gauntlet while being pounded, or may fight one or a number of gang members at the same time for a specified amount of time. One group in Chihuahua, Chihuahua, Mexico in 1985 would throw the new person into a public fountain. In interview #724 in the archives of the University of Texas at El Paso's Institute of Oral History, a *veterano* describes an early practice of one pachuco group in El Paso in which a bucket of water was thrown on the new person.

2. *La teoriqueada* refers to the ability to express oneself in caló and also to the way one handles concepts (*la teoría*, "theory") or the realm of philosophy.

3. For a critique of the portrayal of Mexican and Chicana women in the movie *La Bamba*, see Rosa Linda Fregoso, "The Mother Motif in *La Bamba* and *Boulevard Nights*," in A. de la Torre and B. M. Pesquera, eds., *Building with Our Hands: New Directions in Chicana Studies*, 130-45. Berkeley: University of California Press (1993).

4. The information in this section is based on accounts and comments of males.

5. *Plegaria* carries the meanings "fervent prayer" or "ringing of bells at noon to call the faithful."

6. A *quinceañera* is the Mass or religious service and/or party held for a girl on her fifteenth birthday.

References

Acuña, Rodolfo F.

1984 *A Community under Siege: A Chronicle of Chicanos East of the Los Angeles River, 1945–1975.* Los Angeles: Chicano Studies Research Center, Publications, UCLA.

Aguilar Melantzón, Ricardo

1981 Diccionario de caló de la región de Ciudad Juarez, Chihuahua. Unpublished manuscript in possession of the author.

1989 *Glosario del caló de Ciudad Juarez.* Las Cruces, NM: Joint Border Research Institute.

Alvarez, George R.

1967 Calo: The "Other" Spanish. *ETC: A Review of General Semantics* 34(1): 7–13.

Alvarez de Williams, Anita

1975 *Primeros pobladores de la Baja California.* Mexicali: Gobierno del Estado de Baja California.

Arizona State Industrial School

1948–49 *Annual Report.* Fort Grant Archive.

1954–55 *Annual Report.* Fort Grant Archive.

Bakhtin, Mikhail N.

[1929] 1984 *Problems in Dostoevsky's Poetics.* Edited and translated by Caryl Emerson. Minneapolis: University of Minnesota Press.

Barker, George C.

1947a Recordings of Pachuco conversations in the archives of the Southwest Folklore Center, University of Arizona, Tucson.

1947b Social Functions of Language in a Mexican-American Community. *American Anthropologist* 76(2): 457–58.

1950 *Pachuco: An American–Spanish Argot and Its Function in Tucson, Arizona.* Tucson: University of Arizona Press.

Barrera Bassols, Dalia

1979 Los cholos: Notas sobre el desarrollo del pandillerismo juvenil en Tijuana. *Boletín del Instituto Nacional de Antropología e Historia,* no. 28 (Oct.–Dec.).

Baugh, John

1983 *Black Street Speech: Its History, Structure, and Survival.* Austin: University of Texas Press.

Bixler-Marquez, Dennis, Jacob Ornstein-Galicia, and George K. Green

1989 *Mexican-American Spanish in Its Societal and Cultural Contexts.* Brownsville, TX.: University of Texas–Pan American at Brownsville in cooperation with the University of Texas at El Paso.

Black, Donald J.

1976 *The Behavior of Law.* New York: Academic Press.

1984 *Toward a General Theory of Social Control: Fundamentals.* New York: Academic Press.

Bogardus, Emory S.

1943 Gangs of Mexican–American Youths. *Sociology and Social Research* 28(1): 55–66.

Briggs, Charles L.

1988 *Competence in Performance: The Creativity of Tradition in Mexicano Verbal Art.* Philadelphia: University of Pennsylvania Press.

Brown, Penelope, and Steven C. Levinson

1978 Universals in Language Usage: Politeness Phenomena. In *Questions and Politeness,* edited by E. N. Goody, 56–289. Cambridge: Cambridge University Press.

Carreras de Velasco, Mercedes

1974 *Los mexicanos que devolvió la crisis, 1929–1932.* Colección del Archivo Histórico Diplomático Mexicano. Obras Monográficas / 2, Tercera Epoca. Tlatelolco, Mexico, D.F.: Secretaría de Relaciones Exteriores.

Chabram-Dernersesian, Angie

1992 I Throw Punches for My Race, but I Don't Want to Be a Man: Writing Us—Chica-nos (Girl, Us)/Chicanas—into the Movement Script. In *Cultural Studies,* edited by L. Grossberg, C. Nelson, and P. Treichler, 81–95. New York: Routledge.

Clavería, Carlos

1951 *Estudios sobre los gitanismos del español.* Madrid: Consejo Superior de Investigaciones.

Cobos, Rubén

1983 *A Dictionary of New Mexico and Southern Colorado Spanish.* Santa Fe: Museum of New Mexico Press.

Coltharp, Lurline H.

1965 *Tongue of the Tirilones: A Linguistic Study of a Criminal Argot.* University of Alabama Press.

Corrigan, Philip D., and Derek Sayer

1985 *The Great Arch: English State Formation as Cultural Revolution.* Oxford: Blackwell.

Cuellar, Jose B.

1982 The Rise and Spread of Cholismo as a Border Youth Subculture. Paper delivered at the Third Annual Binational Border Governors' Conference of the Southwest Border Regional Conference. Tijuana, Baja California, September 21.

Cummings, Laura

1972 Tape-recorded conversation with Zeferino Diego Ferreira. Ejido La Misión, Baja California, Mexico.

1986 Some Observations on the History, Lexicon, and Use of Los Angeles Black Street English and Tijuana Caló. Unpublished manuscript in the possession of the author.

1990a A Comparison of Tijuana's Cholo Slang and Los Angeles Black Teen-Age English. In *Memoria de la Asociación Cultural de las Californias, XXVII Simposio Anual en Playas de Rosarito, Baja California, México*, 38–54. Tijuana: Centro de Investigaciones Históricas, UNAM-UABC.

1990b Una comparación del caló de los cholos de Tijuana y el inglés de los adolecentes negros del centro de Los Angeles. *Memoria de la Asociación Cultural de las Californias, XXVII Simposio Anual en Playas de Rosarito, Baja California, México*, 38–54. Tijuana: Centro de Investigaciones Históricas, UNAM UABC.

1991 Carne con Limón: Reflections on the Construction of Social Harmlessness. *American Ethnologist* 18(2): 370–72.

1994 Que siga el corrido: Tucson Pachucos and Their Times. PhD diss., Department of Anthropology, University of Arizona.

2004 Cloth-Wrapped People, Trouble, and Power: Pachuco Culture in the Southwest. *Journal of the Southwest* 45(3): 329–48.

Daniels, Douglas H.

1997 Los Angeles Zoot: Race "Riot," the Pachuco, and Black Music Culture. *Journal of Negro History* 82(2): 201.

Domer, Marilyn

1955 The Zoot-Suit Riot: A Culmination of Social Tensions in Los Angeles. Master's thesis. Claremont Graduate School, Claremont, CA.

Dozier, Edward P.

1964 Two Examples of Linguistic Acculturation: The Yaqui of Sonora and Arizona and the Tewa of New Mexico. In *Language in Culture and Society: A Reader in Linguistics and Anthropology*, edited by D. Hymes, 509–20. New York: Harper & Row.

Duran, Javier

2001 Border Crossings: Images of the Pachuco in Mexican Literature. *Studies in 20th Century Literature* 25(1): 140.

2002 Nation and Translation: The Pachuco in Mexican Popular Culture: German Valdez's Tin Tan. *Journal of the Midwest Modern Language Association* 35(2): 41–49.

Eble, Connie C.

1977 If Ladies Weren't Present, I'd Tell You What I Really Think. In *Papers in Language Variation*, edited by D. L. Shores and C. P. Hines, 295–301. Tuscaloosa: University of Alabama Press.

Folb, Edith A.

1980 *Runnin' Down Some Lines: The Language and Culture of Black Teenagers.* Cambridge: Harvard University Press.

Fregoso, Rosa Linda

1993 The Mother Motif in *La Bamba* and *Boulevard Nights.* In, *Building with Our Hands: New Directions in Chicana Studies*, edited by A. de la Torre and B. M. Pesquera, 130–45. Berkeley: University of California Press.

Fuentes, Dagoberto, and José A. Lopez

1974 *Barrio Language Dictionary: First Dictionary of Calo.* La Puente, CA: El Barrio Publications.

Galindo, D. Letticia

1981 Perceptions of Pachuquismo and Use of Calo/Pachuco Spanish by Various Chicana Women. *La Red/The Net*, no. 48 (November): 2, 10.

1992 Dispelling the Male-Only Myth: Chicanas and Calo. *Bilingual Review* 17(1): 3–35.

Giroux, Henry A.

1983 *Theory and Resistance in Education: A Pedagogy for the Opposition.* South Hadley, MA: Bergin & Garvey.

Goffman, Erving

1974 *Frame Analysis: An Essay on the Organization of Experience.* New York: Harper & Row.

Goldsmith, Raquel

1994 Seasons, Seeds, and Souls: Mexican Women Gardening in the American Mesilla, 1900–1940. In *Women of the Mexican Countryside, 1850–1990*, edited by H. Fowler-Salamini and M. K. Vaughan, 141–56. Tucson: University of Arizona Press.

Gómez Maillefert, Eugenio

1920 La marijuana en México. *Journal of American Folklore* 33 (127): 28–33.

González, Rafael J.

1967 Pachuco: The Birth of a Creole Language. *Arizona Quarterly* 23(4): 343–56.

Griffith, Beatrice
[1948] 1973 *American Me.* Westport, CT: Greenwood Press.

Gumperz, John J.
1971 *Directions in Sociolinguistics: The Ethnography of Communication.* New York: Holt, Rinehart, & Winston.

Hagedorn, John, and Perry Macon
1988 *People and Folks: Gangs, Crime, and the Underclass in a Rustbelt City.* Chicago: Lake View Press.

Hill, Jane H.
1988 Language, Genuine or Spurious? In *On the Ethnography of Communication: The Legacy of Sapir, Essays in Honor of Harry Hoijer, 1984,* edited by J. H. Hill, D. Tedlock, and A. L. Becker, 9–53. Los Angeles: Department of Anthropology, UCLA.
1993 Hasta la Vista, Baby: Anglo Spanish in the American Southwest. *Critique of Anthropology* 13(2): 145–76.

Hill, Jane H., and David M. Coombs
1982 The Vernacular Remodeling of National and International Languages. *Applied Linguistics* 3:221–31.

Hill, Jane H., and Kenneth C. Hill
1987 *Speaking Mexicano: Dynamics of Syncretic Language in Central Mexico.* Tucson: University of Arizona Press.

Hinojos, Francisco G.
1975 Notes on the Pachuco: Stereotypes, History and Dialect. *Atisbos: Journal of Chicano Research,* Summer, 53–65.

Hoffman, Abraham
1974 *Unwanted Mexican Americans in the Great Depression: Repatriation Pressures, 1929–1939.* Tucson: University of Arizona Press.

Iglesias Serafín, Federico
1992 *Monumento 204, San Luis Río Colorado.* San Luis Río Colorado, Sonora: Artec Publicaciones.

Institute of Oral History, University of Texas at El Paso, Archives.
1976 Interview #724, with anonymous pachuco.

Kochman, Thomas
1984 The Politics of Politeness: Social Warrants in Mainstream American Public Etiquette. In *Meaning, Form, and Use in Context: Linguistic Applications,* edited by D. Schiffrin, 200–209. Georgetown University Roundtable on Linguistics (GURT). Washington, DC: Georgetown University Press.

Limón, José E.
1989 "Carne, Carnales," and the Carnivalesque: Bakhtinian "Batos," Disorder, and Narrative Discourses. *American Ethnologist* 16(3): 471–86.

Lingenfelter, Richard E.
1978 *Steamboats on the Colorado River, 1852–1916.* Tucson: University of Arizona Press.

Lomawaima, K. Tsianina
1994 Talk on her interviews with individuals who had attended the Chilocco Indian School. Faculty Lecture Series, Department of Anthropology. University of Arizona.

Madrid-Barela, Arturo
1973 In Search of the Authentic Pachuco—An Interpretive Essay. Part I. *Aztlán* 4(1): 31–60.

Martin, Patricia Preciado
1992 *Songs My Mother Sang to Me: An Oral History of Mexican American Women.* Tucson: University of Arizona Press.

Mazón, Muricio
1984 *The Zoot-Suit Riots: The Psychology of Symbolic Annihilation.* Austin: University of Texas Press.

McWilliams, Carey
[1948] 1968 *North from Mexico: The Spanish-Speaking People of the United States.* New York: Greenwood Press.

Meigs, Peveril
1939 *The Kiliwa Indians of Lower California.* Berkeley: University of California Press.

Melville, Margarita B., ed.
1980 *Twice a Minority: Mexican American Women.* St. Louis: C. V. Mosby.

Menchaca, Martha
1993 Chicano Indianism: A Historical Account of Racial Repression in the United States. *American Ethnologist* 20(3): 583–603.

Mendez, R.
c. 1983 *Chicano Street Gangs.* N.p.: Arizona Department of Corrections.

Michalowski, Raymond J.
1985 *Order, Law, and Crime: An Introduction to Criminology.* New York: Random House.

Mixco, Mauricio J.
1985 *Kiliwa Dictionary.* Salt Lake City: University of Utah Press.

Molina, Alonso de
[1571] 1970 *Vocabulario en lengua castellana y mexicana y mexicana y castellana. Estudio preliminar de Miguel Leon-Portilla.* Mexico: Editorial Porrúa.

Mooney, James
[1898] 1979 *Calendar History of the Kiowa Indians.* Washington, DC: Smithsonian Press. Reprinted from the *Seventeenth Annual Report of the*

Bureau of American Ethnology, 1895–96, Part I, 129–445. Washington, DC: Government Printing Office, 1898.

Moore, Joan W.

1978 *Homeboys: Gangs, Drugs, and Prison in the Barrios of Los Angeles.* Philadelphia: Temple University Press.

1985 Paper presented at the annual meeting of the American Anthropological Association, Oaxaca, Mexico.

Morales, Armando

1972 *Ando Sangrando/I Am Bleeding: A Study of Mexican American–Police Conflict.* La Puente, CA: Perspectiva Publications.

Ochoa Zazueta, Jesus A.

1978 *Los kiliwa y el mundo se hizo así.* Mexico D.F.: Instituto Nacional Indigenista.

Officer, James

1987 Talk on the history of Tucson's Barrio Anita. Faculty Lecture Series, Department of Anthropology. University of Arizona.

Ornstein-Galicia, Jacob

1995 Features and Functions of a U.S. Southwest Mexican-American Argot. *Orbis* 38:113–29.

Ortega, Adolfo

1977 *Calo Tapestry.* Berkeley: Editorial Justa.

1991 *Calo Orbis: Semiotic Aspects of a Chicano Language Variety.* New York: Peter Lang.

Ortner, Sherry B.

1976 The Virgin and the State. *Michigan Discussions in Anthropology* 2:1–16. Reprinted 1978 in *Feminist Studies* 4:19–37.

Pagán, Eduardo O.

2003 *Murder at the Sleepy Lagoon: Zoot Suits, Race, and Riot in Wartime L.A.* Chapel Hill: University of North Carolina Press.

Painter, Muriel T.

1986 *With Good Heart: Yaqui Beliefs and Ceremonies in Pascua Village.* Tucson: University of Arizona Press.

Paz, Octavio

1951 [1961] *The Labyrinth of Solitude: Life and Thought in Mexico.* New York: Grove Press.

Peñalosa, Fernando

1980 *Chicano Sociolinguistics: A Brief Introduction.* Rowley, MA.: Newbury House.

Pfohl, Stephen J.

1985 *Images of Deviance and Social Control: A Sociological History.* New York: McGraw-Hill.

Philips, Susan U., Susan Steele, and Christine Tanz, eds.
1987 *Language, Gender, and Sex in Comparative Perspective.* Cambridge University Press.

Poudevida, Antonio Raluy
1986 *Diccionario Porrúa de la lengua española.* Mexico: Editorial Porrúa.

Reisman, Karl
1970 Cultural and Linguistic Ambiguity in a West Indian Village. In *Afro-American Anthropology: Contemporary Perspectives,* edited by N. A. Whitten and J. Szwed, 129–44. New York: Free Press.
1974 Contrapuntal Conversations in an Antiguan Village. In *Explorations in the Ethnography of Speaking,* edited by R. Bauman and J. Sherzer, 110–24. London: Cambridge University Press.

Robinson, Cecil
1971 *With the Ears of Strangers: The Mexican in American Literature.* Tucson: University of Arizona Press.

Rubel, Arthur J.
1965 The Mexican-American Palomilla. *Anthropological Linguistics* 7(4): 92–97.

Sacks, Harvey, Emanuel A. Schegloff, and Gail Jefferson
1974 A Simplest Systematics for the Organization of Turn-Taking for Conversation. *Language* 50:696–735.

Saiz, Flor
1973 *La Chicana.* N.p.: Flor Saiz.

Sanchez, Rosaura
1983 *Chicano Discourse.* Rowley, MA: Newbury House.

Sanchez-Tranquilino, Marcos
1987 Mano a Mano: An Essay on the Representation of the Zoot Suit and Its Misrepresentation by Octavio Paz. *Journal: A Contemporary Art Magazine,* Winter, 34–42.

Sanchez-Tranquilino, Marcos, and J. Tagg
1992 The Pachuco's Flayed Hide: Mobility, Identity, and Buenas Garras. In *Cultural Studies,* edited by L. Grossberg, C. Nelson, and P. A. Treichler, 556–70. New York: Routledge.

Santamaría, Francisco J.
1974 *Diccionario de mejicanismos.* Mexico: Editorial Porrúa, S.A.

Scollon, Ron, and Suzanne Scollon
1979 *Narrative, Literacy and Face in Interethnic Communication.* Norwood, NJ: Ablex.

Sheridan, Thomas E.
1986 *Los Tucsonenses: The Mexican Community in Tucson, 1854–1941.* Tucson: University of Arizona Press.

Silverstein, Michael
1976 Shifters, Linguistic Categories, and Cultural Description. In *Meaning in Anthropology*, edited by K. H. Basso and H. Selby, 11–55. Albuquerque: University of New Mexico Press.
1985 The Culture of Language in Chinookan Narrative Texts; or On Saying That . . . in Chinook. In *Grammar inside and outside the Clause*, edited by J. Nichols and A. Woodbury, 132–71. Cambridge University Press.

Spitzer, Steven
1975 Toward a Marxian Theory of Deviance. *Social Problems* 22(5):638–51.

Sturtevant, William C., ed.
1988 *Handbook of North American Indians*, vol. 10. Washington, DC: Smithsonian Institution.

Thorne, Barrie, Cheris Kramarae, and Nancy Henley, eds.
1983 *Language, Gender, and Society*. Rowley, MA: Newbury House.

Trejo, Arnulfo D.
1968 *Diccionario etimológico latinoamericano del léxico de la delicuencia.* Manuales UTEHA #365/Doble, sección 12, Linguística. Mexico, D.F.: Unión Tipográfica Editorial Hispano-Americana.

Trujillo, Larry D.
1974 La evolución del 'bandido' al 'pachuco': A Critical Examination and Evaluation of Criminological Literature on Chicanos. *Issues in Criminology* 9(2): 43–67.

U.S. Commission on Civil Rights
1970 *Mexican Americans and the Administration of Justice in the Southwest—United States Commission on Civil Rights—Report, March.* Washington, DC: United States Commission on Civil Rights, 1970.

U.S. Office of Indian Affairs
1907–1938 *Superintendent's Annual Narrative and Statistical Reports from Field Jurisdictions of the Bureau of Indian Affairs, 1907–1938* [microform]. Washington, DC: National Archives and Records Service, General Services Administration, 1975.

Urciouli, Bonnie
1985 Bilingualism as Code and Bilingualism as Practice. *American Linguistics* 27:363–86.
1991 The Political Topography of Spanish and English: The View from a New York Puerto Rican Neighborhood. *American Ethnologist* 18: 295–310.

Urla, Jaqueline
1993 Cultural Politics in an Age of Statistics: Numbers, Nations, and the Making of Basque Identity. *American Ethnologist* 20: 818–43.

Vasquez, Librado K., and Vasquez, Maria E.
1975 *Regional Dictionary of Chicano Slang.* Austin: Jenkins.

Vigil, James D.
1988 *Barrio Gangs: Street Life and Identity in Southern California.* Austin: University of Texas Press.

Voloshinov, V. N.
[1927] 1973 *Freudianism: A Marxist Critique.* New York: Academic Press.

Walby, Sylvia
1990 *Theorizing Patriarchy.* Oxford: Blackwell.

Walther Meade, Adalberto
1983 *Origen de mexicali.* Mexicali: Universidad Autónoma de Baja California.

Webb, John T.
1982 Mexican-American Calo and Standard Mexican Spanish. In *Spanish in the United States: Sociolinguistic Aspects,* edited by J. Amastae and L. Elías-Olivares, 121–31. Cambridge University Press.

Weigle, Marta
1976 *Brothers of Light, Brothers of Blood: The Penitentes of the Southwest.* Albuquerque: University of New Mexico Press.

Williams, Brackette F.
1989 A Class Act: Anthropology and the Race to Nation across Ethnic Terrain. *Annual Review of Anthropology* 18:401–44.

Winfrey, Dorman H.
1971 *Indian Tribes of Texas.* Waco: Texian Press.

Zatz, Marjorie S.
1987 Chicano Youth Gangs and Crime: The Creation of a Moral Panic. *Contemporary Crises* 11:129–58.

Index

About the Author

Laura L. Cummings received her PhD degree in cultural anthropology from the University of Arizona in 1994. Her principal focus is the U.S.–Mexico border, its cultures, sociolinguistics, and history. Dr. Cummings has conducted research and applied projects in both urban and rural settings on both sides of the border. She resided in Baja California, Mexico, for ten years, where she was a consultant to the state government while employed as an anthropologist with the Universidad Autónoma de Baja California commissioned to Mexico's Instituto Nacional de Antropología e Historia.

Dr. Cummings has carried out fieldwork on border youth cultures in Tijuana, Baja California; Nogales, Sonora; Ciudad Juarez and Chihuahua, Chihuahua, in Mexico, and in the United States in Los Angeles, California; Tucson, Arizona; and El Paso, Texas. As an administrator with the South Texas Council on Alcohol and Drug Abuse in Laredo, Texas, she adapted and directed prevention programs in four south Texas border counties. She has also worked with the Hopi Tribe in Arizona as a linguistic consultant on the Hopi Dictionary Project and on cultural issues related to disability.

She has published in the United States and Mexico on substance abuse trends as a member of the National Institute on Drug Abuse Border Epidemiology Work Group, coauthored a program adaptation manual for the CDC for HIV prevention programs working with Hispanics, and has published numerous articles and monographs on U.S.–Mexico border cultures, language, and history.